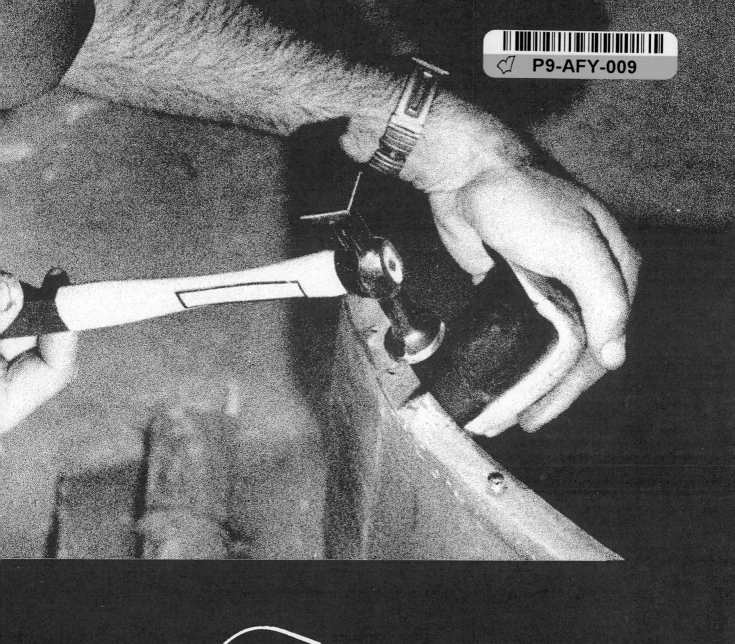

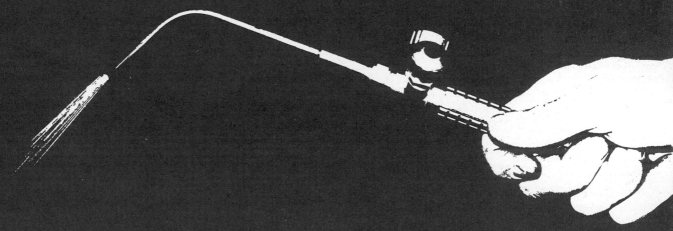

BASIC BODYWORK
AND PAINTING
NO.4

Introduction

Many people consider bodywork and painting fields of endeavor where nothing that is really new ever comes along. Dents, they assume, can be knocked out today just as they were a generation ago. And painting an automobile is a chore unchanged since the spray gun was invented. But, nothing could be further from the truth. There are new wrinkles—pun intended—in straightening bodywork damaged by collision, in repairing areas of rust, in patching body panels. Painting, too, is an art that has enjoyed much progress. New developments in both of these closely-related fields are the stock-in-trade of this 4th edition of Basic Bodywork and Painting.

As has been pointed out in earlier versions of this book, bodywork and painting are among the more thankless tasks in automotive repair work. After all, no one can appreciate a perfectly repaired and paint-blended dent for the simple reason that he can't see it! But if the bodyman and the painter can satisfy their personal egos by learning to ply these crafts, then the reward lies in the customer's inability to find fault with the handiwork.

The point of this book is twofold; to reveal to those who have a metalworking or painting aptitude the ins and outs of body repair; and what they'll face if they "hire on" at a bump shop. Too, the experienced pros will appreciate our "refresher" course as they look over the newer developments and techniques presented on these pages.

But this book is not aimed solely at those who wish to take up a new career. We are also catering to the custom bodywork clan, the do-it-yourselfers who are into old car restoration, and the lovers of "trick" painting. Each faction will find something of interest and value between these covers. As an example, if you're not up on "gop" art, including the application of "acrylustrations" for real eye-appeal on the body of a car or van, then you had better thumb on back a few chapters. Or, how about customizing, with frosted glass following your own design? If such things strike your fancy, then the book you're holding is right up your alley. Good reading!

Spence Murray

SPECIALTY PUBLICATIONS DIVISION

Erwin M. Rosen/Executive Editor
Dick Fischer/Art Director
George Fukuda/Artist, Design
Angie Ullrich/Secretary, Administrative
Pamella Rogers/Secretary, Editorial

Automotive

Spencer Murray/Editor
Mike Criss/Managing Editor
Jay Storer/Feature Editor
Jon Jay/Technical Editor
Eric Rickman/Special Assignments
Jim Norris/Associate Editor

General Subjects

Al Hall/Editor
Ronda Brown/Managing Editor
Richard L. Busenkell/Managing Editor
Allen Bishop/Associate Editor
John T. Jo/Associate Editor

Special Projects

Don Whitt/Editor
Steve Amos/Art Director
Ann C. Tidwell/Managing Editor
Harris Bierman/Associate Editor

Library of Congress Catalog Card Number 73-79967

Spencer Murray/Editorial Director
Jay Storer/Editor
Dick Fischer/Art Director
Jim Norris/Managing Editor
Jon Jay/Technical Editor
Mike Criss/Associate Editor
Eric Rickman/Special Assignments

ART SERVICES

Robert I. Young/Art Director
Celeste Swayne-Courtney/Artist, Design
Kathy Philpott/Artist, Design
Wanda Satow/Artist, Design
Carol Winet/Artist, Design

COVER

Steve Young of the "Crazy Painters" of Bellflower, Calif., shows us spot disc-sanding with an air-driven sander (top). Then, as you'll discover while you peruse the pages of this book, there are a lot of new things in "trick" painting. Steve shows in the lower photo how to shoot a "blow-out." Both photos by Eric Rickman. Cover design by Dick Fischer.

BASIC BODYWORK AND PAINTING No. 4

ISBN 0-8227-0105-7

PETERSEN PUBLISHING COMPANY

R. E. Petersen/Chairman of the Board
F. R. Waingrow/President
Robert E. Brown/Sr. V.P., Corporate Sales
Herb Metcalf/V.P., Circulation Marketing
Dick Day/V.P., Automotive Publications
Philip E. Trimbach/V.P., Finance
Al Isaacs/Director, Graphics
Bob D'Olivo/Director, Photography

Spencer Nilson/Director, Administrative Services
Larry Kent/Director, Corporate Merchandising
William Porter/Director, Circulation
Jack Thompson/Assistant Director, Circulation
James J. Krenek/Director, Purchasing
Thomas R. Beck/Director, Production
Alan C. Hahn/Director, Market Development
Maria Cox/Manager, Data Processing Services

Contents

Metalworking Fundamentals

Analyzing the dings and dents—what's bent and how badly—makes the repairs easier.

1

2

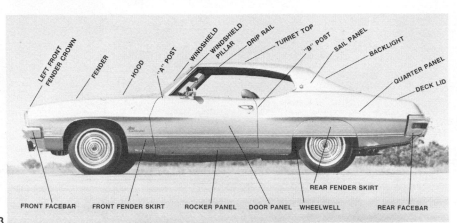

LEFT FRONT FENDER CROWN — FENDER — HOOD — "A" POST — WINDSHIELD — WINDSHIELD PILLAR — DRIP RAIL — TURRET TOP — "B" POST — SAIL PANEL — BACKLIGHT — QUARTER PANEL — DECK LID

FRONT FACEBAR — FRONT FENDER SKIRT — ROCKER PANEL — DOOR PANEL — WHEELWELL — REAR FENDER SKIRT — REAR FACEBAR

3

1. *Would the '73 "5-mph" bumpers have prevented this? Maybe, maybe not. But the fact remains that a car's cosmetic covering, otherwise known as the body, is fragile and easily damaged. The career body man must know how to repair all manner of bumps and scrapes; from relatively minor ones like this, to severe smash-ups.*

2. *Many body men sand tight contours with a standard flat grinding disc, but cones or mushroom discs are better suited, are available in a sequence of grit numbers.*

3. *Every part of an automobile has a specific name, a name that is common to any make of car. This illustration displays many of these.*

Any car that has suffered damage to its body can be fixed, no matter how wiped out it may appear on cursory examination. Once the damage has been examined and repair costs evaluated, of course, it may turn out that fixing it is economically inadvisable. This makes the car a "total" in bodyworking jargon. But if the estimate proves that fixing the car is advisable, then its up to the body man to do the job at hand. From this point, there are two ways to dig into the repair. The body man can carefully consider such things as the first point of impact, the direction of force, whether or not to replace certain damaged parts, and so forth. Or, he can dive headlong into the job and indiscriminately begin wielding his hammer and torch.

Obviously, the best way to proceed is with forethought and care, as the wealth of material in this book will show. While we don't pretend to give you a step-by-step sequence of repairs on every conceivable type of damage to all makes of cars, we will give you plenty of in-depth chapters to provide you with a good grounding in fundamentals.

THE NATURE OF AUTOMOBILE BODIES

It would be totally unwise for any body and fender mechanic, whether he be a complete professional or rank amateur, to contemplate sheetmetal modification or repair without a fundamental understanding of the medium to be worked. That is, the worker must have certain basic information about steel and learn how to apply this to various aspects of the job at hand.

Because of the requirements of forming and later use, the sheetmetal used in a car body is of low-carbon steel. If a higher carbon metal were used, the parts might resist certain impacts better, but the panels would be very hard to form at the factory and extremely difficult to repair in the field. Special car bodies have been made from rather exotic steel and other metals through the years, usually as a publicity stunt or part of a research program, but ordinary mild steel remains the leader in automotive body construction. Strength for mild steel body panels can be achieved by design with extra reinforcements,

strong shape, or a little more thickness in the metal.

Although the enthusiast is restricted to working with what he has, it is wise to understand what the factory strives for when making the original metal. Things the foundry must keep in mind are properties that will allow the metal to be formed and welded, give it excellent strength and enable it to meet surface texture requirements. All these properties are covered under three headings: plasticity, work hardening and elasticity.

Plasticity is the sheetmetal property permitting a shape change when enough force is applied. In the beginning, the sheetmetal is a large flat sheet that becomes a fender or a hood or a top panel. When the flat sheet is modified by the press, the change is called plastic deformation. The amount of deformation possible without breaking is relative to the metal hardness. This plastic deformation occurs under both tension and compression. Deformation under tension is ductility, deformation under compressive force is malleability. The end result of tension deformation is stretching, and the result of pressure

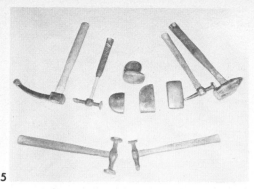

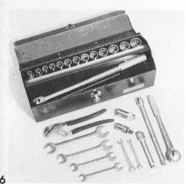

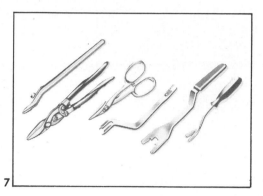

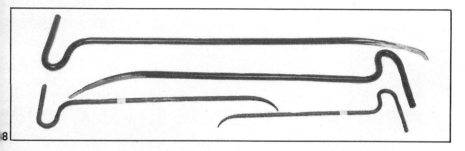

4

5

6

7

8

4. Metalite cloth cones can be had in coarse, medium and fine grits (24,36,50) and are ideal for sanding tight body contours.

5. Displayed here are a number of bodywork hammers and dollies offered for the repairman. The different styles are necessary to facilitate ease of making repairs.

6. Naturally, the body man must have access to a complement of ordinary hand tools and know how to use them.

7. Typical of specialized tools a body man will gather are these. From left to right: manual panel cutter, aviation tin snips, regular tin snips, molding clip and door hardware tools, clip and tack bar.

8. Pry bars prove invaluable in performing body repairs as they allow leverage to be applied in hard to reach areas, often pulling panels out where they can be repaired more easily.

When a body panel is made in a press, or die, residual stresses are left in the panel. That is, there will be areas of stress that remain in the panel. Cut through the edge of a hood panel and the two pieces will pull apart slightly; the residual stress from the original stamping causes this. Such stresses will usually be greater the more complicated the panel shape. Thus, when a panel is repaired, it will probably be restored to a state of minor tension.

Heat is a part of body repair, whether from the torch or from the grinder, and will have three separate effects: scaling, grain structure change, and expansion/contraction. The three effects happen at the same time during a repair operation.

When steel is heated to 430°F., if the steel is clean and bright, the color will be a pale yellow. As the heat is increased, the color will change through straw, brown, purple, light blue and dark blue, with the latter reached at around 600°F. The color will then fade to a gray or greenish tone until the first reddish color comes at about 900°F. Various colors of red are then apparent until approximately 1550°F., when the red increases in brightness through orange and yellow to white. Steel melts at around 2600°F.

Scale forms when the heated area is attacked by oxygen; therefore this scale will form faster on the side away from the torch. When the torch is removed, however, scale will immediately form on the near side. This scale is not a major problem. A definite and progressive change in metal grain structure occurs when steel is heated toward the melting point, with a consequent result in hardness and strength. There is not enough carbon in sheetmetal to harden from heating, but it can be annealed. When a piece

deformation is upsetting. The enthusiast is interested in both aspects of deformation, since both stretching and upsetting take place in body panels during modifications and repair work.

When metal is bent, stretched, upset, or changed in shape at a temperature less than red heat, it has been cold worked. That is, plastic deformation has taken place without the use of heat. Of course, how much a piece of metal can be worked cold has a limit, beyond which it will break. As the metal is worked toward this limit, it becomes harder with an increase in strength and stiffness. This is called work hardening. A good example of work hardening is supplied by bending a flat piece of sheetmetal double without creasing the bend. When the metal is flattened out again, the original bend remains and two new ones are added, one on either side of the first. The metal stretched at the first bend and became work hardened, thus stronger than the rest of the metal.

Some work hardness will be found in all body panels, caused by the original press forming. When a panel

has been damaged, additional hardness will occur, and still more hardening will accompany the straightening process.

Elasticity of sheetmetal is the ability of the metal to regain its original shape after deflection. When a panel is warped slightly, it may spring back into original shape when the restraining force is removed. This is elasticity. Of course, the harder the steel the greater the elasticity, which means elasticity will increase as work hardening increases.

When the metal has been bent to the point where it will not spring back completely to the original shape, it has reached the elastic limit, or the yield point. When a damaged fender is removed from a car, both the fender and the inner splash panel will have a tendency to spring back toward original shape slightly. All sheet steel will retain some springback no matter how badly damaged. This is of significance to the body repairman, since a badly "waved" panel may return to normal shape when a single, simple buckled spot is removed, the buckled spot having held the panel out of shape.

Metalworking

of metal has been work hardened, it can be returned to the soft stage by rearranging the grain structure. If the metal is heated to the salmon color just above bright red (about 1600°F.), the metal will reach the critical temperature where the grain structure is reformed.

When metal is heated it will expand a given amount; when it cools it will contract. The coefficient of expansion in automotive sheetmetal up to 1500°F. is six-millionths of-an-inch per degree, which seems infinitesimal. But this is the reason metal will warp when heat is applied. There is a significant difference between heat distortion and stretching.

There are four basic classifications to the crown of a particular panel, with "crown" as a definition of the curvature of that given panel. There is the low crown (low curvature), high crown (high curvature), combination high and low crown, and reverse crown.

Panels with low crowns have very little curvature, and consequently, very little load-carrying ability. The roof panel is a good example, with slight curves at the edges and a mid-section that is nearly flat. At the extreme edges near the drip molding, the top panel will usually curve rapidly with a high crown.

A high crown is often considered a shape that curves rapidly in all directions. Such surfaces are quite common on older cars that the enthusiast is likely to work with, and will usually resist deformation due to damage. Such a high-crown area would be the top and front portions of a Model A fender, the body roll at the rear of the top, and so on. The tendency has been away from this type of "tight" styling during the last two decades, until the modern car is made up of very large low-crown panels. Obviously, a high-crown area is very strong in itself and will not need reinforcements as will the low-crown panel.

The combination high- and low-crown panel which is very common to the modern car—examples are fenders and door panels—provides a very strong structure. A door panel is usually much stronger than a roof panel.

The reverse crown shows up in the complicated areas of design, as an inside curve on a hood or fender. A typical example of an inside curve or reverse crown would be the taillight area of a Corvair, where the metal is "pooched" out to accept the taillight assembly. These areas have very high-strength concentrations, the reason damage to such an area is usually severe but localized. To the body

man, such damage usually means use of some kind of filler.

When the metal of a high-crown area is struck, the metal can always be expected to push outward from the point of impact. When a low-crown area is struck, the metal will tend to pull inward. A combination panel will include both outward and inward forces.

When a collision occurs, damage will then be dependent upon the area affected and the force of the collision. The damage can be separated into five types: displaced areas, simple bends, rolled buckles, upsets, and stretches.

A displaced area is a part of the metal that's been moved but not damaged. If a door panel is smacked sharply, for instance, the entire panel may buckle inward. But there will be actual damage only around the edges of the larger buckle. If the panel is lightly pushed from the back, it may snap back into place, and repair is needed only around the small buckles, or edges. If a fender is hit slightly

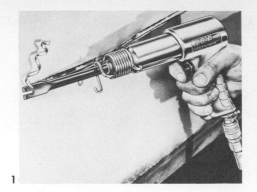

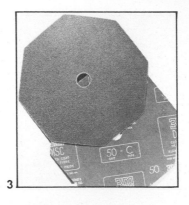

1. An air-operated panel cutter is extremely handy when replacing panels or doing custom work, but hand power will work in a bind.

2. This operator is grinding down a weld on a torn fender. He is using a Bear Closekote Green-Bak fiber disc, in No. 16 grit.

3. This octagonal disc by 3M is used for reverse-crown work, where the sharp edge of a regular round disc would dig into the metal. The points of disc allow it to flex with the metal shape.

4. A number of different types of backup pads are available. The average home craftsman will want a rather firm pad and a flexible unit that will follow contours.

5. These pads are molded from soft material and are useful for grinding concave areas where they must flex accordingly. The smaller size may be chucked in a standard drill motor.

6. A grinding disc may be scalloped like this to make it "floppy" so its edge won't catch in a crevice or seam.

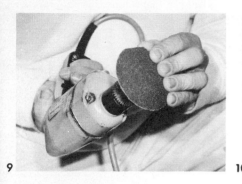

7

8

9

10

7. Paste-on discs are for drill motor pads, come in handy when working in tight areas and when doing finish of soft fillers.

8. PSA discs and pads are small and flat for sanding recesses difficult to reach with other devices. PSA discs are treated with Pressure-Sensitive Adhesive.

9. Very coarse-grit discs are usually not available for drill motor pads, but a used large one can be trimmed down to the smaller size required.

10. Here we find the body man using an Openkote Green-Bak fiber disc, No. 24 grit, to remove old paint with broad grinding strokes.

near the headlight, it may cause slight waves down the side of the fender toward the door. There may be a small buckle in the fender somewhere that is holding the metal down. If the fender is pushed or pulled in a reverse direction from the impact, the displaced metal reverts to original shape and only the small buckled places need repair.

Whenever collision occurs, there is usually some form of simple bending involved. In the above case, if the fender is struck hard enough, the small-buckled area may turn into a simple bend, where the metal makes a kind of S-shape as it is forced out of place. As the severity of the simple bend increases it becomes a rolled buckle. In the simple bend, the outside of the bend includes metal-under-tension and the inside of the bend under-compression. This is in a very small area as sheetmetal is so thin, but there is a distortion of the metal involved.

In the rolled buckle, the S-shape of the bend is pronounced, with the metal trying to tuck under itself. Such damage is not unusual to front- or rear-end collisions, and indicates a rather severe impact. For the enthusiast, such a buckle indicates a considerable amount of metal work, starting with pulling or pushing the panel back into some semblance of shape and then working the buckled area carefully with hand tools.

An upset in metal happens when opposing forces push against an area of metal causing it to yield. Because of this yield, the surface area of the metal will be reduced and the thickness increased. An upset area will tend to gather the surrounding metal and does not, to a large extent, occur in automotive bodies. However, a very small upset can cause the panel to react strangely, sometimes even as though the panel had been stretched. Unless the metal shows signs of having been worked before, chances are the panel has an upset area somewhere on its surface.

Stretching is the result of tension rather than pressure, as in upsetting, with stretching typical of the gouge type of damage. When a car bumper rakes down a door panel, it will probably cause a gouge in the panel. This is stretched metal and the repair procedure is usually one of filling the gouge as there is seldom a raised bump anywhere near. A false stretch can result from a nearby upset, but it usually takes an expert to see this.

When making the decision as to what kind of repair procedure to follow, the body man must determine the angle of impact; speed of the im-

pact object; size, rigidity and weight of the impact object; and construction of the panel damaged. Trying to visualize how the metal folded during the impact is the first step to repair, since applying an opposite force will pull much of the damage out.

The impact angle will be either a direct or a glancing blow with a resulting effect on all the other areas of the car. A big impact on the front end can cause misalignment at the rear of the body, and so on. If the impact angle is not too great, much of the impact force will be absorbed by the panel. If the angle is high, the impact energy may be diverted, leaving small damage. In some cases, the impact object may be sharp, driving some of the metal before it. This pushes the metal up in front of the object and stretches it behind. A typical sideswipe condition includes such a possibility making repair difficult.

TAKING THE BODY APART

It is vital to understand that time spent trying to repair or modify a piece of body sheetmetal will have a direct effect upon cost. If an untrained metal man spends three hours repairing a 30-minute dent, the cost will likely be too high. Learning to assess the damage is important and not too difficult. A few minutes spent looking at a crumpled fender may save many hours of labor later on.

One typical consideration would be determining how much of the crumpled front end must be removed for a straightening operation, with the amount of time spent on the total project relative to the amount of body tear-down required. It is often easier

Metalworking

to straighten a particular panel if it is removed from the vehicle, perhaps an inner splash panel, and sometimes the removal of an adjacent panel makes repair of a specific panel easier and faster.

As a general rule, a large amount of damage to the front end means most of the front end should be disassembled. If the impact has been severe, chances are that the frame has been damaged, as well as parts of the body farther back, such as a doorpost or cowl section. However, if one fender is in relatively good shape, it need not be removed unless extensive frame repair on that side is necessary.

When the body parts are being taken apart, save all the nuts and bolts, as well as small brackets. These parts are seldom included on replacement panels, and as a result, are difficult to obtain individually.

The front sheetmetal can sometimes be removed from the chassis as a unit, by removing bolts down either side of the cowl and one or two bolts holding the radiator core support to the frame. When the electrical wiring and radiator hoses have been disconnected, the front fenders, grille, radiator and core support can be detached as a single piece. Nothing else on the body is so easily removed. The doors and deck lid are removable at the hinges.

Automobile bodies are welded together in giant jigs at the factory, with the outer panels welded or crimped in place over supporting framework. The top panel and drip molding are spot welded in place, the cowl section may be a separate unit, the quarter panels are spot welded at the door posts and deck lid opening, etc. Removal of all these welded parts must be done carefully and with forethought to preclude unnecessary work. We cover panel replacement in another chapter.

THE FRAME

Anytime a vehicle is damaged, it is possible that the frame or frame structure has also been damaged. While some of the damage may be obvious, misalignment can be involved to a great extent without being seen.

Frame checking is usually done at three stages: in assessing how much damage is involved, during the repair, and as a final repair check. The frame can be considered in three parts—front, center and rear—with the front being from the firewall forward, the center portion covered by the passenger compartment, and the rear what is left.

Frame damage can run the gamut from twisting, to collapse of one section, to slight misalignment. In all cases where frame damage is suspected, the enthusiast should entrust the vehicle to a frame shop for repair. Such shops are completely equipped with necessary gauges and equipment to check and repair the frame. Repair of the major frame is not a backyard project. It is possible to replace small front frame extensions, called frame horns, but nothing larger should be attempted in the home garage.

It is possible to save considerable money on a frame repair by removing all sheetmetal that might be in the way. If the frame shop does not have to spend time just getting to the job, the resulting cost savings will be large.

WORKING WITH JACKS

The average enthusiast will not purchase anything as specialized as a body jack, with all the attendant pieces, but such units can be borrowed or rented. It must be kept in mind that jacks offer a steady pressure—a very high pressure—that can restore buckled metal to near factory-fresh shape quickly.

If a dent is banged out with a hammer, the metal will tend to be upset. A similar effect will occur with pushing a dent out with a hydraulic jack. It is usually easy to push a crumpled fender back into some semblance of shape, but getting the final good repair job may be impossible because of the excess force used with the jack. In areas where the primary concern is alignment, such as door posts, the push-method of jack use is acceptable if done correctly.

Pulling the wrinkles from a piece of sheetmetal is better than pushing. This is particularly true where the section features low-crown construction, such as a top or quarter-panel. When tension is applied to a panel, the dented area is pulled back to shape rather than pushed. Pushing or driving a dent tends to concentrate the force in small areas with a resulting upset in the metal. This means the upset areas must then be taken out if the final job is to be a success. By pulling the metal straight, there are no upset areas, thus less work.

Learning where to attach jack points for pulling a dent from sheetmetal is a matter of recognizing the proper leverage angles, lift reaction, work hardening of the damaged place, variations of the surface crown, and alignment with the panel crown. Attachment of the jack ends should be done so that the most leverage is applied directly to the bent area. As an example, it is not too difficult to straighten a steel bar bent double by simply pulling the ends apart. But as the ends are pulled farther apart, more effort is required to pull the bar straight. The leverage has decreased.

At the same time, lift reaction enters the picture. For every action there is an equal and opposite reaction. When a jack is attached on either side of a dent, there is an action to pull the dent up and a reaction through the jack to force the metal

1. After paint is sanded from metal, the fender must be conditioned by right angle grinding with a No. 50 grit Closekote Green-Bak disc.

2. Hand-held, powered sanders come in several types and sizes, are most often used in pre-paint preparation. But often the body man will use one to show up high or low spots instead of a regular body grinder that might cut too deeply into the metal.

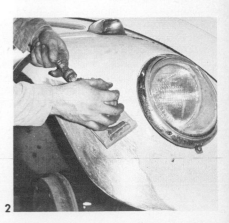

downward at the attachment points. This reaction force will cease when the dent is pulled out, although the jack can still be bumped to increase tension on the metal being straightened. When looking for attachment points for securing a jack in tension-straightening, these points should be strong. The edges of the door or fender would be good examples.

When a panel has been crumpled from collision, the area most affected will have work hardened due to upset of the metal. When tension is applied to pull the metal back into a rough shape, as much of the area as possible should be worked out with hand tools before the tension is released. The reason is simple enough, since any work done to the metal will tend to stretch it back to the original shape.

Learning to work areas of high-crown or combination-crown design will take a little more time than the simple low-crown repair, but the jacks can still be used effectively. The key is to go slowly at first. In fact, this should be the maxim of any jack work. "Proceed with caution as it is easy to overdo a good thing!"

TOOLS AND HOW TO USE THEM

Hand tools used to straighten sheetmetal accomplish the job in one or more of the following ways: by striking a direct blow on the metal surface, as resistance to a direct blow struck on the opposite side of the metal, and as a lever prying against the surface. For the enthusiast, this means bumping hammers, dolly blocks, bumping spoons, body spoons, pry tools and caulking tools. Unfortunately, none of these tools is automatic. Each requires some semblance of dexterity, and the body man must practice before learning to strike a blind dolly or slap a spoon just right.

HAMMERS

Hammers come in a variety of styles, sizes and combinations. There are many small manufacturers of body tools, but most auto parts stores carry a reasonable supply, as do the larger mail order houses (Sears Roebuck, Montgomery Ward, etc.). This is especially true of hammers.

The large, flat face of a body hammer spreads the hammer blow force over a fairly large area of the metal surface. This is essential when working with sheetmetal, and is one of the reasons a metal man will visibly wince when he sees metal being struck with a ball-peen hammer. It is difficult for the beginner to accurately strike a hidden dolly (one that is being held behind the panel), so the large, flat-body hammer face reduces the chance of a miss. The best hammers have a dead flat spot in the center of the head, blending into a slight curved edge to prevent making sharp edges.

For the home enthusiast, the number of body hammers necessary may be as few as two, this is usually determined by what is on the opposite end of the head from the flat surface just described. The combination hammer is the most common, and may include a slightly smaller, more rounded head, or a picking end. The rounded head is great for working out raised sections of metal without a backup dolly, and the picking head is used to raise stubborn low spots.

Under no circumstances should a carpenter's or claw hammer be used for metal working. It's head is rounded to help prevent bending a nail if it is struck off-square. Using it on sheetmetal will only tend to give you stretched round areas.

DOLLIES

Dolly blocks come in every possible shape and size, but the most common are the general-purpose; low-crown general-purpose; heel; and toe. The general-purpose dolly is often nicknamed the railroad dolly because it is shaped something like a piece of railroad track, with a variety of curves. The low-crown, general-purpose dolly has a flatter main working face, better suited to working flatter panels. When working in narrow confines, the special designs of the heel and toe dollies come into play because they are thinner. These dollies have sharp edges for working flanges.

A dolly can be used as a handle-less hammer. Watch a good body man at work and note how he will strike a low dent from the back with a dolly during the hammer and dolly phase. This raises a low spot so the hammer work will be effective as the dent is being raised. A dolly is not an anvil. That is, it is not intended as a place to smash the sheetmetal. Instead, it serves to raise metal with its working face, whether struck directly by the hammer or from a nearby blow. The correct dolly will weigh about three times as much as the hammer, and when used by a good body man, the dolly/hammer com-

3

4

5

3. All bodywork procedures are not limited to hammers, dollies and sanders. Weatherstrip adhesives are used for bonding weatherstrip to doors, trunks, trim, etc.

4. Bear's spray undercoat in aerosol can is used effectively for rust prevention and sound deadening of underparts of door panels, fenders, decks and hood panels.

5. Most specialized body tools come in a variety of shapes and sizes, and the body files are not exceptions. Some are steel, like a machinist's file but with far more widely spaced teeth, while others accept long strips of very coarse sandpaper.

Metalworking

bination is hard to beat for near perfect surface finishing.

SPOONS

If the enthusiast contemplates any kind of extended body repair or modification, a selection of spoons is desirable. A spoon is a bar of steel, forged flatter and thinner on one or both ends. It may be bent in a number of shapes, with the forged end serving as a working face to use against the metal. A spoon can serve as a means of spreading the force of a hammer blow over a large area, as a dolly block where access to the inner face of the panel is limited, and as a prying or driving tool.

When working on badly damaged panels, or when modifying panels such as in customizing, the pry or pick tool is an invaluable ally. When inner panels restrict access to a panel area, the pry or pick can be inserted and used to push metal around slightly.

ROUGHING THE METAL

The initial step of any body repair after disassembly of destroyed pieces is roughing the metal into shape. This first step will be followed by bumping (hammer and dolly work) and finishing (filing and grinding). Aligning is also part of the repair and is usually included with roughing, but it is so full of tricks that we have treated it separately in another chapter.

Repair of sheetmetal is something like building a house in that each step builds upon those taken previously, with a mistake made at first likely to be magnified several times at the finish. With automotive bodies, roughing means bringing the particular piece of sheetmetal back into general contour, including supporting members and reinforcements. When a panel is being roughed into shape, it may have force applied by using a hammer and dolly, by pushing with a jack, or pulling with a jack. Sometimes a combination of these methods will be required, or all three may be involved.

The vital importance of initial roughing cannot be over-emphasized, since the newcomer to bodywork will have less tendency to make mistakes if the roughing is reasonably successful. The cardinal rule is to always pull if possible, and never push or hammer major damage unless absolutely necessary.

Once the rough shape has been attained and the panel at least looks like part of an automobile, the second and third phases of repair start. This begins with the hammer and dolly, two hand tools that can easily be misused if the workman is not careful.

1

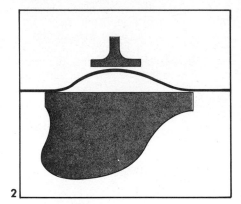

2

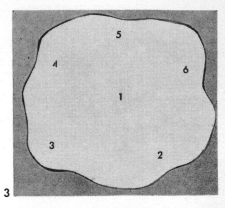

3

While the dolly can be used as a hammer, it is primarily used in conjunction with a hammer in both the hammer-on and hammer-off methods.

HAMMER-ON TECHNIQUE

When the neophyte begins to learn metal work, the hammer-on method seems the most difficult. This entails placing the dolly behind the panel and striking it through the metal. It is very difficult at first, but can be mastered with brief experience. It is advisable to practice hammer and dolly coordination on a discarded piece of metal before attempting an actual repair.

At first the force of the hammer blow on the dolly is not nearly so important as hitting the dolly at all. It is important to learn a technique wherein the hammer hits with just the right amount of force, time after time. Further, the hammer is allowed to "bounce back." That is, the dolly should remain in constant contact with the metal, with the hammer rebounding from the blow. Improper

use of the hammer and dolly can be expected at first, with the hammer striking the metal, causing the dolly to bounce away and restrike the backside of the metal. The dolly will bounce away slightly when the hammer is used properly, or snapped with a definite wrist action, but it will not be a pronounced "limp-wrist" bounce.

The hammer-on technique is especially effective for raising a low point in metal, as the hammer first tends to flatten the metal being struck. This is followed by the reaction of the dolly as it slightly rebounds from the hammer blow. If the hand holding the dolly increases its pressure, then the tendency of the dolly to raise the low spot also increases.

It is advisable to use the hammer-on technique sparingly until the body man knows just about how much the metal can be expected to "stretch" during the operation. It is not entirely correct to say the metal stretches during hammer-on work, but this is the common body shop term. At any rate, too much use of the hammer-on technique will cause the beginner to end up with too much metal in the right places.

HAMMER-OFF TECHNIQUE

In the hammer-off technique, the dolly is placed adjacent to the hammer blow, but not directly under it. Learning the hammer-off style is easy after learning the hammer-on. The spot struck by the hammer drives the metal down, since it is not being supported by the dolly. Movement of the metal transfers the hammer-blow force to the dolly, making it rebound the same as with the hammer-on technique. The effect is to drive the low spot up (from dolly force) and the high spot down (from hammer force) with a single hammer blow.

1. This fender has been repaired with a plastic filler, which rises slightly above adjacent metal, and is being cut down to contour with a 36 grit Openkote Blue-Bak disc.

2. Shrinking with heat is an essential of bodywork. For shrinking high spot, metal is heated and backed with dolly, hammer is applied on the high spot itself.

3. This is the sequence for heated high spot to be struck with the hammer, using light blows. Work around edges more than middle.

4. How off-dolly work straightens a damaged high-crown fender.

5. Shrinking a low spot starts with heat, then a blow from behind with dolly. High spots are worked off-dolly as shown, then on-dolly.

6. Shown is hammer-on dolly versus hammer-off dolly technique.

When using the hammer-off technique, the hammer blow should always be on the high metal adjacent to the low spot, never anywhere else! Learning to "see" with the hand palm is part of metal work experience, and feeling to locate the low and high parts of the damage becomes a natural reaction. The dolly should be of the high-crown type, or the portion used should have minimum contact with the metal, and hammer blows should be just enough. Too much hammer effort will cause extra damage. Normally the dolly would be about ¼-inch away from the hammer blow, depending upon the metal "springiness."

The bumping spoons are used differently than dollies in that they are really methods of spreading out the force of the hammer blow. They are used to straighten long, smooth buckles. There is a paradox in the type of spoon to be used with a particular panel, in that a high-crown or combination panel needs a very low-crown or flat spoon, and a low-crown panel needs a high-crown spoon. This is so because the high-crowned panels are stiff and need lots of force spread over quite an area for straightening purposes. The low-crown buckle has springy metal on either side, so the force should be concentrated directly on the buckle.

When using a spoon, place the center directly over the area to be worked, then strike with a ball-peen or similar hammer. Never use the body hammer. Grip the spoon only lightly to allow the spoon face to conform to the panel. If the spoon is gripped too tightly the hammer blow

force will be transferred to an edge, causing damaging marks at that point. Move the spoon over the entire buckled area, striking it with the hammer as it is placed in a new spot, starting as far from the main damage as there is sign of distortion. A common mistake is trying to use the bumping spoon on too sharp a buckle. If this is the case, the area must be roughed into near shape and finished off with the spoon.

Unlike the bumping spoon, the body spoon is used like a dolly, held behind the metal being hammered. It is really just a form of dolly for getting into very tight places or for prying, and should not be used as a dolly substitute if the latter can be used. The body spoon can be left in the toolbox until the hammer and dolly are mastered.

PRY BAR

Another tool the beginner should understand, but does not necessarily need at first is the pry bar. A pry tool is used when the damaged area cannot be reached from the inside, such as the lower portion of a door panel. A prying tool is usually considered a kind of last resort, because the surface will always be roughened. When using a pry bar, avoid too much force; it is better to work up the area with a series of low force pries than with a single pry that may raise a bump. The problem with the bump distortion is that it may grind down too thin (or even clear through). Go slow with pry tools!

FINISHING

After the hand tools have been

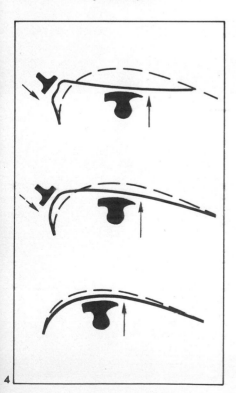

4

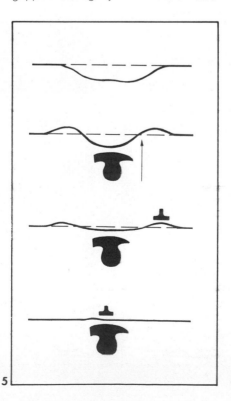

5

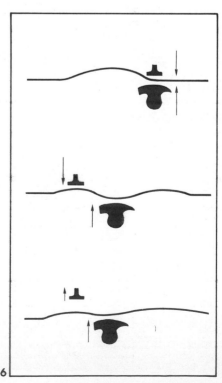

6

Metalworking

used to straighten a damaged section, the metal must be finished preparatory to painting. In bodywork, metal finishing means restoration of final surface smoothness after straightening has been carried as far as practical. This means that areas which are still too low (or too high) can be picked up or lowered—whichever is necessary.

The file and disc sander are the two prime tools of metal finishing. The beginner should become thoroughly familiar with the file first, since it does not work as fast as the sander, and consequently will not make as great a mistake. For the budding customizer, the file should become extremely familiar, as it is an integral part of any professional customizer's bag of tricks.

FILES

Body files are usually fitted with flat, 14-inch blades, with the wooden file holder preferable. Metal file holders are available, some with adjustable blade surface. The beginner who

contemplates extended bodywork in a customizing vein should also equip himself with files of various shapes that will conform to the sometimes odd curves he will be working.

When a file is used correctly, the many cutting blades down its length remove minor surface irregularities. When a file is drawn over a freshly straightened surface, the blades will cut on the high or level spots and leave the low spots untouched. So, the file becomes a sort of tattle-tale straightedge.

The file should always be moved in the general direction of the flattest crown of the panel in order to show up the greatest imperfection in the panel. At the same time, the file must be shifted to one side slightly during the stroke to get maximum area coverage. During the filing stroke, the area covered will not be as long as the file, usually, and several inches wide. At the same time, the blade is curved very slightly so that the stroke starts with the front of the blade in metal contact and ends with the rear. But customizers can take note that a perfectly flat file can be used to en-

sure maximum smoothness of a panel. The flat file will cut slower, but the finished job is better.

After the file has been passed over a straightened area, any excessively high spots will show up as sharp cuts from the file and should be worked more. Usually, however, the appearance will be of low spots spread throughout the filed area. These spots can be lifted with any blunt-ended tool, but the best is the pick hammer. Here is where the home body man can do an excellent job—or get into serious trouble and ruin a panel.

Coming under the heading of a file, but actually a tool that uses coarse sandpaper as a cutting medium, is a relatively new piece of equipment called an air file. It works off air pressure and will run up to 3500 strokes per minute, with each stroke ½-inch long and moving straight back and forth. Different sandpaper platens are available; one with both shoulders "hard," another with one "soft" for use in tight, concave areas.

PICK HAMMERS

It is very difficult to "hit where you

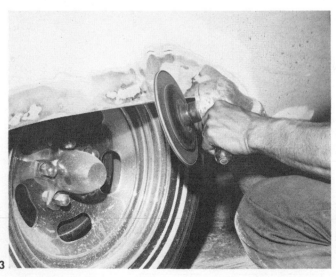

1

2

3

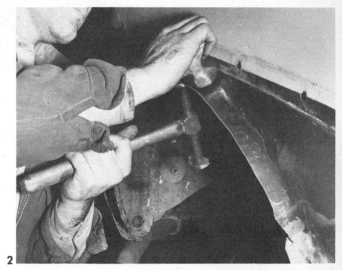

4

6

7

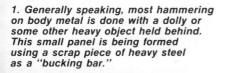

5

1. Generally speaking, most hammering on body metal is done with a dolly or some other heavy object held behind. This small panel is being formed using a scrap piece of heavy steel as a "bucking bar."

2. The all-purpose dolly is just that; its many curves and shapes provide a back-up for just about any shape that can be found on a car.

3. A rotary sander is lighter than a body grinder; hence, it's used during pre-painting steps. Here one is being used to featheredge a paint edge and smooth down filler used during repair.

4. Vixen file has rows of saw-like teeth, instead of individual teeth. It actually shaves metal off the high spots. It's being used here to take the "highs" off a heavy frame member to be used on a street/show car.

5. Remember the assortment of pry bars shown on a previous page? Here's where such things are used. Dent in this car's quarter panel couldn't be reached from behind due to interference of inner structural members, so hole is poked up through inner wheel house and pry bar is then inserted so damage can be worked out.

6. It is often convenient to lightly dust a coat of primer over a damaged area, then file surface so that high and low spots needing more rework are easily visible. But, real pro with "educated" hands could "see" the same thing by running palm over area.

7. Fillers, like the plastics and lead (also referred to as body solder), are handy for filling a dent where it cannot be reached from behind. This fix-it method is discussed in detail in another chapter of this book.

look" when learning to pick up low spots. Since the pick hammer is being driven toward the user and is out of sight behind the panel, the normal reaction is to hit below the desired spot and often off to the left side. Learning to use a pick hammer is a matter of practice, but the way to begin is to bring the hammer into view at first, then move it up to about where the low spot should be. A good guide to keep the hammer working in the same spot is to rest the arm on an available piece of metal, which will keep the hammer from wandering during use.

Start with a gentle tap to the metal and see where the blow lands. It may be difficult to locate this spot at first, so lay the flattened hand against the metal as a guide. The small bump can usually be felt and the pick adjusted to then hit the low spots. Low spots will feel like high spots on the inside of the panel, so the pick head can be rubbed against the metal to locate the spot if the touch is sensitive. As with the pry bar, go easy and slow with the pick hammer, as too much metal can be hammered up.

Use a blunt pick unless the area to be lifted is very small, then a sharp pick may be desired. In any case, it is possible to create a pick dolly which will limit metal displacement.

These dollies are not normally sold in stores but we have seen several being used by customizers. After the area has been picked up lightly, use the file again. Repeat the pick and file operation until the damaged surface is smooth.

DISC SANDER

Any hot rodder worth his salt will consider a disc sander an invaluable part of the toolbox. This is one of the most versatile of power tools, and fills the need for a lightweight, heavy-duty grinder on the toughest of jobs. Good used sanders can often be purchased at very low prices from a body shop with newer equipment. Often, broken sanders require only minor repairs, and can be bought at bargain prices.

The sanding discs are fiber discs coated on one side with an abrasive grit, usually an aluminum oxide. The grit size is identified by number. Disc size refers to the disc diameter, with 7 and 9-1/8 inches the common sizes, smaller discs being made by cutting down the larger units.

Grit size is designated by a number, such as #34 or #36, etc., and refers to the size of screen which the grit will pass through. These discs are available in open- or closed-coat types, with the open-coat discs commonly used as paint removers. The

Metalworking

closed-coat discs have a heavier layer of abrasive for heavy-duty use in metal grinding. The open- and closed-coat discs are available in glue bonding only, as the resin-bonded discs come in a single style.

Grit size determines how the disc will be used, with the coarse #16 selected for paint removal and coarse cutting. A #24 disc is most commonly used as an all-around grit since it will cut paint and finish off the metal smoothly. However, a #36 grit is better for finishing.

A professional body man will use the disc sander as a file substitute, but the beginner should not. At any rate, the sander is intended as both a substitute and as a method of finishing off the rough file marks. Learning to use a disc sander on sheetmetal is a skill not easily picked up, but seldom forgotten.

When using the sander rather than a file, the disc is run across the surface at such an angle that the grit swirl marks will bridge across the low spots. This allows the low spots to stand out as with the file, and is accomplished by moving the sander back and forth across the panel following the flat direction of the panel as with the file. The sander is held so that the disc approaches the metal at an angle, and pressure applied to cause the disc pad to flex slightly. This will produce the best cutting action but the sander motor will not be loaded so much it will slow down. During the side-to-side strokes, the

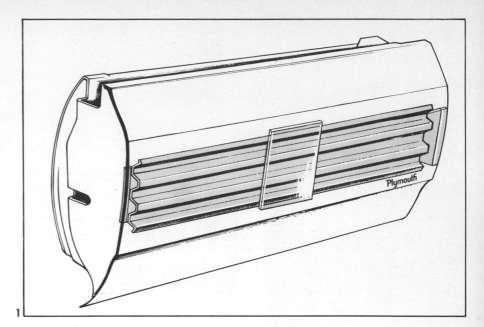

1

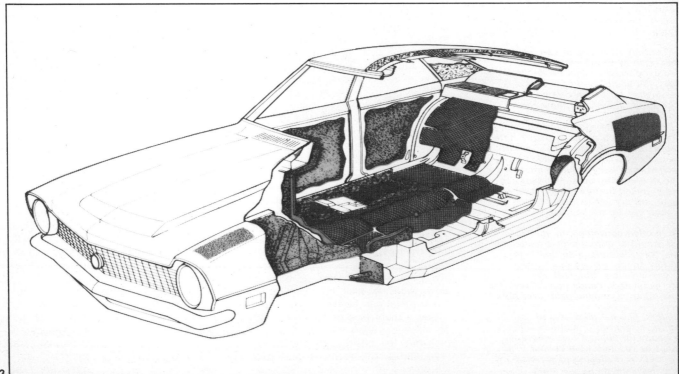

2

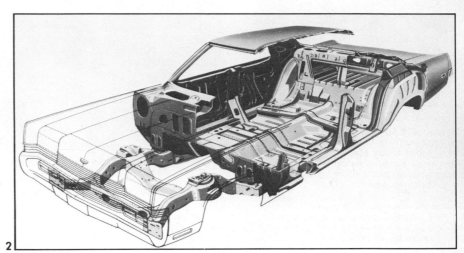

3

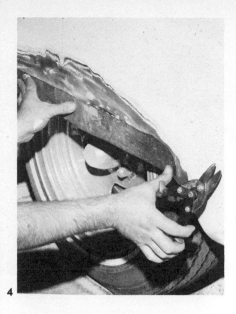

1. The safety precautions being taken by Detroit will result in increasing difficulty for the body man. Here's a Chrysler Corp. example of side impact structure for '73 Satellites and Valiants. Some models have an increase in door weight of up to 25 lbs. A small dent in outer door panel directly behind this beam will probably be filled with plastic or lead due to difficulty of access with this interfering member.

2. By their very nature, automobile bodies are very complex. Most outer panels today are double-thickness for body strength, especially in the case of a unit-construction car without a supporting frame. However, advanced body fabrication techniques produce consistently uniform openings for doors, deck lid, etc., which will gladden the heart of many an old-time metal man when it comes to repairs.

3. The trend today is toward quieter cars, usually accomplished through increased amounts of sound deadening material. Cutaway of '73 Maverick body shows where blanket-like material is applied, and which must be peeled back or scraped off when damage necessitates hammer and dolly work.

4. Rusted-out areas are the bane of a body man's existence, yet automobile fabrication, materials, and techniques have yet to cope with salted roads in winter. One "popular" rust-out area is around wheelwells where salt collects in the rolled-under panel edge. Since rust "grows" like cancer, filler cannot be applied right over it and be expected to adhere for the rest of the car's life. Solution is to cut offending area away, form a replacement piece from sheetmetal.

5. New piece of panel is brazed in place, area ground down to eliminate old paint, weld scale, then a coating of plastic filler is squeegeed on.

6. When the material has set up, it can be shaved with a carrot grater-like file to bring it to desired contour. This kind of work is detailed in another chapter, and while it was once frowned upon, it is now being accepted as normal bodyworking practice and technique is being taught in bodyworking shops and trade schools.

sander is tilted first to one side and then to the other. That is, when going toward the right, the left side of the disc is working; when moving back to the left, the sander is twisted slightly and the right side of the disc is working. Moving the sander this way will cause a criss-cross pattern which will show the low spots better.

If there has been considerable metal work involved in an area, it is advisable to go over the area with a file after the sander has been used. This is a final check for low spots and is particularly suited to the beginner.

After the area is smooth, a #50 or #60 grit disc can be installed on the sander and the metal buffed. While the sander follows the flattest plane of the panel, usually lengthwise with the car, the buffing is done across the greatest crown, usually up and down. The sander is not tilted on the edge quite so much, so that a much larger part of the pad contacts the metal surface during a stroke. The final buffing cuts down the deeper scratches of coarse discs or a file and is a preliminary to the painting operations.

When using the sander around a reverse-crown area, it is advisable to cut the disc into a "star" shape. The round disc edge will have a tendency to dig into the reverse crown, while the floppier corners of a star-shaped disc will follow the crown contour. A disc may have any number of points, depending upon how severe the reverse crown is, but as a guide, the more severe the crown, the more points on the disc.

Never use the disc sander without some kind of eye protection. Although the flow of particles may be away from the face, they can and do glance off other surfaces and can cause serious eye damage. Also be careful how the sander is handled, as

the disc will cut a nasty wound in a leg or arm. Be especially careful when resting the sander on the leg during work, as the disc can wind-up loose clothing (such as coveralls) rapidly.

SHRINKING

As far as the body man is concerned, shrinking really means the use of heat from an oxygen-acetylene torch to soften metal for a specified upset. A propane tank without oxygen will not give enough heat. When an area is being shrunk, a spot—or group of spots—is heated and worked with a dolly and hammer, then cooled. While shrinking looks easy, it is a precision job and requires more "feel" than ordinary bodywork.

Damage at any part of a car body may require shrinking to some degree, but it is usually more prevalent in the low-crown sections, such as door and quarter panels, top and hood.

Stretched metal will have an increase in surface area, either in length, width or both. In collision damage, the stretched area may be confined to a rather small section, and may show as either a depression or bulge in the panel. If a large section of the panel is stretched, it is usually advisable to replace the entire panel.

A panel can have a false stretch which is easily confused with a true stretch because the false stretch will tend to "oil can" or have a raised hump. A false stretch will always be smooth and unworked and next to an area that has been upset; the raises are being caused by the gathering effect of the upset. A false stretch is usually found around the reinforced edge of doors, hoods and deck lids where there has been a rolled buckle and the upset has not been relieved completely. Beating out a stiff buckle

Metalworking

which should be straightened under tension is a typical cause of false stretch.

When an area of sheetmetal undergoes the shrinking operation, the high crown, or bulge, must be upset to bring the bulge back down to its original contour. If a bulge is struck cold, the hammer force is transmitted out through the metal toward the edges and little or no effect is usually noted. However, as the bulge is heated the metal at the hot spot will tend to upset readily. When the heat is first applied, the bulge will grow noticeably, but will return to the bulge shape as the metal cools. If the metal is upset while the spot is still hot, the metal will shrink to a state smaller than the bulge. Of course, the hot spot will tend to begin cooling as soon as the torch is removed, so hammer and dolly application must be immediate. The hammer does not drive the bulge completely away, leaving a perfectly level surface while the metal is still hot. If this were to happen, the metal would be overshrunk as it cooled.

The rate at which the metal cools will have an effect on the total shrink; therefore it is possible to use a sponge or wet rag as part of the

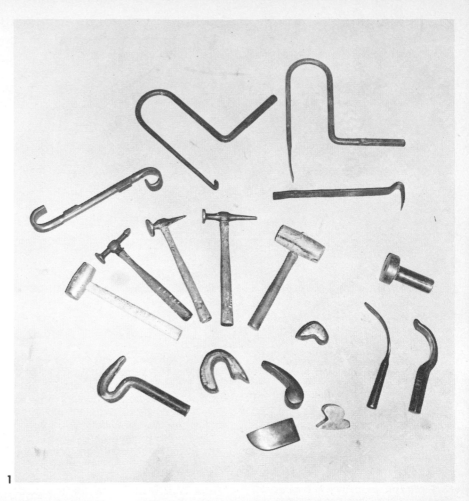

1

2

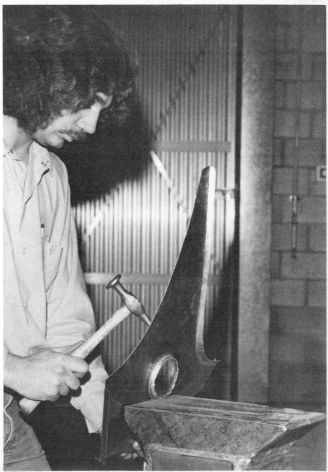

3

shrinking procedure. If the heated spot is cooled faster than normal, more of the upset can be retained. That is, the shrinking can be more effective if the metal is quenched immediately after working with hammer and dolly. The rapid cooling stops the yield of the heated area to contraction-tension, but must be done while the metal is still quite hot (the water will steam on metal contact). It will take a little experience to learn when and when not to use quenching. If the metal appears to be approaching the original contour during the hammer and dolly work, chances are that little or no quenching will be necessary. If the area receives too much quenching, buckles will often appear in the surrounding panel and must be worked out with the hammer.

When an area is overshrunk, this will have a puckering effect on the surrounding metal. If an area has been overshrunk, some hammer-on dolly technique will often stretch the spot just enough to relieve the stress. Space the hammer blows well over the area and do not apply heavy pressure to the dolly from the back side. As the hammer strikes the metal it will tend to spread it just enough to compensate for the overshrinking.

A gouge in a door or quarter-panel is typical of the type of shrinking job the metal man will encounter frequently. Shrinking a gouge is similar to shrinking raised metal, but it is done from the backside. The customizer is well acquainted with shrinking raised surfaces, for they are quite common when installing top panels in older cars, chopping tops or making section cuts, or radiusing wheel cutouts. The gouge is more common in

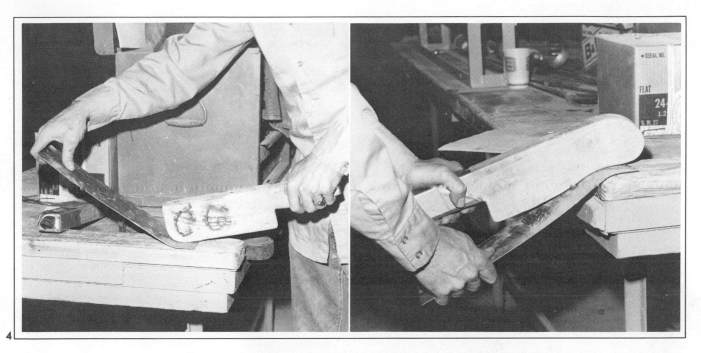

4

1. As an amateur bodyman, you won't need every tool we have pictured here, but all of them serve a purpose for the pro who must work on many types of cars. From the top we have various pry bars, rubber mallets and steel body hammers; several shapes of dollies, and (lower right) spoons.

2. Pry bars have many uses, and are often used in conjunction with other tools, such as here where a wooden block gives the pry bar leverage in pulling out this fenderwell lip.

3. A good anvil, either homemade or store-bought, can be an invaluable aid in working on panels that you can remove from the car. A good anvil has a different angle on each edge for hammering shapes into sheetmetal.

4. Not all bodyworking tools need be expensive or elaborate. You can often make a tool from wood which, while not a long-lasting one, will do the job you want because you can make it any shape you need and use it as a dolly or hammer; or one of each.

5. Gene Winfield of the Traditional Coach Works, Chatsworth, Calif., is using one of the more elaborate tools for metalworking: a plemishing hammer. It has various dies for the hammers which can put into a panel a compound curve that by hand would take several hours.

5

Metalworking

collision repair and the stretch tends to be more severe and concentrated in a smaller area.

When shrinking a gouge, the dolly must supply the force to upset the metal from the backside. A small gouge can be bumped out from the back and then shrunk as a raised bulge, but this is limited to very small damages. The more common gouge will require use of the hammer and dolly as follows: The gouge is heated to above 1400°F., or good and red, which will deepen the gouge. The dolly is used as a hammer from the backside, knocking the gouge outward at the deepest point and driving the metal adjacent to the gouge higher than the original contour. The dolly is then held hard against the low point and the hammer used in a hammer-off technique to drive down the surrounding high metal. When the gouge is very close to the original contour, the hammer should then be used directly against the dolly to relieve some of the stress that might cause overshrinking.

A small gouge is usually removed with one or two heatings; a long gouge may require a number of heatings down its length as the hammer and dolly work progresses. Usually, quenching is not needed for a gouge shrink.

Learning to get the proper heat application will be the hardest part of shrinking for the novice, as heat requirements will differ with each type of shrink. The problem is getting just the right amount of heat in just the right size and spot. If a large bulge is involved, the heat should be spread out, but not necessarily red hot. Sheetmetal will begin to soften where the first color begins to form, so the large bulge can be shrunk very well (the upset will be considerable) when the metal just begins to turn blue. On large areas the shrinking spots may be spaced out over a wide pattern, but the temperature should be kept relatively low.

In a severely stretched area, such as a gouge, the temperature must be higher, usually to the bright red range, and must be concentrated in small areas. Several of these bright red heatings may be necessary in a typical gouge. Incidentally, much of the crease in a minor gouge can be removed without heat, but requires the hammer-off dolly technique, with the hammer striking very close to a high-crowned dolly. Keep heavy pressure on the dolly and tap both sides of the crease lightly for an inch or so. Then tap the crease directly over the dolly for an equal space, and again revert to the hammer-off technique. Slapping the crease in this way will remove most of the damage rapidly.

Shrinking is not difficult to master, but it definitely requires patience and practice. After a few gouges have been attempted with success, the be-

ginner will learn to remove much of the gouge with one heat application and rapid use of hammer and dolly.

INSPECTING THE DAMAGE

There is much that can be learned about a damaged panel during the initial inspection, and the following hints will apply to all types of collision damage. First, locate the point, or points, of initial impact. Then decide if there are two or more points of impact. If so, are they equal or is there a significant major impact point with others secondary? How are the secondary areas of impact related to each other, and will repair of any area be related to the others? Should any specific area be repaired first? When looking at a collision damage, categorize the type of damage involved (buckles, displaced metal, etc.) and then decide how each will be best repaired.

Obviously, proceeding with a repair plan without some kind of organization will be chaotic, something a beginning customizer soon learns. For this reason, the best way to go after the inspection is to decide where to start, and whether the repair should be roughed out by driving, pushing or pulling. Thought must be given as to what the panel or area will look like after the initial roughing, and which panel should be repaired next. After some kind of organized plan is formulated, the problems of doing the job are quickly dispatched.

1

WHAT KIND OF JOBS TO TACKLE

To the beginning body man, whether he plans on making a simple repair or an extensive modification, the question of just how big a job to tackle invariably crops up in the light of reality after the initial glow of enthusiasm subsides. It is one thing to dream of building a radical custom or restoring a damaged car, and quite another to actually do the work successfully. Still, because bodywork is a step-by-step proposition, whether straightening a fender or making a custom grille, the average enthusiast can expect to achieve at least acceptable results if he plans well and takes time with the work. Unlike building a high-performance engine, the hot rodder chopping a top can see immediate results as he progresses with the job.

The beginner can chop a top or section a passenger car, or even repair a very badly wrecked vehicle if he has the patience to stick with the job. There are no particular areas he cannot do, at least reasonably well, but it is suggested that some amount of practice be included before a major customizing or repair job is attempted. For instance, learning how to form metal takes practice, but much of this experience can be gained in straightening bent metal. Any customizing job is going to require the use of both lead and plastic fillers, items well known to many repair jobs. Therefore, before a major repair job or customizing project is begun, take the time to make several repairs. There will be plenty of little jobs available, on friends' and relatives' cars. With some minor experience, don't be afraid to branch off into greater challenges.

Who knows, maybe you will become the next great customizer. At the least, you will have learned the rudiments of a valuable new skill. 🦀

1. Gene demonstrates the use of the "English roller," which although it doesn't hammer the metal, can roll a curve into metal because of the shape of the dies that the metal rides in.

2. Edges of panels can be curved in quick fashion with this tool, which by the action of the foot-operated jaws can stretch or shrink the edge. This is very handy for putting a curve into the edge of a rolled panel.

3. Another edge tool that is often used in body and sheetmetal shops is the Pexto roller. With different dies in the end, you can roll lips and stiffening ribs in sheetmetal edges.

4. A Beverly shear is a fixture in most any sheetmetal shop. It makes long straight trims of sheetmetal a lot easier than with hand shears.

Welding and Brazing

Light your fire and burn through welding basics in a hurry.

Whether you're building or rebuilding a car at home, or just like to dabble in plain bodywork or customizing, there are perhaps two pieces of equipment that belong in your garage. The first item is an oxyacetylene welding and cutting outfit. This tool is a must if you plan to do any bodywork. If you plan to do any chassis work, then you'll need a good shop-type arc welder.

While both of these products cost in the neighborhood of $100 each new, they shouldn't be beyond the means of most of us. Sure, you have probably gotten along without them in the past, but at what cost and inconvenience? How many times did you have to drive across town to get some work done, at someone else's convenience? The money and time you have probably blown over the years could have been well spent on buying your own welding rigs. The answer is clear that the opportunities to do so much of your own work, at a tremendous savings, is present ev-

eryday. Not only that, but you can do work for your friends, friends that aren't as enterprising as yourself.

Say you can find the means to come up with the money to buy your own welding outfits. What then? The next step naturally is to learn how to use them. Many high schools and colleges offer shop classes that teach welding, in both day and night classes. I've seen instances where private businesses also teach welding; for a fee, of course. There is, therefore, little reason why an interested person should not be able to learn how to weld. As a last resort, one can also learn by reading books on the subject, or even articles such as this. But regardless where you learn the basics, you must *practice* to attain the skill necessary to become a good welder.

Two manufacturers of arc welders also provide both beginning and advanced classes in gas or arc welding. For further information and free literature regarding classes, locations

and rates, you might contact Lincoln Electric Company, Attn: Richard Sobo, 22801 St. Clair Avenue, Cleveland, Ohio 44117, and Hobart Brothers Company, Attn: Harry Prestanski, Hobart Square, Troy, Ohio 45373.

When it comes to doing body work on any car, the accepted method of joining sheet metal together is with oxy-acetylene welding utilizing a steel filler rod. When steel rod is used, the body metal is actually fused together. Some bodymen prefer to braze-weld sheel metal panels together because less heat is required, and therefore there is less chance of panel warpage. However, in most instances, brazing is referred to as "hard" soldering, as it merely bonds the metal together (like glue), rather than fusing it together. One brazing rod that I'm familiar with is known for its super holding ability. It is Chemetron's All-State No. 101 general purpose silver brazing rod. There are other brands on the market similar to it, and they all work great.

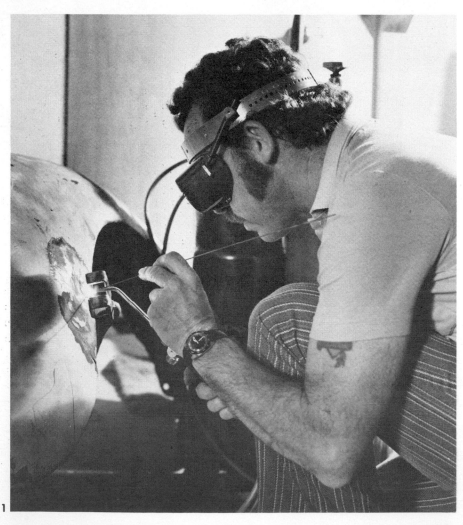

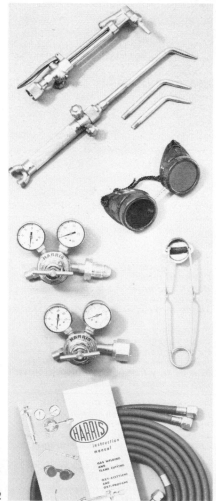

1

2

3

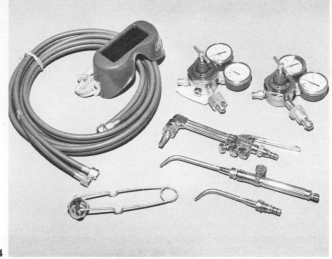

4

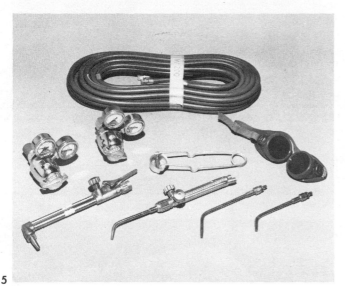

5

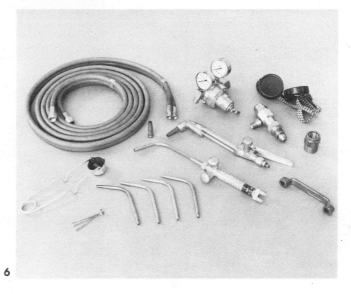

6

1. To really do professional-quality bodywork at home, or build specialty projects, you need welding equipment. A basic gas welding setup to start is an investment you'll never regret.

2. The Harris Calorific Co. offers a full line of oxyacteeylene welding and cutting outfits. This is one of their better sets, which features brass parts in torch and regulators.

3. This Sears Craftsman two-stage set is one of their best. It comes with siamese hose, regulators, a cutting head, welding tips, torch handle, goggles, striker, all-purpose wrench and a set of instructions.

4. Here is one of Smith's welding/cutting outfits without the extras; though other tips, etc. are available.

5. Purox Division of Union Carbide offers the amateur welder a line of welding/cutting outfits, too. This set is ideal because it's lightweight.

6. This Airco Handicrafter set comes with a full line of tips. A heating tip is in the torch, and is used for most heating (for bending, etc.) of plate and tubing. A pre-set regulator is furnished for the acetylene tank, so that only oxygen need be regulated.

GAS WELDING SETS

Because of its great versatility, an oxy-acetylene welding outfit should have priority over an arc welder if you feel you can't manage purchasing both at the same time. There are quite a few different brands on the market today, with prices for a basic starter set ranging from below $100 up to around $200. Generally, a welding set will include a pair of oxygen and acetylene regulators that attach to the cylinders—or bottles as they are often referred to—in addition to a welding torch and a few tips (sometimes a cutting torch or cutting attachment are included in the set); fuel and oxygen hose, goggles and striker for lighting the torch. Some sets are available with a number of optional welding and cutting tips, in addition to heating tips designed for heating metal plate and tubing. About the only other items one would want to buy would be tip cleaners and welding gloves.

Oxygen and acetylene cylinders come in different sizes, and the size you should select will depend upon your needs.

Depending upon where you live and the welding supply dealer with whom you do business, you will normally find three options open to you. One, you can buy a set of cylinders outright, with price and size depending on the dealer. Two, you can lease a set of cylinders under a plan called a lifetime lease. You might have to pay $100 for this lease, in addition to the cost of the contents each time the cylinders are refilled. You can use these cylinders personally for 5, 10, 20 years or whatever, but usually 20 years may be figured as the lifetime limit. If at any time during this period you wish to return the cylinders, you'll get part of your lease fee back, pro-rated over the period you used them. Or, you can "sell" your lease to a friend, who will pay you for your "un-used" time remaining on the lease, though you must make it official with the leasing agency by getting his name on the documents as new leasee: otherwise you will be held responsible for the cylinders.

Welding and Brazing

The third option open to you is to pay for the contents (oxygen and acetylene) of a pair of cylinders and use them on a sort of borrowing plan. If you use the contents before one month is up, you return the cylinders for a re-fill, again paying for the contents. But, if you retain them for more than one month without having them re-filled, then you pay what is called demurrage for each day the cylinders are used until they are again re-filled. The demurrage fee varies, but it may be as much as 8¢ per day per cylinder, or a total of 16¢ per day. This is like a rental fee on the cylinders for each day you keep them over 30 days without re-filling. A few days of demurrage won't hurt anyone, but if it takes you a couple of months to use a set of bottles, it may be cheaper to get a smaller set or lease them.

Oxygen cylinders are very high strength cylinders because of the very high pressures involved. A standard-size cylinder may have as much as 2200 psi pressure at 70°F., a pressure that will increase if the cylinder is located near a heat source (heater, furnace, etc.) or parked out in the hot sun. So beware! Keep this cylinder cool, and be safe. The bottle is topped by a bronze shut-off valve with a safety device to release pressure under emergency conditions. One of the regulator gauges on the oxygen bottle informs you as to how much pressure is remaining in the cylinder at any given time. The other gauge tells you how much pressure is passing through the hose and torch during use, and is regulated by a screw handle on the regulator body.

Always keep in mind that oil and grease are not compatible with oxygen. Just a drop of oil on an oxygen valve can be a source of a fire and/or explosion. Keep in mind that diesel engines operate by highly compressing air (which contains oxygen). One shot of oil into a cylinder full of hot, compressed air is all it takes to cause an explosion, and the same is true with high-pressure oxygen cylinders. So keep all oily rags and oil cans away from the scene of action.

You'll find it impossible to install one of the two pressure regulators on the wrong cylinder because the oxygen regulator features a large nut, whereas the acetylene regulator features a threaded male fitting. The acetylene cylinder is remarkably different from the oxygen cylinder and operates under a lower pressure. Acetylene cylinders are filled with Acetone as well as acetylene, the former to stabilize the acetylene gas, which is highly flammable. For reasons of safety, you should take care

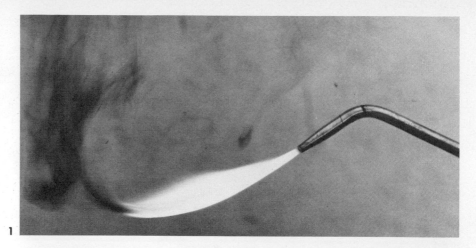

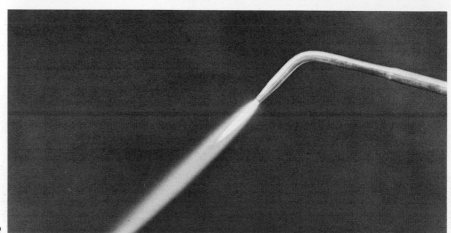

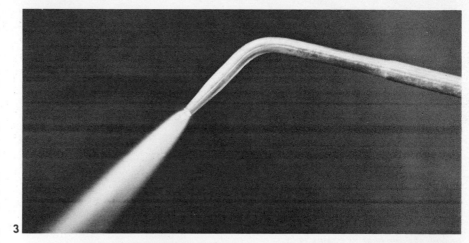

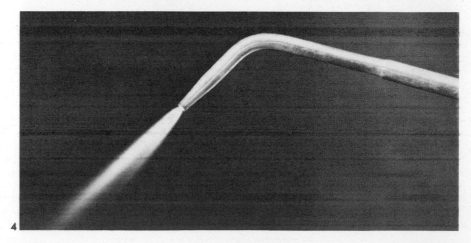

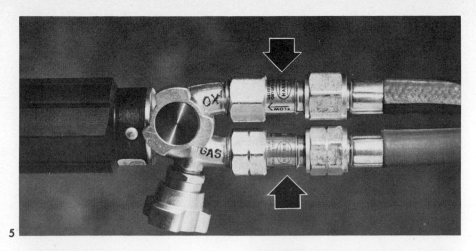

5

6

7

1. *When an acetylene valve is first opened and the flame lit, heavy soot will pour out. Continue opening the valve until soot stops, then start oxygen into the flame for proper mix.*

2. *Some oxygen has been added here, but the flame is still acetylene-rich. Note the flame's long central cone.*

3. *A neutral flame is achieved when the center flame is about ¼-in. to ⅜-in. long. Introduce oxygen until the inner cone just starts to become needle-sharp, then back it off until it is the desired size.*

4. *If you bring the inner cone out to a needle-like point and leave it there, you will have an oxidizing flame which will leave the weld weak. Note how the outer flame is ragged.*

5. *A good investment is a pair of reverse-flow check valves. The units shown here installed between the hose and the torch are Harris Flash Guard valves. They prevent oxygen or acetylene from backing up into the other hose, which could cause an explosion.*

6. *There are several of these solid-oxygen welding setups now available. They use a small tank of propane; and oxygen is supplied by burning pellets in a tray under the box. These are fine for welding/brazing sheetmetal.*

7. *With the cylinder valve opened one turn, the regulator gauges on this acetylene cylinder tell you that there are 230 lbs. of pressure remaining. The pressure valve on the regulator has been turned in (clockwise) until the regulator will permit acetylene to flow through the hose at 7 psi.*

that neither cylinder gets banged around or knocked over, but especially the acetylene cylinder.

Acetylene is easily dissolved into acetone and the acetone is replaced as needed when the cylinder is refilled. You should never use an acetylene cylinder until the regulator shows that the cylinder is void of pressure (and thereby completely empty of acetylene gas), or until the flame refuses to light. If you try to milk the cylinder of every last cubic inch of gas, you may end up drawing acetone through the regulator, hose and torch. This could cause you a heap of trouble, so avoid it.

Some manufacturers fill acetylene cylinders with an inert, porous filler to help reduce shock from rough handling. Because of the acetone, you should never place an acetylene cylinder in any position but vertical. This means don't lay it down when transporting, storing or using it. If a cylinder with regulator attached is placed on its side, some of the acetone can find its way into the regulator and through the torch. Aside from being a dangerous practice, as previously described, it can possibly ruin the seals in both regulator and torch. These cylinders have been known to explode when transported or stored in a horizontal position, so heed our warning: Keep them upright at all times.

Before you consider buying an oxy-

acetylene welding and cutting outfit, make sure the unit you acquire will perform the jobs you will be doing. In other words, don't buy the least expensive set if you're going to be trying heavy welding or cutting; this set may not cut it, literally. If you have any doubts about what you need in the way of equipment, give your job requirements to your welding supply dealer. He should be able to help you make a proper decision.

Here's something else to consider, too: There appears to be a shortage of cylinders in some parts of the country. I've learned from hot rodders in other states that some dealers will not lease or loan you cylinders if you have your own welding or cutting outfit (usually purchased elsewhere), only making cylinders available to you if you buy your welding outfit from them. It might, therefore, be wise to check out all sources of cylinders in your area before you lay out any bucks for a welding outfit, new or used. It pays to be careful!

TORCHWORK BASICS

If you're unfamiliar with oxy-acetylene welding procedures, you might be interested in some basics before you fire up that new torch for the first time. Initially, it takes a very high degree of heat to melt or cut steel, or even metals with a lower melting point. We need a "needle-like" flame which will burn consistently, with its maximum heat concentrated at the tip. Therefore, we use acetylene as fuel, and use pure oxygen to "feed" it. When acetylene is combined with oxygen, it will burn the hottest of all gases (approximately 6000°F.). Acetylene gas is highly flammable, but it is perfectly safe if used with reasonable care. *Never* apply heat to the cylinder, or drop it. *Always* keep the cylinder upright (valve at the top).

Oxygen is not harmful in any way. It can, however, "puff" a tiny spark into a roaring flame—can even cause oily or greasy rags to burst into flame from spontaneous combustion. *Never oil or grease any part of the equipment, the cylinders or the valves— under any circumstances.*

The first step you should take before any attempt at welding is undertaken is to secure your acetylene and oxygen cylinders in their cart, or to a permanent post, etc. This will prevent their being knocked over. After removing the valve protection caps from the cylinders, examine the cylinder valve threads and wipe them clean with a *clean* cloth. Next, slightly open (called "cracking"), then close, both the oxygen and acetylene cylinder valves—to make sure they do not stick and also to blow out any dirt

Welding and Brazing

or moisture that may have lodged in the valves.

Loosen both regulator adjusting screws (turn them counterclockwise) until they turn freely, then install the regulators on their appropriate cylinders, tightening firmly but without force. You can't make a mistake here, as the oxygen regulator is fitted with a female fitting, the acetylene with a male fitting. Standing to one side of the oxygen regulator, open the cylinder valve very *slowly* so the high-pressure gauge needle will move up slowly until full pressure is registered. Now the valve should be opened completely. The acetylene cylinder valve should be opened slowly a *maximum* of one complete turn only. This is so you can turn it off rapidly in the event of any mishap.

Connect the green (oxygen) hose to the outlet of the oxygen regulator. This hose has a right-hand thread connector. If this hose is new, it probably contains talcum powder to protect it in storage. If it's used, it probably contains dust. In either event, before connecting the torch up to the hose, turn the adjusting screw on the oxygen regulator clockwise until a reading of five pounds shows on the low pressure gauge. Allow the oxygen to escape until you are sure the hose is clean.

Connect the fuel hose (red) to the acetylene regulator outlet. This hose

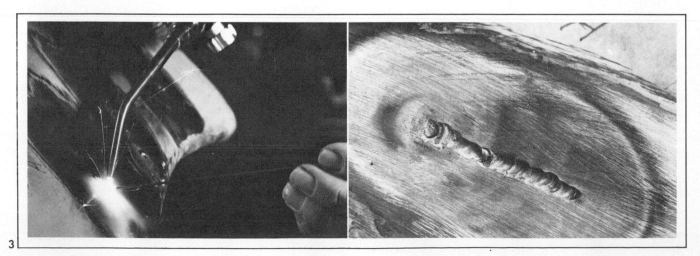

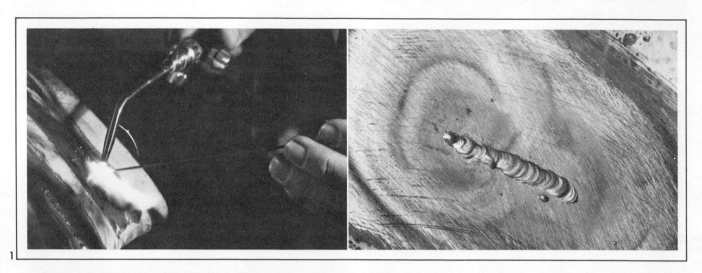

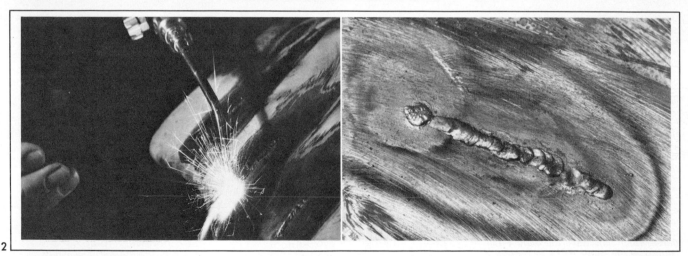

1. *A forehand weld is being applied on this fender. The flame is neutral, with the proper mix of oxygen and acteylene for welding mild steel. The puddles should be uniform.*

2. *An oxygen-rich flame is used here. Such a flame is noted for the sparks it puts out, but the resulting weld is burned, pitted, and weak.*

3. *An acteylene-rich flame is used here, which introduces excess carbon into the weld. This is a carburizing flame, which produces a weak weld, but this type flame is preferred when brazing instead of welding.*

4. *Quite a few books, brochures and catalogs are available from makers of arc welders. They tell you how to arc weld, what's available in their line of equipment; how to select the proper electrode and heat range, etc.*

5. *A cutting torch attachment is a handy tool when you need to cut plate for making engine mounts or for doing frame work. To start a cut, you heat the edge 'til almost molten, then cut in the oxygen with the lever (arrow).*

has left-hand thread connections. Blow out the acetylene hose in the same manner as you did the oxygen hose. Remember that this gas will burn. Keep it away from open flames as you are blowing out the hose. Now you can connect the welding torch to the hoses. In addition to having right-hand threads, the oxygen side will usually be marked "OXY" or "Oxygen," or some similar key. The fuel side of the torch will be marked "FUEL," "ACY," "Acetylene" or some similar marking, and will feature left-hand threads. Select the welding tip size that is recommended for the size job you're doing. Now you can install the tip in the torch, snugly, but not too tight.

LIGHT YOUR FIRE

Let's assume for the sake of illustration, that you wish to weld sheet-

metal 1/32-in. thick. Your welding manual states a size "O" tip is required, and maximum oxygen and acetylene pressure should be at 3 psi. Now partially open the torch oxygen valve and adjust the oxygen regulator until the pressure rises to 3 psi. Close the torch oxygen valve. After being careful that no flame is about, partially open the torch acetylene valve and adjust the regulator pressure to 3 psi; then close the valve. All pressures in welding and cutting charts are flowing pressures with the torch valves open. If you change tip sizes in the middle of a job, and must change pressures, do so with the torch valves open.

You have finally arrived at the point where you can light that fire. Open the torch acetylene valve approximately ½ turn and ignite the acetylene with your striker, pointing the flame away from people, pets, the cylinders or any flammable materials. Keep opening the torch valve until the flame stops excessive smoking and leaves the end of the tip about ⅛-in.; then reduce slightly to bring the flame back to the tip.

Open the torch oxygen valve now until a bright inner cone appears on the flame. The point at which the feathery edges of the flame disappear and a sharp inner cone is visible is called the "neutral flame." Adjust the torch oxygen valve back and forth until you are sure you have a neutral flame. If too much oxygen is flowing, you'll have an "oxidizing flame" that will burn the metal you're trying to weld, making it brittle and weak. It will have a flame that is pale blue in color without the clearly defined inner cone of the "neutral flame." Should you attempt to weld with a flame that is acetylene-rich, you will have a "carburizing flame," distinguished by its long carburizing feather. This is

the flame you have just before reaching the neutral flame. A carburizing flame introduces excess carbon into the metal.

There are two methods one may employ in oxy-acetylene welding: forehand and backhand welding. The forehand method is usually used where you're welding material under ⅛-in. thickness. It is performed by pointing the torch down at an angle, toward the direction that you plan to lay the bead, with the rod preceding the torch. The flame tip preheats the edge of the joint; and the oscillating motion you use with both rod and torch, moving them in semi-circular paths along the joint, will distribute the heat and molten metal uniformly.

In backhand welding, the torch is moved along in front of the rod in the direction of welding, with the flame pointed back toward the molten puddle and completed weld. The end of the welding rod is placed in the flame between the tip and the weld. The torch needs to be moved slowly along the joint in front of the weld puddle, while the rod may be merely rolled from side to side in the puddle. Better fusion between the metals at the root of the weld is normally achieved with this method.

Enough emphasis cannot be placed on the need to achieve full penetration to the bottom of the materials being joined together, and complete fusion along the sides of the joint. Where two pieces are being joined together and the joint is quite long, you must take into consideration the expansion of metals in heating and contraction on cooling. For steel plate being welded together, you should tack the pieces lightly where you are going to begin welding, then space the pieces out on down the joint, figuring about ¼-in. per foot. Tack the two pieces very lightly at frequent int-

Welding and Brazing

ervals. This will hold them in alignment, but still allow closing of the joint. It's what you want.

In the long run, you're going to have to practice, and practice a lot, if you're going to learn how to gas weld. There is no other way out. All the books in the world can't be of assistance if you don't apply yourself. As a guide to get you started on the right foot, listed here are a few good welding rods that you might be interested in, along with their recommended applications.

Chemetron's No. 101 high silver content rod has a tensile strength of 52,000 psi, and a low working temperature of only 1125°-1145°F, making it ideal for sheet metal work. A slight carburizing flame is used with this rod. Relative to arc welding electrodes, *Coor-Alloy 303, Lincoln Fleetweld 37, Hobart 413* and *Arcweld Satinarc 13* are all recommended for welding mild steel. Working with chrome moly? Then consider *Arcweld 351, Hobart LH-4130* or *LH-4340, All-State No. 275* and *Lincoln Jetweld LH-70* should fill the bill. Welding supply centers carry electrode and welding rod guides. Ask them.

SOLID-FUEL WELDING

Just by chance you may be interested in *brazing* metals together with brass fill rod rather than fusion welding with steel, and don't care to purchase a complete gas welding rig. Well, the answer to your dilemma could be one of the solid oxygen sets available at many welding shops, parts stores, etc. These outfits are much smaller than common oxy-acetylene welding setups, and cost somewhat less. Like any other welding outfit, though, you must read the instructions and use regulated pressures according to the tip size you're using for a specific job.

With one particular set I've used, once the cylinder valves are turned on and pressure set, you're ready to light up. The acetylene valve on the torch must be opened ¼-turn, and the gas must be lit with your striker. The acetylene will burn with a long, yellow flame emitting heavy soot. Some people get around this sooting problem by opening the oxygen valve on the torch at the same time they open the acetylene valve; but this isn't recommended. The torch could pop, and flame can backup up into the acetylene hose and cause a disastrous explosion.

This might be a good place to mention a safety device developed to prevent such tragedies. These are reverse-flow check valves that can be attached between the fuel and oxy-

gen hoses and the torch. They prevent oxygen or acetylene from backing up into the opposite hose, which could conceivably happen when the pressure in one line is greater than that in the other. It is even wiser to install a set of reverse-flow check valves both at the torch and at the regulators, as sort of double insurance. These units are recommended for both standard oxy-acetylene setups and solid oxygen types.

Okay, back to lighting our torch. Continue opening the acetylene valve until the yellow flame is rushing from the torch and just barely begins to pull away from the tip; then back off on the valve until the flame touches the tip again. Open the oxygen valve and note that the flame begins to include several cones of blue flame, all of different shades. As the oxygen valve is opened further, the flame cones will seem to recede back into the torch tip until finally only one very sharply defined dark blue cone remains. By having the regulators adjusted to similar pressures, this will give a neutral flame—the kind a body man will use most of the time. At this point, with the proper tip installed for the size of work you're going to be doing, and with pressure set correctly

1

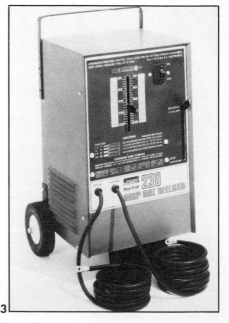

2

and flame set, you're ready to weld as with any other outfit.

One problem that occurs with irritating frequency is that of momentary loss of flame while welding. This is usually caused by a hot particle popping into the tip opening, temporarily cutting off flow of gas. The particle immediately cools, however, and is ejected. The gas then re-ignites. All of this happens rapidly, and sounds like a sharp pop. Sometimes, it will be repeated in rapid succession. If such a situation persists, go to a large tip size which will generally clear up the problem. Learning to adjust the flame until the welding operation goes smoothly is a big part of the battle in learning how to gas weld.

BRAZING AND BRAZE WELDING

Learning to braze is easier than welding, but the beginner is cautioned to learn fusion welding first, before attempting brazing. There is a difference between braze welding and brazing, although both use nonferrous filler rod that will melt above 800°F. In braze welding the filler rod of brass or bronze fills an open-groove joint or makes a definite bead. In brazing, a closely fitted joint is filled by capillary action of the filler material (as in furnace brazing). Such a connection is really just a thin film of filler metal between the two surfaces, but it can be extremely strong. Furnace brazing is necessary when outstanding strength of precision parts is required. Around a body shop, the term brazing is used to mean brazewelding, and brazing is used primarily in repairing a joint that was originally spot welded. Brazing of

3

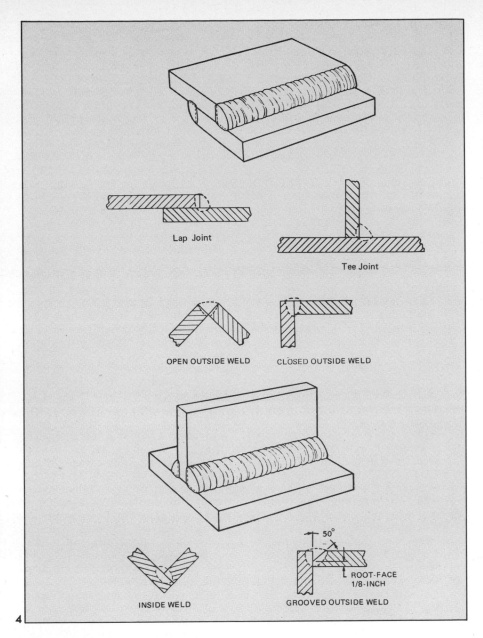

Lap Joint

Tee Joint

OPEN OUTSIDE WELD   CLOSED OUTSIDE WELD

INSIDE WELD   GROOVED OUTSIDE WELD

50°

ROOT-FACE
1/8-INCH

4

1. Sears Roebuck's Craftsman Color-matic welder can easily be moved around your garage on its wheels. A popular unit, it provides an infinite number of heat ranges from 40-230 amps.

2. Hobart's Miami T-225 arc welder is compact, and ideal for general automotive work. Dial control offers 18 different current settings.

3. Montgomery Ward's offers this 230 amp welder and a 295-amp welder, too. Unit comes complete with electrode holder, ground cable and clamp, face shield, power cable, electrodes of various sizes, and instructions.

4. A fillet-weld joint forms a right angle pocket for weld metal deposit. Squaring of edges is usually all the preparation needed. Lap joints are formed by overlapping edges that must touch surface-to-surface on entire joint for best results. Corner joints are formed by two pieces perpendicular to each other at the edges. On heavy material, the corners must be open or grooved as shown. Tee joints are similar, usually requiring welding on both sides of heavy material.

such joints may not be as strong as perfect-braze welding or fusion welding, but the joint's strength is usually sufficient. It also requires less heat, which means less heat distortion. For this reason most bodymen will steel-weld body panels together, so that the joint is strong even after grinding. Braze welding is done mostly on panels where you can't get at the backside to hammer and dolly it after welding.

Brazing is possible because many nonferrous metals will diffuse and/or penetrate into other metals when temperature and surface conditions are right. This means the copper-base filler material must be melted while the parent metal must be kept at the same temperature. This permits the filler metal to flow over the joint being brazed.

The parent metal must be clean, which can be accomplished by grinding, scraping or using a wire brush.

An easier way—chemically—is to use a strong flux, but such a flux leaves a residue that is difficult to remove. The bodyman may use a combination of the two, cleaning the joint to be brazed and then using a flux with a low chemical residue.

On a good brazed joint, the penetration is called diffusion since the two metals intermix to cause an alloying action at the joint's interface. Such an alloy is sometimes stronger than the parent metal, especially with the newer high-strength brazing rods. The strongest brazed joints are made when the parent metal surfaces are between .003-and .005-in. apart. For the bodyman, that means flush.

Flux is both a chemical cleaner and a protective shield for the heated metal surface which allows the molten brazing material to wet and diffuse into the parent surfaces. Such a flux can be a powder or a paste, or you can buy flux-coated rods. Naturally, the coated rods are more expensive to buy than the plain ones, but I find them much more handy to use. After you have spilled a few cans of brazing flux, while attempting to stab a hot rod into its contents as you find yourself simultaneously blinded by a pair of goggles, you'll learn the meaning of this. All the time you lose poking the plain brazing rod into the flux can, plus the cost of the flux itself, brings their cost to a par with the coated variety. With powdered fluxes, you have to heat the end of the brazing rod so it will "pick up" the flux. This isn't true with the paste fluxes, however.

A good brazed joint should be smooth and bright, with edges that blend smoothly into the parent metal. A pitted or blistery surface or an edge that seems to stand on top of the parent metal means an unsatisfactory job. This doesn't mean the joint won't hold, it just means you need more practice. A very common mistake is to overheat the surface, as shown by a fine white powdery material left on both sides of the joint.

Brazing is particularly applicable to sheet metal work, where you wish to keep excess heat to a minimum, thereby preventing warped panels. But it should not be used for critical suspension parts, even where high-strength brazing rod is going to be the one that's used.

ARC WELDERS

While an oxy-acetylene outfit makes it possible to weld, braze, cut and heat metal, an AC arc welder lets you do these same things, but in *grander* style. *Only* an arc welder will let you, as an amateur, build your own chassis, install a rear end, engine mounts, front axle; build an en

Welding and Brazing

gine stand, or you name it. It's an item that you'll soon discover you can't do without. Used in conjunction with your acetylene torch, you'll find there is little that this team, if properly used, can't do for you.

Funny thing is, of all the equipment you've probably gathered up, an electric arc welder will probably be the first one to pay for itself. True, you can perform "money-making" jobs for your friends, but we're talking about the money an arc welder can *save* you. Four, five or six small jobs in your garage will probably save you enough in welding fees alone to pay for your own welder; while welding-up just one frame will do the same trick. Anyway you look at it, you can't go wrong owning one of these machines.

New shop-type electric welders cost in the neighborhood of $125, complete and ready to weld. Some dealers may even have good used welders in stock (possibly trade-ins or repossessions); therefore investigate this possibility if you're kinda' hurtin' for bucks or want a good bargain. These units don't wear out like some products.

Generally speaking, most of the smaller home or shop arc welders are nearly identical in size, cost, amperage range and features. Still there are some differences. To give you an idea of what to look for in an arc welder, we'll cover some of their features and learn what we're getting for our money. Then we'll delve into arc welding basics themselves.

As hot rodders, interested in working with chassis and maybe making shop equipment, or even a car trailer, our needs for an arc welder are limited. The material we'll be working with will usually vary between 1/16-in. and ½-in. Therefore our needs dictate use of an electric welder capable of

producing, at most, 225-250 amps. All of the small shop welders discussed and illustrated here fit into this category and are suitable for the work discussed. There *is* one type of electric welder that you should shy away from, however. This is the little buzz box-type that is frequently advertised at prices around $25-$35 or so. Buy one of these and you've blown some good money. Any of these tiny welders have to operate at maximum capacity and will quickly overheat. Even the larger shop-types we're covering here can't be operated continuously at many amperage settings.

Most electric welders come complete, ready to be plugged into your 240-volt electrical receptacle. If your garage or shop isn't wired for 240-volt, single-phase, then you'll have to have this done. You'll need a circuit with at least a 50-60 amp fuse or circuit breaker to handle the welder.

One area in which some arc welders vary is in the type of ground and electrode cables supplied, as well as the ground clamp and electrode holder (torch). Some welders feature heavy-duty equipment, others don't. Generally, we have found that face shields supplied with most shop-type arc welders aren't of good quality. They do work, but you'll probably want to spring for a better quality helmet later on, preferably one with a flip-front lens holder.

An accompanying chart lists the minimum and maximum available amperage figures for all the welders discussed. It also lists a *duty cycle* for each, which refers to the length of time you can weld without overheating or damaging your welder. A 20% duty cycle means that one can weld for two minutes out of ten, or 20% of the ten-minute period. A 100% cycle means you can weld ten minutes out of ten, but you'll seldom be that busy. Experience has proven that a 20% duty cycle is sufficient for

just about any work with which you will be involved.

There are many welders rated at a maximum of, say, 180 amps, or even 100 amps, they are good units; but we would recommend units of more amperage, as the price difference isn't that much. From a personal standpoint, I have used two of the 225-230-amp arc welders listed here for many years. I have built many a chassis from the ground up and have never experienced any trouble with overheating. Unless you're doing a lot of production work, it's highly unlikely that you'll be welding for more than a few minutes at a time.

While most of these welders offer a maximum amperage setting of 225-235, it is seldom that you would ever rely on such amperage for your work. I have welded ½-in. thick rear radius rod brackets on many an axle housing and never found need to go over 180 amps. Where ¼-in. stock was involved, 130-145 amps usually sufficed; and when it came to ⅛-in. steel, the amp setting I generally used was 75-90 at most. These figures would vary somewhat, depending on the application. Even though I never used a higher amperage setting than 180, the extra 45 or so amps capability of my welder was sort of a buffer zone: it was never taxed to its maximum capability and therefore it would run cooler. While some of these welders offer fixed amperage settings, between 12 and 21 individual choices, others offer an infinite number of amp settings via a sliding lever or control wheel. If you're interested in an arc welder, have a talk with your local welding supply dealer or other knowledgeable store personnel. Whatever you do, buy a unit that will satisfy *your* needs, not his.

USING THE "STINGER"

Okay, let's get down to the basics of what arc welding is all about.

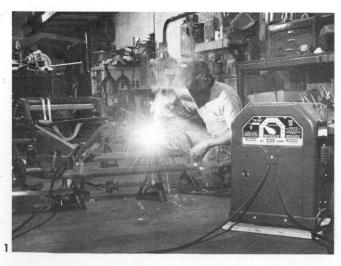

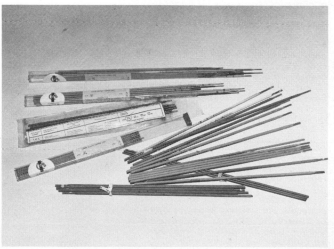

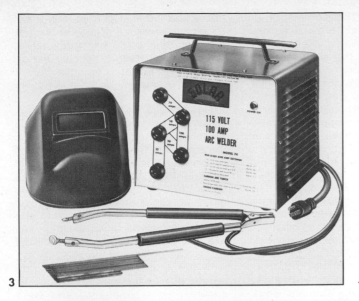

3

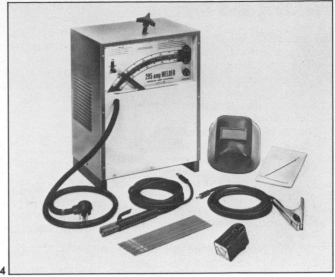

4

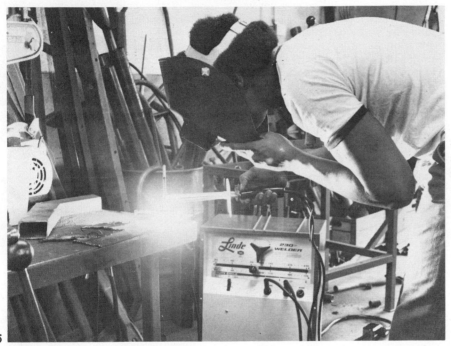

5

1. *Quite a few chassis shops use an AC/welder, such as this Lincoln 225, in performing custom chassis work.*

2. *There is a wide choice of arc welding electrodes on the market; for every type of material, including cast iron. Make sure you use the proper electrode for the job.*

3. *This Solar 100 amp arc welder can be used on household 115-120-Volt circuits, with a 30-amp fuse or 20-amp time-delay fuse. It is one of the smallest welders you can use for general automotive repairs.*

4. *Twentieth Century manufactures wide line of arc welders. This model is their 295 amp version, with infinite amp settings. It offers a 100% duty cylce up to 143 amps and comes with everything you need to start welding.*

5. *A carbon arc torch is being used here to heat a piece of sheet steel. Unit plugs right into AC arc welder, in this case a Linde 230-amp machine.*

There's nothing mysterious about arc welding, and as long as you select the right electrode for the material you intend to weld, and set the welder at the right heat range for the gauge of metal involved, the battle is half whipped. Practice will teach you how fast to move the electrode, how high to hold it above the work, which angle is best and so forth.

The first time you try arc welding, and before you plug the power cord into a 240-volt receptacle, turn off the main switch in the light meter box, then check the receptacle to make sure *its* ground wire will be connected to the welder's ground wire. Also make sure that the fuse, or circuit breaker, on the particular circuit is sufficient to handle your welder. As previously mentioned, a 50-amp fuse should suffice. If the fuse or circuit breaker is too light, the fuse will blow

or the circuit breaker will jump when you weld for any period of time.

After your welder is connected, connect the ground clamp to the work to be welded. Make sure the connection is super-good, or you'll waste power and heat up the ground clamp. Use clean, dry welding rods (electrodes), and be sure of a positive grip on the electrode by the electrode holder. The thickness of the metal to be welded and the diameter of the electrode will determine the amount of heat required for welding. In general, the heavier and thicker a piece of metal is, the larger the electrode and the more heat (amps) it requires. Many welders come with guides that give you an idea as to what diameter of electrode to use for specific metals, metal thicknesses as well as amperage required. But because conditions vary in line voltage, rod coatings, speed of the operator, type and condition of the metal worked on, no hard-and-fast rule will tell you the exact amperage to use. Your own experience after following these initial guidelines will tell you whether you are using too much or too little heat.

If you use too much heat, you will burn holes in light metals, or the bead will be flat and porous. Also, the bead will likely "undercut" the work (caused by rapid movement of the rod along its surface, due to the high heat and insufficient time for the crater to be filled).

Using too little heat will result in beads that are too high, as though they lay on top of the work. The bead will also be irregular because of the difficulty you'll have in holding an arc. Also, with the amperage too low, you'll have trouble striking an arc; the electrode will tend to stick to the work, and, what is more, the arc will frequently "go out."

But where you use the right heat,

Welding and Brazing

the bead will lay smoothly over the work without ragged edges. The "puddle" will be at least as deep in the base metal as the rod that lies above it. The sound of the welding operation will "crackle," like the sound of eggs frying.

Your rate of travel over the work affects the weld as much as the heat setting. Move the arc slowly to ensure proper penetration and enough weld metal deposit. Rod movement must be at a *consistent* speed, too. But first let's delve into the act of "striking" an arc.

The purpose of the arc is to create an intense heat between the end of the electrode and the surface of the metal to be welded (called the work or base metal). The heat energy generated by the arc is so great that the base metal almost immediately is heated to a liquid state at the point where the arc is directed. This creates a molten pool (puddle) of metal which is always present on the base metal during the welding process.

MAKING A BEAD

This same heat also melts down the electrode. As it melts, the metal from the electrode falls through the arc into the molten pool, or puddle. This adds additional molten metal, which mixes thoroughly in the puddle, resulting in complete fusion of the two metals. As more metal from the electrode is added and the electrode is moved forward, the material added from the electrode forms a uniform pile of metal along the base metal. This is known as the "bead."

Now that you have a general idea of what happens when you are arc welding, let's find out how you actu-

ally start to weld. The first thing to do is to "strike an arc." This is accomplished by scratching the end of the electrode across the surface to be welded. With a short stroke, scratch the rod end across the base metal, close to where you want to weld. You will soon hear a sputter and see an arc. You *must* be wearing a protective helmet at this time, or any time you are welding. There is no way you can see what is going on without one, and you'll burn your eyes severly trying to weld without one. The minimum density of lens you should use in the welding helmet is a No. 9, while a No. 10 is ideal for most arc welding. The darkest lens you should use is a No. 14. Protective gloves will keep your hands from being burned, too, and are recommended, along with a heavy, long-sleeved shirt. Welding with a T-shirt on will get you a sunburn on your arms equivalent to a long day on a hot beach!

As soon as an arc begins burning between the electrode and the base metal, raise the electrode about ⅛-in.

above the work. If you do not, it will stick to the work. If it does stick, rock the electrode back and forth until it breaks loose. Keep practicing the art of striking an arc, using different gauges of metal, and, at different amperages too.

Now you're ready to lay a bead. Strike an arc, hold it at the starting point for a short time before moving the electrode forward, to ensure good fusion and to allow the bead to build up slightly. Bear in mind that the electrode continues to melt off as you move across the work, so you must move the electrode down into the puddle as well as along the path you are following. The electrode should be held at an angle (see illustrations), with the end held at a maintained height above the work surface. To ensure proper penetration and evenness of the weld, learn to watch the molten pool of metal forming just behind the arc.

The easiest bead to lay is called a stringer bead. It is made by making one continuous pass over the work

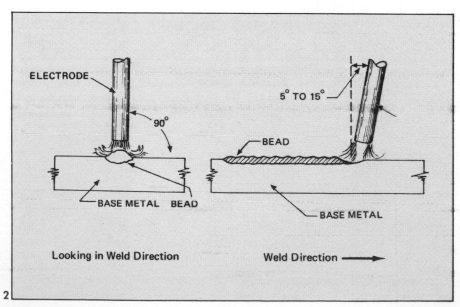

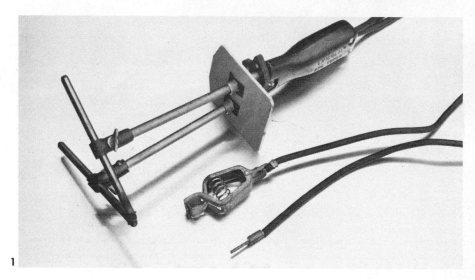

1. *Lincoln's carbon-arc torch is inexpensive, and allows you to heat, braze, solder and bend metals.*

2. *When arc welding, hold electrode perpendicular, but tilt the top or holder end in the direction it is moving (weld direction). Feed your electrode at a uniform rate down to the plate as it melts and forms bead.*

3. *When the electrode contacts the work a high-temperature arc forms. The heat is controlled by current and space between the rod and the work. The flux coating provides a gas shield against contamination from the air.*

4. *The completed weld should be thoroughly fused to the base metal throughout the groove area. The weld metal should penetrate to the root of the joint with a small amount extending below the surface to assure a full section weld. At the face of the weld, there is usually a buildup known as "reinforcement."*

ELECTRODE

90°

BASE METAL   BEAD

Looking in Weld Direction

5° TO 15°

BEAD

BASE METAL

Weld Direction →

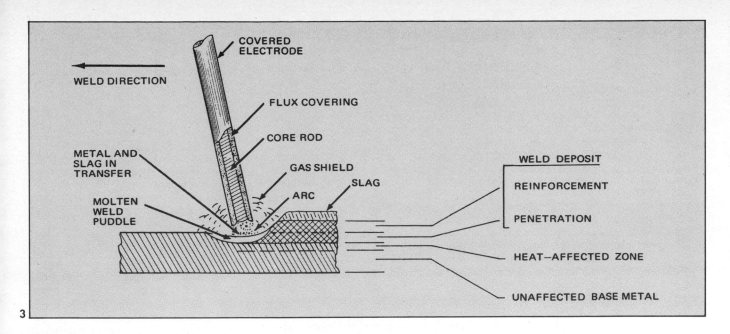

COVERED ELECTRODE

WELD DIRECTION

FLUX COVERING

CORE ROD

METAL AND SLAG IN TRANSFER

GAS SHIELD

SLAG

ARC

MOLTEN WELD PUDDLE

WELD DEPOSIT

REINFORCEMENT

PENETRATION

HEAT—AFFECTED ZONE

UNAFFECTED BASE METAL

3

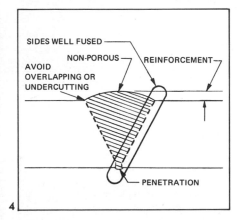

SIDES WELL FUSED

NON-POROUS

REINFORCEMENT

AVOID OVERLAPPING OR UNDERCUTTING

PENETRATION

4

metal, without trying any weaving or oscillating movements. If you are right-handed, move from left to right when you start practicing. If left-handed, reverse the process. With the electrode tipped back toward the direction of travel (about 15 degrees), the arc will throw the molten metal of the puddle away from itself, ensuring good penetration. The average bead, when using a ⅛-in. electrode, will be about ⅛-in. high and ¼-in. wide. Practice the stringer bead until you are able to make a smooth weld of consistent width and height, with uniform ripples.

Another bead that is commonly used is known as a weave bead. Its purpose is to deposit metal in a wider space than would normally be possible with the stringer bead. It is accomplished by weaving from one edge of the space to be filled to the other edge and continuing this motion, along with a forward speed of travel that will give the most satisfactory results. It is a good policy to hesitate momentarily at each edge of the weave so you will provide the same heat at the edges as that which is obtained in the middle.

It is recommended that any time you butt-weld two pieces of metal together, where their thickness is 3/16-in. or more, that the edges be beveled by grinding. This will permit a much better weld, as you are ensuring complete penetration of the weld filler metal (electrode). Where necessary, you can even make a second or third pass over an initial weld as long as you remove all slag from previous beads. It is seldom that we will be making butt welds in construction of our street rods, but Tee joints and lap joints are very common. About the only place I can think of a butt weld being used on a rod is where a channel frame is being boxed in. Here you would find the boxing metal fitting tightly against the main frame rails.

It will often happen that you're laying a beautiful bead, and before you're finished, you run out of rod. For best results, the crater, or depression, remaining at the end of the weld should be thoroughly cleaned with a wire brush before you again start to weld. After this has been done, a new arc should be struck just ahead of the crater and then moved nearly to the back of the crater. After the crater is filled, the weld can be carried on as before.

An arc welder can be used to weld aluminum, stainless steel, cast iron and galvanized steel, and for heating, burning holes, brazing, soldering and so forth, in addition to welding mild steel. While the electrode holder and various types of electrodes will take care of most of these jobs, a rather convenient accessory, a carbon arc torch, is used in conjunction with your arc welder to permit brazing, soldering, heating, bending and the welding of aluminum and copper alloys. Rather than delve too deeply into how to operate a carbon arc

torch at this time, let us just say we have used them, and they do work.

ARC WELDING RODS

Let's touch on mild steel electrodes for now, as these are the most common types used by rodders. There are fast *freeze* electrodes which have a snappy, deep penetration arc and fast-freezing deposits. Some of these can be used with an AC welder. They are used for general-purpose all-position welding. *Low hydrogen* rods get their name from the fact that their coating contains little hydrogen in either moisture or chemical form. They offer these benefits: outstanding crack resistance, elimination of porosity on sulphur bearing steels, and X-ray quality deposits. There are also what the trade calls *fast-fill* electrodes that feature a soft arc and fast deposit rates, too. Other rods are designed for short or irregular welding, downhill fillets and laps, etc. There are so many different types of electrodes available, unless you are positive of the type you need, check with your welding supply dealer. Tell him what you're planning on welding, and he'll help you choose the right electrode for the job.

Whatever you do, never fabricate a chassis or other component that will be stressed, or upon which someone's safety must depend, until you *know* you're proficient at the art of arc welding, or gas welding, for that matter. It's most important.

Before you can practice arc welding, you must be able to select the best electrode for the particular job at hand, and you must know how to use them properly. These are important considerations, because the quality and appearance of your work will depend upon proper electrode selection and application. ♟

Replacing Panels

Sometimes it's easier (and cheaper) to put on new "skin" than try to fix the old one.

Whenever a fairly sizable body panel has been severely damaged, as a door, turret top, quarter panel, etc., it is often quicker and easier to replace it completely rather than try to hammer and dolly all the kinks and bends out. However, it is generally left up to the body man to determine if the cost of replacement is sound economy. Replacement panels, whether new or garnered from a salvage yard, can be expensive, and the labor cost of fixing the old one just might turn out to be the way to go.

Many times a panel replacement is purely an economic consideration. Recently, we investigated the repair of a dented door on a late model car. From a wrecking yard, the complete door would cost $145, because the yard man knew those doors were scarce. At the car dealer, a new door was priced at $110, but the dealer didn't have any in stock (the wrecking yard man must have known this). We priced just the outer panel, and it was only $45 from the dealer, so that's the way we fixed it.

Practically every portion of a car's body is available in replacement form from its manufacturer or body parts specialist, but the exterior panels are normally the only units replaced. Such external sheet metal may include the front fenders, hood and deck-lid panels, quarter panels, door panels, top panel and rocker panels. All these units are available directly from the factory and are listed in collision manuals.

It depends largely upon the factory as to how the various panels are attached to the substructure, but as a rule large panels that can easily distort from heat, such as the top, are spot welded. Areas that are not easily distorted, or where stress may be concentrated, such as quarter panels, are usually fusion welded in several related seams. Fender panels are bolt-on and require no welding. There may be a combination of welding methods involved, such as the quarter panel which is fusion welded where it meets the top panel and is spot welded along the door post and deck opening.

If a panel is to be replaced, or even if a partial panel replacement is required, the general area must be roughed into alignment before the panel is removed. Panels may be removed in several ways. If spot welding is involved, each spot may be drilled. A ¼-inch drill bit is normally big enough for this job, but there will be many welds to break loose. The area near a fusion weld may be cut away with a torch if distortion can be limited and there is no danger of fire (inside a door, inside the headliner, etc.), but the best tool for cutting large areas of sheet metal is the panel cutter.

Panel cutters (chisels) were usually moved by a well placed hammer blow until recent years, when the air chisel came into prominence. Such chisels are great time savers, with the advantage of producing little panel distortion, and are considered imperative by any professional custom shop. The home craftsman can still do a good job with the older-type cutters, especially if they are kept sharp.

Also easy to use and inexpensive to buy are the popular electric sabre saws. They are widely available and most hardware stores stock metal-cutting blades for them. They operate much like a jigsaw, but use a special blade that secures to a chuck at one end only. They will cut starting from an edge, or they can be started in mid-panel if you first drill a hole, usually ¼-inch.

When a fusion weld is to be parted, it is wise to cut below the weld, that is, toward the damaged panel, about one inch. This is particularly true if the torch is used. The final trim up to the original weld is made with a pair of right- or left-hand aircraft-type tin snips. If the replacement panel is new there may be a lapping lip where fusion welds are required, but not always. If the replacement panel has been cut from another car, the area near the fusion weld must be trimmed to fit the vehicle being repaired. In the case of a partial replacement, this trimming must be careful and precise.

Collision damage is not the only reason a panel might need replacement, since rust is such a great factor in metal cancer. Rust is particular-

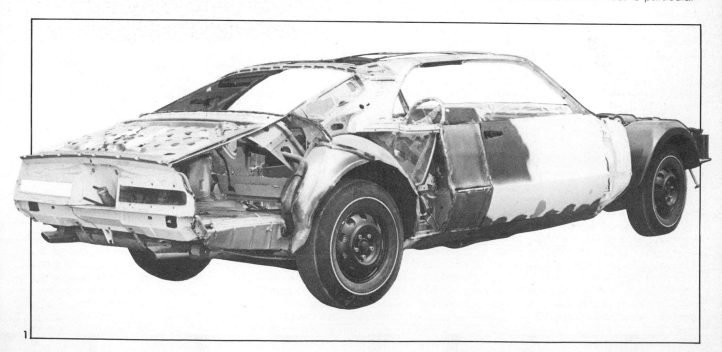

1

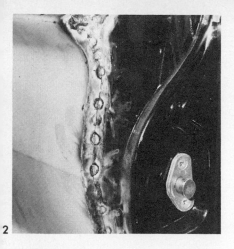

2

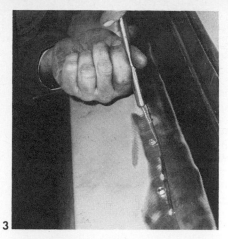

3

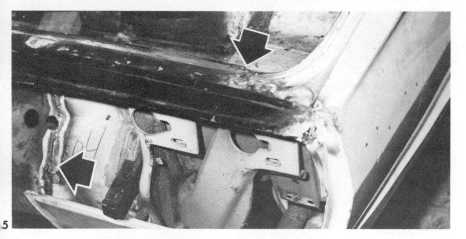

4

5

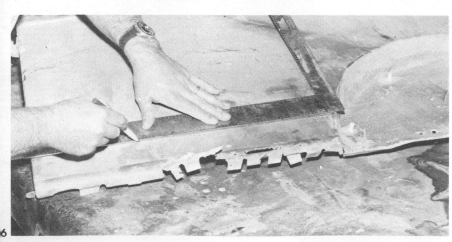

6

ly prevalent in areas where salt is used to control snow on the streets, and it attacks new cars as well as slowly nibbling on older vehicles. Such attacks are generally limited to areas where the salt slush can gather, as on lower-door panels, rocker panels, and the skirts for both front and rear fenders. In any of these cases, a partial panel may be considered the best replacement.

LEADING

It may be economically more advantageous to lead small, rusted areas, especially if the rust can be controlled from spreading. Leading is quite common in areas where rusting is not a major problem, and even extends into special hot rod bodywork. As an example of the latter, old Model T and Model A bodies (that have gone unused for years) tend to gather rust at the base of the quarter panel, the cowl panel, and the doors. In the western states, the rust spots will be limited to a thin line near the extreme bottom edge of the panel, but in locations where there is salt or considerable moisture, the rust may extend well up into the surrounding panel. It is possible to lead these areas (where less than a perfect job is required) by thoroughly cleaning out all the rust scale and treating the cleaned metal with a rust inhibitor. Coarse steel wool may be packed behind the panel as an initial support, and lead used to bridge the gap. Keep in mind that lead will not have

1. A car's skin consists of the outer sheetmetal; the visible body panels. The skin goes over a complex body skeleton, as exemplified by this partially denuded Oldsmobile.

2. Skin sections, as quarter panels, are generally flanged at their edges to fit over substructure to which they are usually electrically spot welded. Because the average body shop does not have such a piece of equipment, panels that are replaced because of damage are generally tack-brazed in position, as in this example.

3. Partial panel replacement sometimes can be accomplished by riveting or bolting overlapped edges where a trim strip or molding will cover them.

4. When an exterior or skin panel must be replaced, the old one is removed by grinding down the edge where it crimps over the substructure. Panel will then come off; spot welded strip can be peeled, chiseled off.

5. Entire right quarter panel of this T-Bird was replaced; deep cuts were made into flooring as damage was extensive. Arrows indicate where parts were welded together.

6. When a panel is only partially to be replaced, such as rust-out at the bottom of a panel, it must be cut off; and a new piece formed in sheetmetal and hammer-welded into the old panel.

Replacing Panels

the strength of a steel panel replacement, but it is the quickest way to clean up a nasty problem. Plastic fillers have not proven satisfactory for this type of restoration, but fiberglass repairs are acceptable.

REPLACING A PANEL

To understand how a partial panel might be repaired, assume a late model car has a large rust area (or critical damage) in the panel between the wheel opening and rear bumper. As a guide, mark off the area that must be cut out and carefully inspect the remaining part of the panel for damage or distortion. Measure to the chalked lines from nearby reference points (molding, door, deck opening, etc.) and transfer these measurements to the replacement panel. This second panel is usually part of a larger panel that was purchased at a wrecking yard.

Cut the replacement section from the second panel, making the edges as straight as possible. Place this piece against the original panel and scribe a mark around the edge. Cut away the fender along the scribe lines. Straighten the edges of both pieces (the original fender and replacement panel), then butt weld the new panel into place. For the most part such repairs will be in low-crown areas, so heat distortion will be high. Therefore tack weld the section in place every 3 or 4 ins., then finish weld. Finish off with lead or plastic filler.

POP RIVETS

An alternative to welding is the pop or blind rivet for any kind of panel repair. This alternative is becoming increasingly popular with professional metal men, since it reduces any chance of distortion and makes the repair job considerably faster. If the

panel just mentioned is to be riveted into place, make the panel to be inserted about ½-in. larger than the section cut from the original fender. Drill holes around the panel edge and insert rivets, then hammer the rivet edge down and fill, usually with plastic filler. Obviously this is not the finest method of repair, but where quality may be sacrificed for speed, it works well.

Replacement of a rocker panel is relatively simple, since it entails drilling spot welds and either riveting or brazing the new panel into place. In the case of a small gouge or rust damage to a rocker, it is better to fill than replace, timewise.

QUARTER PANELS

Replacement of a quarter panel may be easier than repair with a

hammer, especially for the beginner. The panel will usually be riveted along the door post and at the deck opening flange, with a fusion weld where it mates to the top (this may be a lapped spot seam, also). Replacement of such a panel will depend largely upon the damage involved, but a good example would be the quarter panel on a 1957 Chevrolet station wagon. If the panel has been hit in the taillight area, it will have been severely damaged. Removal is by drilling the spot welds along the door post and the tailgate opening. This particular car has a chrome molding between the quarter window and the quarter panel. Remove the molding and cut the damaged panel off at the *bottom* edge of this molding line, either with a panel cutter or by the torch/tin snip method.

1

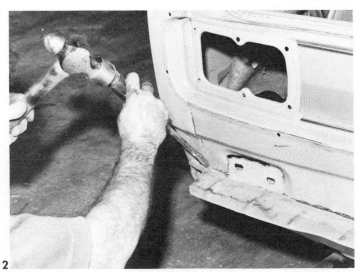

2

3

The replacement panel should be trimmed just *above* the molding line. A small, vertical slot (the width of the molding) is cut at the panel's forward end where it joins the door post, and a similar slot at the rear end where the panel joins the tailgate flange. In this way, the replacement panel may be slid up under the molding line of the original body. This is to keep water from running down between the panels where they lap.

Now align the molding clip holes in both panels and the replacement panel at both the door post and tailgate flange. When the panel is zeroed in, drill holes down the molding line and use rivets to make the connection. Spot braze or weld the door post and tailgate flange. When the molding is replaced it will cover the rivets, while the spot welds can be finished with a grinder and filled if desired (remember, plastic filler will

not take a good bite over brass).

On sedans, replacement of the quarter panel is a bit more difficult, in that the panel does not usually have a chrome molding between the top and quarter panels. Furthermore, the two panels are usually factory welded with the seam running into the rear window lip. This method means removal for panel replacement.

However, most professionals don't wish to take so much time. Therefore the panels are removed as with the station wagon, but the seam cut is made near the original weld to a point just outboard of the rear window. Here the cut skirts the window opening until it meets a line from the deck-opening flange. A butt weld may be used where the two panels meet, but more common is a lap joint with rivets and plastic filler. The customizer is advised to use a butt weld and lead, or a true hammer weld, as the

stress concentration caused by panel modification may be greater than on the original design.

DOOR PANELS

Other than the front fenders and quarter panels, the doors receive more panel replacement than any other part of the car. Replacement is usually due to excessive damage, since the door is susceptible to bad collisions. Rust is a reason on older cars, but usually only because the water drain holes have become plugged. When rust has taken the door panel, chances are good that the lower part of the reinforcing substructure is also badly rusted and in need of repair.

A door may receive a full or partial panel replacement, depending upon the damage. If the lower part of the door has received a severe gouge or is rusted away, replacing the panel below the chrome molding (if one is used) may be all that's necessary. If there is no molding to hide the rivets, it is wise to replace the entire panel, since welding and working the middle of a low-crown panel requires a considerable amount of labor.

Late model cars usually have a window opening structure separate from the panel, which means replacement panels come only to the window. Earlier model cars had panels which carried through the window opening edges. This means earlier doors will need to be cut and welded somewhere near the top of the door panel in a high-crown area, usually just below the window (chrome trim at this point was common). Incidentally, deck lid and hood panels are crimped to the substructure much the same as doors, so replacement would be similar. However, before a door, hood or deck lid panel is replaced,

4

5

6

1. This view of a Toyota shows typical damage incurred from a rear-end collision: rear panel caved in and a quarter panel wrinkled badly.

2. After removal of bumper and all trim pieces from rear of body, a chisel and torch are used to free tack welded panels from main body.

3. Entire corner of body is removed after all tack welds are cut. A torch is used to remove major portion of side quarter panel, though.

4. The body man who did this work obtained new panels first, then knew exactly where to cut.

5. Paint has been ground off where new quarter panel will join main body structure, so parts can be tack welded together for strength.

6. Inner fender edge has been drilled every few inches where it rests against wheelwell, then is tacked in place with acetylene torch.

Replacing Panels

the cost of a good used item should definitely be considered.

PANEL JOINTS

There are four basic types of joints involved in panel replacement, two of which were covered in the quarter panel replacement. These were the butt weld and the rivet lap. Also possible is the recessed lap joint, which is usually made well up on the door panel in a high-crown area. In this method, the upper or lower panel has a recess placed in the edge so the mating panel will be flush in contour, and the joint is then welded or riveted and finished.

The fourth type of joint is the flange joint, where both panels have a 90° flange (approximate) at the mating edge and are joined by welding or rivets. Both the recessed lap and the flange joint can be easily finished off, but are more time-consuming than the first two.

If a panel is to be cut off and a small portion of the original panel is to be left, the cut will be at one of three points: the belt line (just below the window), the belt molding or somewhere below the molding. Of the three locations, under the molding is the most desirable as replacement will require a minimum amount of labor and heat.

On most late model doors, the entire panel is replaced to the window lower edge as a unit, with no panel mating required. However, on older model doors the panel may be mated at the belt line.

The panel can be cut with an air chisel or saber saw, leaving enough material for the lap if a lap joint is to be made. This recessed lap is usually made on the original panel, but some replacement panels include the lap. The perimeter of the door panel is held to the substructure by a crimped flange, which may be easily removed by a disc grinder. Run the grinder along the *edge* of the panel, grinding through to the substructure beneath, then peel off the small piece of flange on the inside with pliers. The larger outer panel will now fall off.

Sometimes accessory replacement panels do not come with the flanges already bent over, so the hammer and dolly must be used, but factory replacements come ready to slip on, tack weld or crimp.

Hold the new panel in place if it must be welded or connected to the old panel, C-clamps being the best for the job. If the joint is made with rivets under the molding, it is a matter of lining up the molding fastener holes as with the quarter panel. The other joints require more work.

If a butt weld is to be made, use a C-clamp or a pair of special vise grips and tack weld as near the clamp as possible—all the way across the door. If speed is the prerequisite, no more welding needed—just fill the crack with lead. Better still is to weld

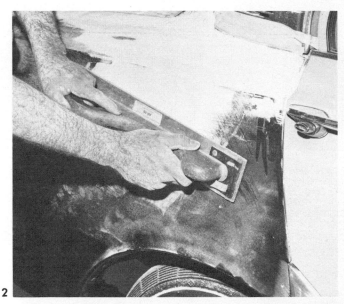

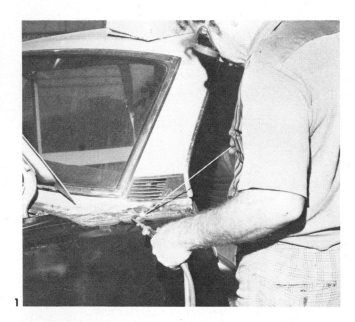

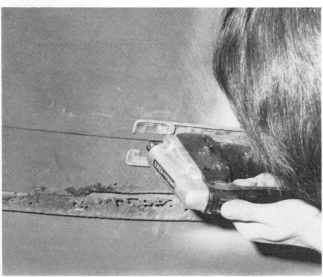

the panels completely, and if this can be done from the inside it cuts down on the amount of work necessary. The weld bead then need not be hammered down, which means less lead or plastic filler will be required. Here is where sheetmetal welding with an arc welder comes in so handy, as the process is very fast and there is less heat distortion in the panels.

With a lap joint, sheetmetal screws are used in the lap to keep everything aligned while the lap ends are welded, then the screws are removed

1. Upper edge of quarter panel is likewise welded to the body panel. Rear panel is also tack welded at intervals, then visible seams filled.

2. After all welds are ground clean, a plastic filler is used to smooth joints. Next operations involve sanding, priming and finish painting.

3. Here a rusted-out section of an early Ford quarter must be replaced with a custom piece; and the bodyman begins by making a straight, clean cut to remove the damaged area.

4. Since a close butt-fit is needed for a good hammer weld on the new panel (see hammer welding chapter), a scissors jack and some wood blocks were used to hold the new panel in place against the quarter panel; the seam is first tack welded.

5. The entire seam is then hammer welded and the low spots picked up. Bodyman Carl Green must resort to brazing the panel in the corners, since the backside can't be reached by a dolly to hammer weld there.

6. Rather than welding the new panel right at the outside of the door opening, where grinding for a perfect look could weaken the weld, Carl carried the fabricated panel around the edge to the middle of the doorpost, where the seam is not so apparent and little grinding is needed.

and the holes filled. Filling with lead or plastic follows. The flange joint matches the two contours of the original and replacement panel perfectly. A clamp is used to hold the flanges, which are then mated with metal screws or rivets. The very tiny crack that remains is filled with lead or plastic.

If the replacement panel has not already been flanged, it is now trimmed. With the door upside down on a workbench, allow ½-in. for the new flange and trim the excess with right- or left-hand tin snips. If the lower door corners are rounded, the remaining flange lip must be notched with triangular cuts about 5/16-in. deep. This will allow the panel to easily follow the rounded substructure frame below.

As the door corner is square, a matching square is cut out of the panel, one line horizontal and one vertical, leaving about 3/16-in. from the cut to the substructure. When the flanges are bent over, the ends will overlap slightly, but will conform to the door corner very well.

When the flange is being bent, it is best to make the bend in two 90° operations. The first step includes hammering the flange 90° to the panel, going a bit down the door, then returning to bend the metal another 90°. If the flange is turned all at one time, there is a good chance of splitting the edge.

TOP PANELS

It is possible to replace the top panel in the same way, and this is where the beginner can do a good job and feel confident of obtaining a good result. All that is necessary is proper alignment of the roof substructure, which can be checked with the tape measure. It is often desirable

to replace a damaged roof panel, since some roll-over accidents and extremely hard hailstorms dent the panel only and leave the rest of the car with only minor damage.

When the substructure has been pushed out and aligned with the doors and front and rear windows, the damaged top panel can be removed. The easiest way is to cut the panel with an air chisel, saber saw or torch about 1 in. from the drip molding. After the major panel has been removed, the small remaining strip can be rolled off like a sardine can lid. An alternative method is drilling out all the spot welds.

After the panel is removed, dress down the sharp edges left by the spot welder and try the new panel for fit. It should drop right in place. But if it doesn't, the substructure probably isn't aligned correctly.

If the drip molding has been damaged beyond spot repair, it may be removed by peeling or drilling out the spot welds. This molding must be placed on the substructure before the top (which laps over the inside of the molding) can be replaced.

The top panel is then welded into position (use metal screws to hold it in place while initial welds are being made) by either spot welding or spot brazing. If the top is brazed in place, a better bond can be achieved by drilling small holes through the top panel, molding and substructure so the brass will flow through.

Once it is realized that an automobile body is really nothing more than a substructure with outer panels tacked in place, the repair or customizing work can proceed at a record pace. There is essentially no difference between panel replacement on cars that have unit-bodies and those with separate frame construction.

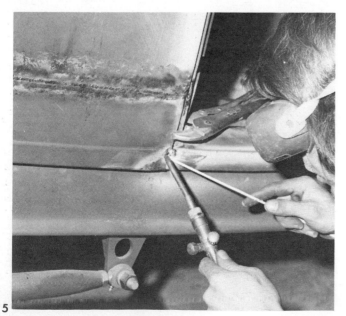

5   6

Making It Fit

A little bending, beating or adjusting will close the gaps in hoods, doors and fenders.

Hammer, dolly, and torch work cannot be the total extent of a body man's knowledge. The alignment of body panels is another area in which the tin-bender will labor, for often a repair will require the readjustment of a door, hood, or deck lid because the force of the collision impact will bend hinges, bracing, etc., without imparting dents to the panel itself. Panel alignment, too, is often the subject of customer complaint. No matter how badly smashed the front end of a car may be, and no matter how much attention is paid to repairing it, the customer will hardly appreciate it if the hood wasn't harmed. The alignment of panels is usually a simple matter—providing the body man knows where and how to tackle the problem, and how *not* to make the alignment worse.

CHECK AND RECHECK

There are two kinds of alignment involved in automotive bodywork: alignment of the basic substructure and alignment of the various panels, both stationary and opening. When some kind of repair or extensive customizing is undertaken, if the reinforcement structure is not exactly perfect, the external panels cannot hope to align. Fortunately, alignment of the substructure can be accomplished by the beginner with a minimum of tools. The secret is in taking accurate measurements.

It is possible for a panel to be completely out of alignment without a visible sign of damage. The quickest way to tell of course, is to look for hidden damage. That is, a slight unnatural kink somewhere in the frame may lead to an entire front or rear body section being out of alignment. The best way to check for this misalignment is with a measuring tape. If a car has had a severe impact, misalignment can be expected, but the same misalignment will occur when a top is being chopped. Always check and recheck with the tape measure. If the frame is out of alignment, it should be trusted to someone with all the necessary corrective equipment. However, merely straightening the frame will not straighten the body.

It doesn't matter whether the car has a unit-body type construction or an individual frame; body measurements are taken in the same places. Usually, any deviation from standard in these measurements will show that the substructure needs repair, and the measurements are really just comparisons since an automobile is basically symmetrical. These comparisons are usually of the diagonal-type, normally called X-checks, and will include the four general body sections. These are: The front section, from the front door forward; the center section, which includes the small area from the front door to the rear door; the rear section, from the rear door

to the trunk; and the trunk, or deck section of the car.

The front section is usually checked first at the immediate forward part of the passenger compartment—that is, from the door hinge posts to the windshield pillars. All measurements must be made from the same point on both sides, which will give results within extremely close tolerances. The farther apart the points being measured, the more accurate the check.

The measurement from the bottom edge of the left door opening to the top edge of the right opening must be identical (or nearly so) to that from bottom right to top left. If there is a slight variation, measure again, and perhaps a third or fourth time. Roadster owners are well aware of how important alignment of these points is since it controls how the doors fit. The same holds true for most cars, and misalignment at this critical point cannot be corrected properly elsewhere. If there is a significant difference in the two measurements, it means the top of the body has been slanted to one side, typical of what is known as a roll-over accident.

It is obvious this same kind of diagonal measurement can be used for X-checking all aspects of the car: from frame, to body substructure, to individual panel openings. Once a starting point has been established, and all other sections have been

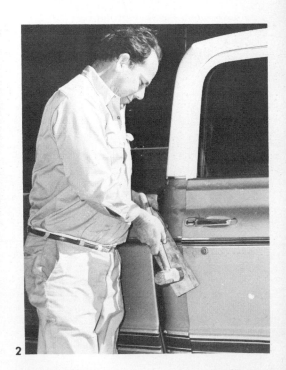

3

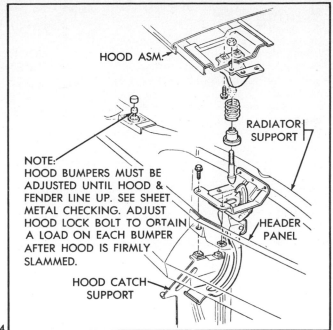

HOOD ASM.

RADIATOR SUPPORT

NOTE:
HOOD BUMPERS MUST BE ADJUSTED UNTIL HOOD & FENDER LINE UP. SEE SHEET METAL CHECKING. ADJUST HOOD LOCK BOLT TO OBTAIN A LOAD ON EACH BUMPER AFTER HOOD IS FIRMLY SLAMMED.

HEADER PANEL

HOOD CATCH SUPPORT

4

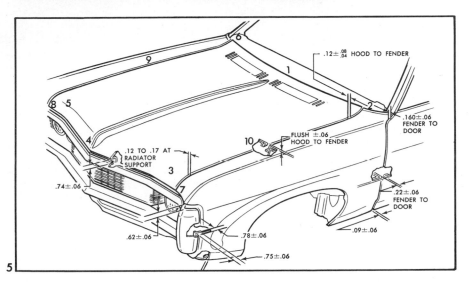

.12±.08/.04 HOOD TO FENDER

.160±.06 FENDER TO DOOR

FLUSH ±.06 HOOD TO FENDER

.12 TO .17 AT RADIATOR SUPPORT

.74±.06

.22±.06 FENDER TO DOOR

.09±.06

.62±.06

.78±.06

.75±.06

5

1. No matter how carefully a panel is de-dented, there will be no customer satisfaction if it doesn't align when you're finished. Cross-measurements should be taken of trunk opening if one quarter panel was smacked hard, for it may have been knocked out of square so the lid won't close.

2. Taking a block of wood and sledge hammer to a new door isn't for the faint of heart, but it is necessary for minute alignment adjustments.

3. If the vehicle has been in an accident, all openings should be measured diagonally as shown, sides compared. When body is being repaired, measurements are taken often; tolerances should be minus ⅛-inch.

4. Hood adjustments include work with latch and tension supports. Alignment may be difficult if front end has been damaged; make small corrections, then check.

5. All factory repair manuals have specifications for alignment measurements, which should act as a guide when repairing collision damage.

checked for alignment, then each section also can be checked against the other.

This type of checking is just an extended version of the individual section checking, in that a specific point is selected on opposite sides. This might be the top of the windshield pillar as when checking the front section, or the lower rear corner of a rear door opening. This measurement must coincide with opposing measurements, and will normally be in alignment if the individual sections are all right. When measurements are taken between sections, it is wise to double-check your work by taking measurements from several different points of reference.

It is not uncommon for the individual sections to be well out of alignment. For instance, a quartering accident to a front fender might include serious damage to the door post. Obviously, this post must be returned to

its original dimensions before the door, front fender, inner panels, etc., can be replaced. This reinforcing substructure can be either pulled or pushed back into shape, and if it's badly damaged, you can expect partial replacement.

As a rule, front or rear collisions do not produce great problems in substructure realignment, but a roll-over or side collision is different. When a vehicle rolls, it is common for the entire top substructure to collapse toward the side away from the direction of roll. Unless the roll is severe, the reinforcing structure can be pushed back into place. In this case, the substructure can be realigned and a new top panel installed. However, if the substructure is severely bent, a new top including reinforcement is usually installed. The latter is the common method of repair on modern cars, since it is rather easy to cut the original top off at the windshield pillars and across the rear panel and weld on a replacement purchased at a local wrecking yard. From a cost standpoint, this procedure is perhaps the most economical. However, when such a new top is installed, diagonal alignment measurements are definitely required.

Rear end damage is more likely to crumple a substructure than a front collision, but here again, the entire reinforcement area can be pieced in from another vehicle as long as the measurements are accurate.

No matter where the damage may occur, or the customizing modification may be initiated, the reinforcing substructures must be in perfect alignment or the exterior panels will not fit right! Welding is the only ac-

Making It Fit

ceptable method of mating reinforcements, as brazing may not take the severe strains imposed (the newer high-strength brazing rods seem to be working well) and there normally is not sufficient space for rivet lapping. Some of the substructure may be made of 20-gauge sheetmetal, but for the most part reinforcements are of heavier gauge.

Alignment of the vehicle extremities, the front and rear ends, is usually a matter of making the hood and deck lid fit. But before these panels can even be tried for a fitting, the openings must be aligned as near perfect as possible. Fortunately, there are built-in guides that make the job easier, especially at the front end.

However, the deck area is harder to align, since the quarter panels are welded to mating panels and X-checking is necessary to get good results. When there is major rear end damage, or the customizer is rebuilding the entire rear section, it is necessary to work from a straight frame. This is essential. Once the frame is straight, it is possible to push or pull the crumpled metal back into place until the trunk flooring again aligns with the frame.

Working from frame/flooring reference points, the inner body structures are straightened until the deck lid opening checks out perfectly by the X-reference. If the deck lid has not been damaged, it should then fit the opening. If the lid must be straightened, it must be repaired to fit the opening. Finally, if the panels surrounding the opening are straightened, a considerable amount of mea-

suring will be required when getting the damaged rear end back into shape.

HOOD AND FRONT METAL REPAIR

The front end is not nearly so difficult, since the entire front end assembly is bolted on. The fenders are attached with several bolts into the cowl structure and the radiator-core support bolts to the frame. If these bolts are removed, all the sheetmetal ahead of the cowl, with the exception of the hood, can be lifted off. Cars with unit construction do not disassemble in this manner, since the front fenders and inner fender panels form part of frame/body unit. However, some cars use unit construction for the main body with a subframe bolting to the firewall. This is common to Chrysler Corp. products of recent date, with the front sheet metal being removable.

As the front sheet metal is not extremely rigid, a quartering front collision will tend to collapse the assembly, leaving the opposite fender relatively undamaged. Impact force is transferred to a much greater degree by unit-construction bodies, but the tendency toward localized damage is still a favorable factor.

Because front end pieces are so easy to remove and replace, it is possible that replacement with used parts will be the most economical. In any case, when a front end is being worked on it must be returned to perfect alignment or the hood will never fit properly.

The front fenders, inner panels, and grille assembly all bolt in place (except in unit construction, where the fenders and grille only are remov-

able), thus alignment is primarily a matter of making the bolt holes line up. While it is possible to have the entire section out of alignment and still have all the bolt holes align, this would be rare. The holes should be utilized for reference only, however, with final judgment reserved for the X-check method.

Quite often a front end collision will cause little visible damage, but the entire panel will be driven out of alignment by the force of impact. A good example would be a fender hit almost head-on near the headlight. The fender may apparently sustain little damage, but the impact can drive the entire fender rearward. The obvious check would include the area around the door to see if the original clearance has been impaired.

There will be room for a very slight change in hood opening size, as the grille work and inner panel bolt holes are elongated, but this is very minor and should not be considered a substitute for proper repair. As a rule, if the core-support panels and the grille assembly do not fit well, realignment is in order. As with most other parts of the body, the flooring or frame provides the basis for most X-checking measurements in the front sheetmetal section.

Any damage to a hood that is reparable will require constant checking, both against itself and against the fender/grille opening. The hood can be checked for correct dimensions with the same X-check procedure of diagonal measurements, but twist or contour damage can only be checked relative to the fenders. At the same time, a new or replacement hood may need minor "tweaking" to fit either a repaired or undamaged front end.

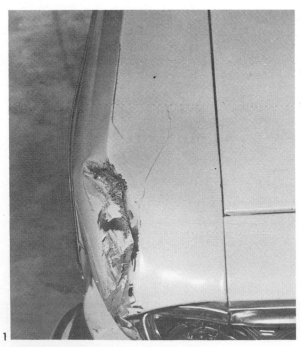

1

2

Hoods are normally held in place by spring-loaded hinges at the rear and a spring-loaded latch at the front. The hinges hold the hood in an open position, but can also be designed to pull the rear of the hood downwards when the hood is closed. In this way the hood is always "loaded" while in a closed position. Small rubber- or lubricant-impregnated fabric buttons along the fenders, cowl, and grille rest form vibration dampeners between the hood and the surrounding panels. Most automobile body opening panels (doors, hood, deck lid) flow into the surrounding panels in a smooth contour. For this reason, the slightest bit of misalignment in any of these panels will stand out. In virtually all cases, the opening panels must be flush with the surrounding panels. There is a considerable amount of built-in adjustment in the hinges to make a hood fit, but only one or two are generally involved during the adjustment process.

Finding that the hood doesn't fit is

1. Note how clearance at right front hood corner has been closed by damage to fender peak. When metal is roughed back into shape, opening should return to normal.

2. If a hood is being removed or adjusted, make a scribe mark around hinge flange as a reference point; make small movements and check, then retighten bolts.

3. Deck lids can be adjusted at the hinges; most common complaint here will be fore/aft alignment.

4. Making the deck lid seal tightly is sometimes a two-man job. Both ends are being forced down slightly; latch will then hold lid securely against the sealing rubber.

no difficult chore. Making it fit is where it gets to be difficult. If the problem lies in the hood opening, it will usually be necessary to shift the fenders and/or the front end sheet-metal-grille to get the right opening.

If a particular fender is too high, too low, too far aft, or too far forward, all the attaching bolts should be loosened and the fender shifted by use of a long lever (a 2x4 makes an excellent bar). In the case of fore/aft movement, a hydraulic jack will do the trick.

The inner panels between the fenders and adjacent to the radiator-core support are called "front end sheetmetal." If the hood opening is too narrow at the front of the hood, loosen the front-end sheetmetal bolts at the fender, jack the fenders apart, and add shims between the radiator-core support and the fenders until the correct fit is obtained. The hood strainer may bolt to the grille, the front end sheetmetal, or both, and then can be shimmed to fit correctly.

Hood hinges can be a "bag of snakes" to the beginner, but they are a delight to the professional, since they allow the hood to be adjusted fore/aft, either corner in/out, and up/down. When a hood has been removed from the hinges, the lock washers usually leave a visible mark on the hinge. Better yet is to scribe around the hinge and the attaching bolts before the hood is removed.

Shifting the hood to the front or back is a matter of slightly loosening the bolts. The bolts should be left barely tight, because the hood can shift on loose hinges as it is raised in order to get at the bolts for tightening. If the hood is adjusted to the rear, make sure the safety latch will

still catch when the primary latch is released.

It is possible to raise or lower the hood corners (assuming all other points of alignment are OK) by bending the hood hinge plate on the cowl. Bend toward the cowl to raise a corner (move it away from the fender/cowl), or bend away from the cowl to bring the corner nearer the fender. On later model cars, there are various hinge adjustments. Fisher bodies, for instance, adjust the hood rear height by special washers between the hinge and hood. Here are some more hints for Fisher body hoods:

If the hood flutters, there is not enough tension, so add special washers between the hood and the hinges at the front hinge bolts. As with many modern cars, hood height at the front is determined by adjustable rubber bumpers, but the latch must be adjusted.

Most cars have similar adjustments at the hinges for both fore/aft, and up/down alignment. In addition, the latching mechanism can be moved both fore/aft and sideways to compensate for alignment shifting. It is easiest to adjust this latching mechanism by loosening the bolts slightly (the latch may be on the hood or on the strainer), then close the hood securely. Carefully open the hood and tighten the bolts. If the mechanism has been bent during a collision, realignment is a matter of minor metal shaping, then following the above indicated course.

Most modern hoods (on cars produced during the last two decades) must rest securely on the rubber bumpers provided. The bumpers help to keep the unit in tension, remove flutter, and dampen vibration. In some

3   4

Making It Fit

1

2

3

4

cases these rubber bumpers are adjustable and should be adjusted up snug to the hood. If the bumpers are not adjustable, the hood should rest on them perfectly.

DECK LID AND REAR PANEL REPAIR

As with doors and hoods, deck lids should fit close and secure, both before and after a wreck or modification. However, the problem of providing and maintaining deck lid alignment is hampered by there being only three points of minor adjustment—the two hinges and the latch. Yet, the deck lid must fit as tightly against the sealing rubber as possible, in order to keep out water and dust.

The deck lid is aligned when it fits the body all the way around, and not until. Usually the lid is in alignment if the gap between the lid and body/fender panels is the same circumferentially; but this doesn't mean the lid is sealing. First chalk the body flange edge (or the lid, whichever the case)

that comes into contact with the lid's rubber weather strip. When the deck lid is closed this chalk will be transferred to the weather strip at all the points of contact. Where the chalk line doesn't show, the lid is not sealing. Check for non-sealing several times before making any corrective action, and make sure the sealing rubber is in good condition and in the correct place. If the lid is not sealing along most of the bottom edge, it can be drawn tighter with the latch, or by loosening the hinge bolts and sliding it forward or lowering it slightly.

As previously mentioned, it is imperative that the deck lid opening be in perfect alignment or the lid cannot be expected to fit. This does not hold true if the lid alone is damaged, but usually rear end damage includes both lid and quarter panel/fender bending. If the deck lid is severely damaged, replace it with a used unit and align the opening to fit the replacement lid. In any case, repair or

1. Older cars, like this '32 Ford roadster, usually need door aligning when undergoing restoration. Panel can be "tweaked" slightly by pulling rear edge against the knee. Doors that are misaligned often ruin the appearance of an otherwise good car.

2. Modern doors are blessed with heavy-duty hinges and a number of adjustments. This is a Chrysler type with fore/aft, up/down adjustment being made on door side of hinge.

3. The 1950 Chevy door hinges did not have as good an adjustment feature as in later models.

4. New cars have longer hinges, full complement of adjustments at door. Bulky, steel hinge arms will bend from door weight after a while, do not need collision to sag.

customizing calls for some tweaking and bending here and there.

If the deck lid seems to be twisted on the hinges—that is, one side seals but the other does not—the lid can probably be twisted by hand to fit.

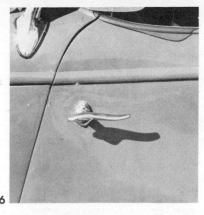

5. Old wooden-frame doors are especially difficult to align. Diagonal brace is supposed to keep doors from sagging, but as wood ages the job gets too big to handle. Framework must be reglued to cure.

6. Where the door opening changes directions there will usually be an alignment problem, since a movement in one place may be all wrong for the other. Note how much wider opening is at top of door than at mid-section.

Open the lid and place something like a rubber mallet between the body and the lid on the side that is sealing correctly. Push downward on the opposite side, but do not use excessive force. After a few test "heaves," check the lid for a fit, then repeat if necessary. This is for a minor misalignment and is not a cure-all for other ills.

Matching the deck lid to surrounding panel contour is the big problem if collision damage has occurred, or if extensive customizing is involved. These places of contour misalignment will be around the lid perimeter, and unless the deck lid has been worked, chances are the opening is out of alignment. If the deck lid opens and closes correctly, but the contour between the lid and top panel is off, the panel must be raised or lowered to fit. This panel will normally be too low, and can be jacked up with light pressure from a hydraulic jack, placed between the hinges.

Along the quarter panels/fenders, chances are the body flange will be too high. If so, tap with a mallet on or very near the flange to bring it into alignment. If this area is too low, use the hydraulic jack. Making the lower edge of the lid fit is a matter of either hammering the lower body panel out or bending the lid. If the lid is not sealing tightly at the latch, adjust the latch. If the center part still does not seal, place two equal pieces of 2x4 (or two rubber mallets) at either side and push forward along the lid center. If one corner is high, place the mallet under the opposite corner and push down on the offending corner. If

both corners are high, place the mallet under the middle and apply equal pressure to both corners.

Making a deck lid fit, especially the modern lids with such large expanses of low-crown metal, is a matter of patience and working with just small areas at a time. The key is to keep watching the crack between the lid perimeter and the surrounding panels, keeping it as equal as possible.

DOOR REPAIR AND ALIGNMENT

Perhaps the most perplexing panels to keep in alignment are the doors, since they can become misaligned through use and age as well as from damage. Even if the beginner is not an accomplished metal man, he can adjust the various openings and panels, which will be especially helpful when working on door alignment.

A door will be out of alignment when the contours do not match the surrounding panels and when the door itself is not exactly centered in the door opening. Remember, contours and centering closely control how the door seals, which is particularly critical on late model cars.

If there has been extensive damage to a door or door area, chances are the opening itself will have sustained some damage, and must therefore be carefully X-checked. At the same time, distortion of the door opening can be caused by frame misalignment, body twist, and other seemingly unrelated factors. If damage is involved, the opening must be X-checked to make sure it is ready for door alignment.

A damaged door can be out of shape in many different ways, enough to cause frustration and hours of seemingly pointless labor in trying to get true alignment. Obviously, the door must be returned to the correct shape or it isn't likely to align with the opening.

The surface contour of the door in all directions must match that of the surrounding panels. When checking for misalignment, the opening gap around the door perimeter should be uniform. Sometimes, there may be a slightly larger gap on one side, but this should also be uniform throughout its length. An unequal gap is abnormal, however, since factories have specialists who do nothing more than align doors in the openings.

While making the visual alignment check, look at the scuff plate to see if the door is dragging (sagging). Open and close the door slowly and note whether the door raises or lowers as it latches. If there is an up or down movement, the door is out of alignment vertically and is being centered by the dovetail.

There are two specific controls that keep a door in position when closed: the striker plate and the dovetail. The striker plate is the latch and the dovetail limits up-and-down movement of the closed door. The dovetail function may be taken by an integral assembly of the latch mechanism, but sometimes must be included to keep the door from jiggling up and down on the hinges.

Striker plates can be adjusted over a relatively wide range, but before any adjustments are made the striker

Making It Fit

should be replaced if worn. A little wear is no problem, but excessive wear, which is visually apparent, or sloppiness in parts (such as rotary latch) dictates replacement. If the door won't close, or fits too loosely, the striker needs adjustment. The striker can usually be moved at an angle which should be avoided.

Types of strikers will vary from year to year within a given model car, but generally speaking the same design principles hold within a certain line. For instance, GM Fisher body strikers are similar, but different from Ford or Chrysler, etc.

If a Fisher body striker is to be removed, mark the original location with a pencil. When the striker is replaced, make sure caulking compound is applied around the striker plate bolts and around the outer edge of the striker back face. This is to eliminate squeaking. It also tends to keep the striker plate from sliding out of adjustment.

Now try the door and see if it closes properly. If spacers are required to shim the striker so the lock extension will engage the striker notch, first add some caulking compound to the striker where the lock extension engages. Close the door to make an impression in the compound, then measure this compound thickness. If the distance from the striker teeth to the rear edge of the clay depression is less than 11/32-inch, spacers and different length attaching screws will be needed, as follows:

Dimension A	No. of Spacers	Spacer thickness	Striker attaching screws
11/32-9/32-in.	1	1/16-in.	original
9/32-7/32-in.	1	1/8-in.	1/8-in.
7/32-5/32-in.	1 each	1/16&1/8-in.	1/8-in.
5/32-3/32-in.	2	1/8-in.	1/4-in. longer

1. This Corvair door has the reverse problem with top of curve fitting tighter than lower area. Very little can be done for alignment.

2. To check how a door is sealing, place strip of paper in it and close. If the paper will slip out of closed door anywhere in opening, that point isn't sealing.

3. A good seal between adjoining glass areas on 4-door hardtops has always been a body man's headache, but starting in '72 all Chrysler Corp. models offer an improved, easier-to-align seal between windows.

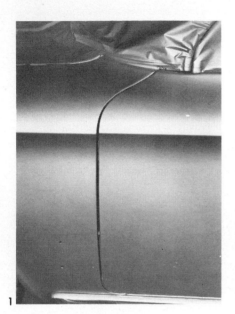

1

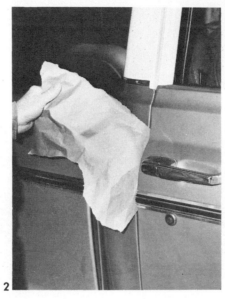

2

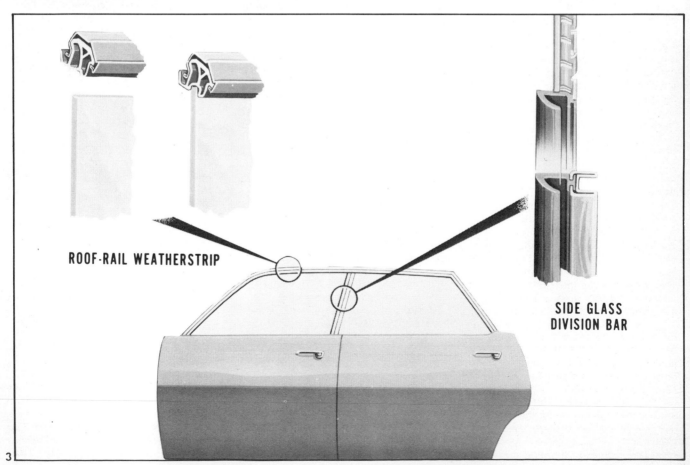

ROOF-RAIL WEATHERSTRIP

SIDE GLASS DIVISION BAR

3

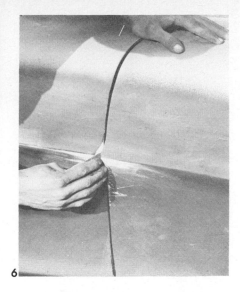

Ford strikers are adjusted differently. The striker pin may be moved laterally and vertically, as well as fore and aft. As with all cars, the striker is not an adjustment to cure door sag. As with the Fisher-type striker, there is a measurable tolerance between striker and lock that should be checked. To get this, coat the striker stub with some dark grease, then shut the door. The lock clips should close over the striker stub with a tolerance between stub cheek and clip of between 2/32-inch minimum and 5/32-inch maximum.

On Chrysler products, the striker plate's top surface should be parallel with the door latch's bottom. The striker plate is in position when there is a very slight lift to the door as it is closed (which will prevent door noise). The latch can be adjusted with shims between it and the pillar— shims of 1/32- and 1/16-inch thickness that bring the latch closer to the door. To check for the door seal, move a piece of paper at 6- to 8-inch intervals around the door opening as the door is closed. If the paper can be removed with no drag, the door is not sealing and the striker adjustment will not ensure sealing, the hinges must be adjusted.

The dovetail is not to correct door sag either, but it will allow slight movement of the door up or down for adjustment. The dovetail on older cars will probably be very worn and should be replaced.

There is considerable adjustment available at the hinges, but no hinge work should be attempted without making sure this is where the problem lies. This is especially important on older cars that did not have hinge adjustment in the fore/aft plane. Such hinges had to be spread or closed. If there is a sag condition, the usual remedy is to spread the lower hinge slightly, which moves the door bottom closer to the pillar. Some-

times, the upper hinge must also be closed to correct sag.

A hinge can be spread by placing some kind of interference between the leaves. There are fiber blocks available that can be stuck to the leaves, but most body men rely on the trusty hammer or screwdriver handle. First the handle is placed between the opened hinge leaves, then the door is pushed toward the closed position. When the handle is tight in the hinge, the door is forced toward the car (sometimes it will close if the interference is slight). Make all force spreading adjustments in small increments to keep from spreading the hinge too far. After each force session, check the door for proper fit. Proceed slowly!

If the top hinge must be closed, the hinge has to be removed. If the door has been damaged and the hinge bent, the distortion will be apparent. Repair is a matter of squeezing the hinge leaves together in a large vise.

If the car has adjustable hinges, as most modern cars do, close alignment is possible with very little labor. Remove the striker and dovetail assembly so they do not interfere with how the door actually hangs in the opening. The major difference between different makes of cars is whether the hinge adjustment is made at the door or the pillar, but in all cases, the door can be adjusted up or down, in or out, or fore and aft. There is a big difference in how hinges are made between the ''Big Three,'' but they all perform the same service. And in all cases, adjustment is a matter of slightly loosening the bolts. This will allow the door to be forced into a new position, otherwise the door will slide all over the place, making it difficult to control.

If the door alignment cannot be taken care of by the hinges or the striker plate assembly, the trouble lies in either door body opening or door

4. A small turnbuckle can often be used to align an early car door which has sagged out of "square" due to its basically wooden construction.

5. Hinges on early model cars have seen a lot of use over the years, probably have worn hinge pins as well as elongated screw holes. Best bet is to remove, pull out pin, drill slightly oversized mounting holes, de-rust, then assemble using new pins, most sizes of which are offered by reproduction parts manufacturers.

6. A door or quarter panel edge that has been damaged near a body contour line, is often difficult to match up even when rest of door fits well. Solution is to reshape the line slightly with plastic filler.

contour. If the door contour is not correct, it could require special tools in severe cases, or nothing more than a knee and two hands in others. If the door is not contoured enough (bowed), the top and bottom must be bent inward while the middle is kept stationary. On older cars with a strong framework around the windows, this can only be accomplished with what is known as a single or double door-bar tool. Most shops have these tools. On late model cars, the window framework (if there is any) is very light and can be bent by placing a knee against the door center and pulling or pushing. As in hinge spreading, use force gently.

Hot rod enthusiasts run up against a very special problem in door contour work, in that some of the older cars were not well made, and some used wood as the major substructure. If the substructure is wood, all rotten sections should be replaced and all joints glued and fitted with wood dowels or new screws. If the inner panels were metal, as on old Model T's, the outer panel may "work" over the inner panel. Force the door to the correct contour, then braze a few spots to hold the two panels together.

Frame Kinks

Repairing a car body is one thing, but don't forget that everything is based on a trouble-free skeleton.

There are two methods used in the manufacture of today's automobiles to provide a substructure or backbone upon which the car is assembled. The first and oldest method uses a heavy steel frame. The second method uses what is called unit construction where all, or a large majority, of the car is built as a self-structuring assembly with myriad channels and double thicknesses that provide the rigidity required. In either case, the body provides stiffness to the chassis, and vice versa.

And in the event of a severe collision, this backbone or skeleton is often twisted, bent, or otherwise misaligned and must be straightened before the component parts of the body undergo repair.

Truck frames are built for strength; they are designed to carry a maximum load without failure. However, a different design philosophy is followed for automobile frames. A passenger car frame is built to contribute good ride characteristics to the car. Suspension, shock absorbers, tires, and

motor mounts all contribute to overall ride performance. But without a satisfactory frame as a starting point, the ride suffers. In addition, the performance of the body—the noise level, and the degree of body shake and vibration—is a function of the rigidity of the frame.

Over the years, the auto frame has been called upon to carry greater and greater proportions of the total vehicle load. In the early days, car design was based on bridge design and strength was built into the roof

1

2

3

1. In order to insure strength and integrity of repairs, it is necessary to arc weld any ripped or cracked areas in a frame that occur during routine frame straightening process.

2. It is often necessary to heat buckled frames to accomplish a normal repair. Bill Chisholm, of Vanowen Brake & Wheel, North Hollywood, Calif., uses a natural gas torch rather than oxyacetylene, as it gives a cleaner heat and allows a larger area to be heated. Care must be taken not to "Spot Heat" when working on frames as this results in overheating and damage to frame. Proper way is start well out on buckles and move towards the center. In this way a large area is heated to a cherry red, rather than just one small spot.

3. In order to make frames accessible for repairs, it's sometimes necessary to strip the frame of bolt-on parts. An exposed frame is easier to work on during servicing.

4. In this view, a buckled frame horn on Olds Toronado is being heated and pulled on frame rack to straighten it out.

5. Tom Powers and Mike Fortier work at task of positioning the door opening to accept stock door, with hydraulic Porto-Power unit, capable of 10 tons pressure. This is used in conjunction with frame rack, but is for more localized work.

6. Specialty equipment companies have a continuing research program into better ways to repair automobile sheet metal and frames. This complex arrangement from Blackhawk Mfg. Co. includes rails imbedded in concrete. Hydraulic jacks and chains are then used to apply pulling forces.

4

5

6

Frame Kinks

and pillars much as it was built into the truss members of a bridge. But that has all changed. Increased glass area, reduction in pillar size for styling and visibility considerations, and smaller, lighter roofs have all decreased the load-carrying capabilities of the upper portions of the car. As a result of these changes, a greater burden has been placed on the frame.

Race car builders realize the importance of the frame for achieving predictable, repeatable handling characteristics. In a car such as a NASCAR stocker or a Trans-Am sedan, where space and styling are not primary considerations, bridge-like roll cage structures are incorporated not only for safety but to increase the rigidity of the basic frame design.

Since the frame has such importance, it should be checked anytime

1

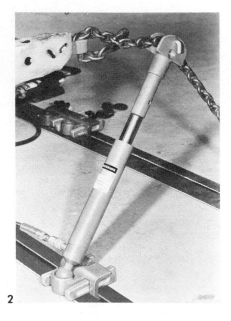

2

3

1. With this type of equipment, the worker can pull frame structures and body metal at the same time, cutting down on labor time and customer cost.

2. The hydraulic jack has long been associated with bodywork, is best used to pull rather than push.

3. The home craftsman is not likely to own specialty hydraulic jacks such as the scissor-jaw head shown, but such items can be rented or borrowed. The body man studies the area of impact carefully before using jack.

4. This is the type of equipment the average body shop will have, with various attachments designed for special or unusual jobs.

5. This is the type of pushing jack commonly associated with body and fender repairs; it is here being positioned to push crushed top back into shape. Base of jack is supported on rigid part of flooring.

Description . . . Diamond is a condition where one side of the car has been moved to the rear (or front) causing the frame and/or body to be out of square . . . a figure similar to a parallelogram.

How To Recognize . . . Diamond is caused by a hard impact on a corner or off-center from the front or rear. Visual indications are hood and trunk lid misalignment. Buckles may appear in the quarter panel near the rear wheel housing or at the roof to quarter panel joint. Wrinkles and buckles probably will appear in the passenger compartment and/or

trunk floor. There usually will be some mash and sag combined with the diamond.

How To Locate . . . Diamond damage is determined by cross checking the diagonal dimensions of the frame with a tram gage. Normally, these diagonal measurements are equal to each other . . . the length from the right front to left rear is the same as the length from the left front to the right rear. If these dimensions are different, diamond is present. Diamond can also be measured from the center of a crossmember diagonally across the car to the side rails.

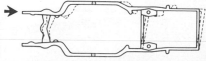

Diamond is caused by an off-center head-on impact.

The damage will extend the full length of the car because one rail has been moved rearward.

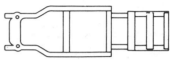

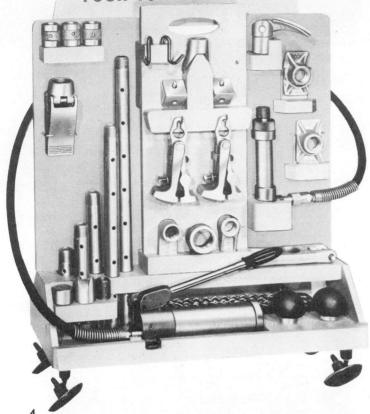

4

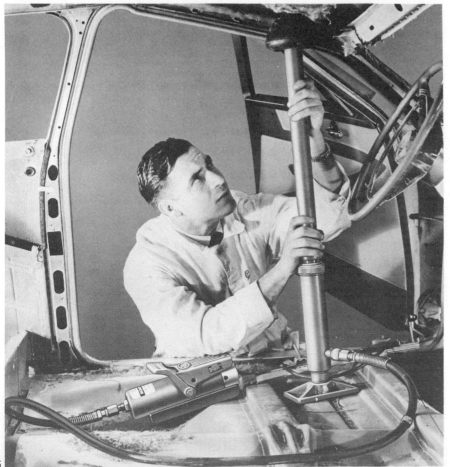

5

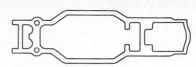

PERIMETER FRAME

This frame is separate from the body and forms a border that surrounds the passenger compartment. It extends forward for power train and suspension support . . . it extends to the rear for trunk and suspension support. Generally, it consists of box or channel-type rails joined by a torque box at the four corners. The torque boxes transfer the primary loads to the frame . . . however, the complete frame relies heavily on the body structure for rigidity.

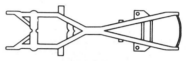

LADDER FRAME

Historically, this type of frame was the forerunner of the various types found on today's vehicles. The ladder frame is similar to the perimeter frame, but the rails do not completely surround the passenger compartment. The rails have less offset and are built on a more direct line between the front and rear wheels. This structure generally has several crossmembers and is reasonably rigid within itself. It forms a strong support on which the body is mounted.

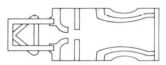

X-TYPE FRAME

Designed as an elongated letter X, this type of frame narrows to a strong junction at the center section. It has considerable front and rear stiffness and a rigid center section. Usually, it has three or more crossmembers to provide torsional stability. However, there are no crossmembers in the center section of the vehicle. This frame forms a rigid structure for the vehicle for mounting the power train, running gear and the body components.

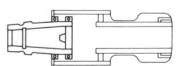

UNITIZED CONSTRUCTION

In this type of construction, every member is related to another so that all sections tend to be load-bearing members. The floor pans, rocker panels, etc. in the lower portion of the body are integrally joined so as to form a basic structure. Heavy reinforcement is used where the engine and suspension are mounted. The front portion generally looks like a separate frame . . . however, the rails are welded to the body structure thereby forming an integral support.

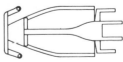

UNITIZED WITH BOLT-ON STUB FRAME

This configuration is found in several models and is particularly noticeable in some front-wheel drive vehicles. A strong, heavy stub frame is utilized to support the engine, accessories, power train and running gear. This frame may have strong, sturdy crossmembers and will extend backward under the floor pan. Back of the cowl, the remaining structure follows the conventional unitized or integral design. The front stub frame is bolted to the unitized body section.

PLATFORM CONSTRUCTION

Somewhat similar to unitized construction, this underbody consists of a reinforced, fairly flat section that forms the entire lower portion of the car. Volkswagon and similar types of cars utilize this construction technique. The lower section which includes the floor pans is a bolt-on assembly which is joined to the body. Therefore, this section depends on the rest of the body for rigidity. It serves as a support member for the engine, running gear and body structure.

Frame Kinks

a vehicle is damaged. This is necessary because of the possibility that the frame or frame structure has also been damaged. While some of the damage may be obvious, misalignment can be involved to a great extent without being seen. In checking for misalignment, diagonal measurements are the quickest method, but in making repairs, referral to original factory information is highly suggested.

1. In the absence of good pulling equipment, the hydraulic jack is used to push frame substructures back into place. When working with jacks measure the amount of progress several times. Do not overdo it.

2. Most body shops are now equipped with this type of lighter-duty beam puller. The beam is attached securely to the vehicle at strong points, then force is applied to pull frame or sheetmetal back into place.

3. In the absence of jacking equipment, the beginner may use this photograph to identify the type of jack head he may need for a particular job and rent or borrow that piece from the local body shop.

4. For straightening frame horns and flanges, Buske Industries makes two wrenches designed to slip onto the flange, utilizing the angled slots, for straightening in many positions.

5. This schematic of a 1970 Ford Mustang is an illustration from the Tru-Way Auto Body & Frame dimension book used by professional frame shops. This is an example of a working chart of the automobile chassis as the repairman sees it, with figures given in inches. These charts are intended to simplify and eliminate error in establishing the location of exact measuring points on the frame.

6. A body-frame straightener such as this rack type is an important piece of machinery in any large body shop. All the major types of damage—diamond, mash, sag, sidesway, and twist—can be repaired on such a straightener.

1

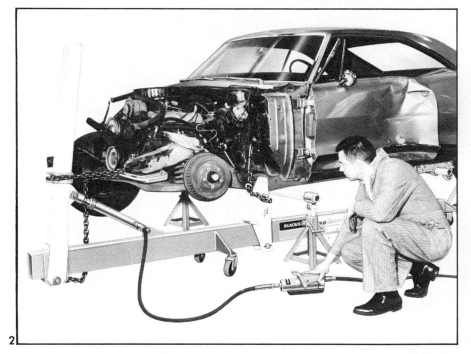

2

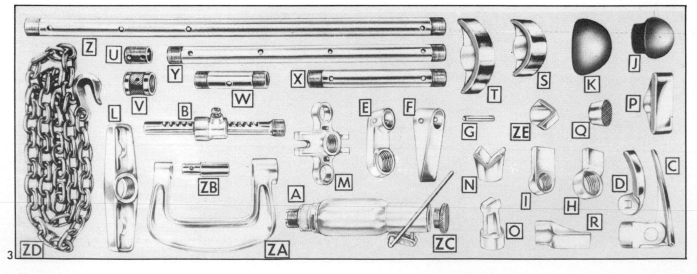

3

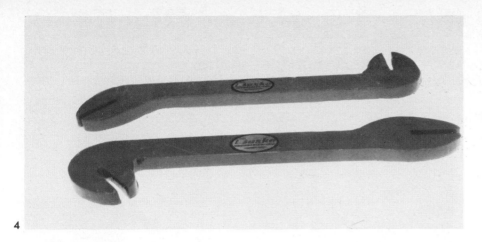

4

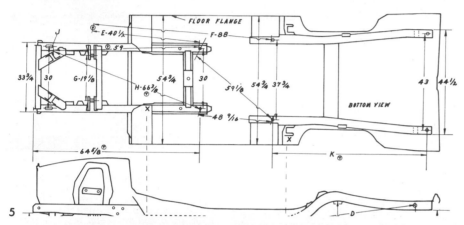

5

Frame checking is usually done at three stages: in assessing how much damage is involved, during the repair, and as a final repair check. The frame can be considered in three parts—front, center and rear—with the front being from the firewall forward, the center the portion covered by the passenger compartment, and the rear what is left.

Frame damage can run the gamut from twisting, to collapse of one section, to slight misalignment. In all cases where frame damage is suspected, the enthusiast should entrust the vehicle to a frame shop for repair. Such shops are completely equipped with necessary gauges and equipment to check and repair the frame. Repair of the major frame is not a backyard project. It is possible to replace small front frame extensions, called frame horns, but nothing larger should be attempted in the home garage.

It is possible to save considerable money on a frame repair by removing all sheetmetal that might be in the way. If the frame shop does not have to spend time just getting to the job, the resulting cost savings will be about eight dollars an hour. And a savings like that is as important to you as a frame is to an automobile. 🔧

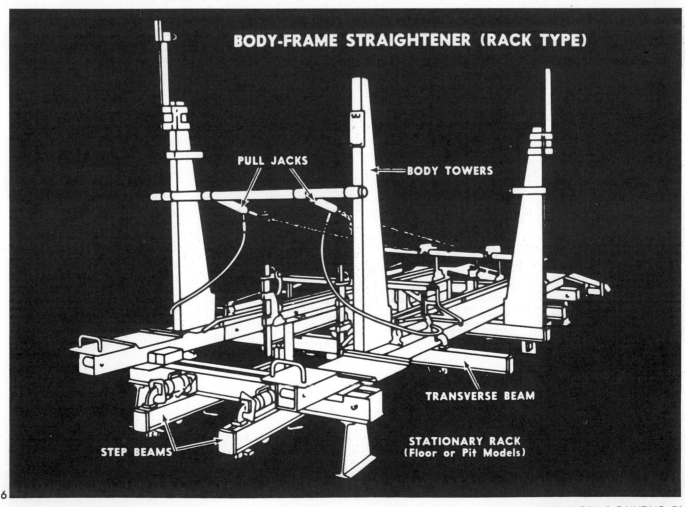

BODY-FRAME STRAIGHTENER (RACK TYPE)

PULL JACKS

BODY TOWERS

TRANSVERSE BEAM

STEP BEAMS

STATIONARY RACK
(Floor or Pit Models)

6

The Cheaters: Lead and Plastic

If you can't repair a damaged panel with hammer and dolly, there's another way—fill it!

1

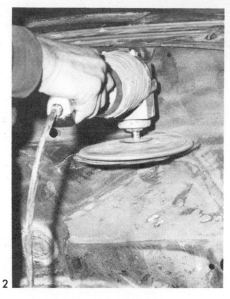

2

3

Body fillers, whether plastic or lead, are perhaps the most abused of all repair materials. It is very easy for a beginner to form the unsatisfactory habit of filling a low spot when very little effort would be required to straighten the damage. In many cases, it would be much faster to repair the metal, and save the added cost of the filler. Excessive use of filler breeds poor work traits and, usually, poor workmanship. This has become especially pronounced with the introduction of quality plastic fillers which can be applied by the very unskilled normally with poor results.

Body fillers also tend to be overused by the pseudo customizer who would take shortcuts to disguise the lack of real customizing talent. The employment of plastic or lead is an essential part of body repair and modification, but their use should be limited. When fillers are used, they must be applied with care. Experience comes with use, and as more experience is gained, the less fillers will be used.

Lead solder has been utilized in basic automobile construction for decades, and will undoubtedly continue for many years to come. Plastic fillers are relatively new, and while they do some jobs quite well, they are not to be considered a total replacement for lead. In this respect, the neophyte customizer would do well to concentrate on learning the use of lead first, then go about picking up the few remaining secrets of plastic.

Practically all automobile bodies use lead to some degree during the initial construction, usually at the visible points of panel mating. This would be where the top panel mates with the quarter panels, where the deck-lid skirt panels mate with the quarter panels, on the cowl panels, etc. However, the amount of lead used here is very small, and it's sometimes necessary for the repairman or customizer to melt this lead when replacing or modifying the panel.

Lead is not an unusual substance, but it does have some peculiar properties when correctly alloyed which make it especially well suited for automotive body application. Lead can be heated and easily shaped, it bonds perfectly and permanently to sheetmetal, it is easy to finish very smooth, and it will accept paint like sheetmetal.

Lead will bond to metals because it will tin the surface with its own properties, although tinning is often accomplished with a secondary compound, but the lead itself can be used. This is made possible by heating the sheetmetal to the melting point of the lead (a point that will vary with alloy), using some kind of flux to clean the metal, and applying a thin coat of lead. If the metal is the right temperature and has been cleaned well, the lead will flow across the metal surface like water.

Lead that is alloyed for body and fender repair has its own peculiar melting characteristics, in that it does not melt from a solid to a liquid immediately. Most body leads start to soften about 360°F. and become

1. The use of lead isn't as common as it once was, but it is still used in customizing and restoring. Plastic is the way to go for a commercial body shop, but the metal man should know the techniques of applying either.

2. The subject at hand is a firewall on a '36 Ford undergoing restoration. It had been drilled full of holes for various accessories over the years, and was dinged up in general. First step is to weld up holes, then grind paint, rust, and scale away. A #24 grit disc is used initially.

3. A small rotary wire brush chucked in a drill motor is used to clean all foreign matter from welded seams. Cleanliness before leading is a must.

softer as the temperature is raised. The point at which a particular lead compound will melt is determined by the percentage of tin in the mixture. Furthermore, the body lead alloy will melt below the melting point of pure lead, 620°F., and it may be below the melting point of tin at 455°F. The higher the amount of tin in a compound, the lower the melting point, and this must be understood when lead is being purchased.

LEAD ALLOYS

For all-around shop use, especially where considerable customizing is involved, the 70-30 alloy is best (70% lead and 30% tin). This alloy melts just under 500°F., which gives a wide latitude or plasticity for working in prolonged areas. Lead is available in a wide range of percentages, but anything other than 70-30 or 80-20 is not easy to use. A good example of

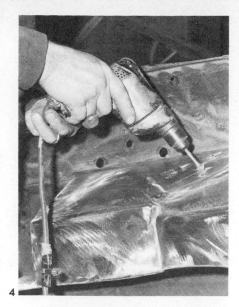

4

6

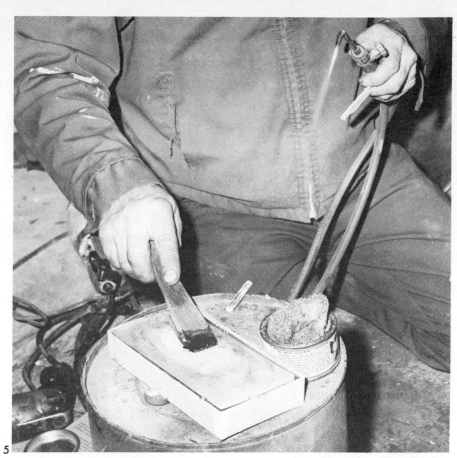

5

4. A small indentation left when a hole was welded shut is similarly cleaned with a rotary deburring tool.

5. A lead alloy comprised of 70% lead and 30% tin, and available in stick form, is used in car bodywork. Lead will be heated then spread like butter with a wooden paddle, but beeswax (or oil) should be on paddle surface to keep lead from sticking.

6. Note flame adjustment of torch. Tip of flame is allowed to lick over end of lead stick until it softens and begins to crumble. Stick is then pushed onto metal into a low "pile."

this is the solder (lead is really a solder) used for other types of repair work, such as radiators. This particular compound is normally of the 50-50 variety, and the temperature range between where it becomes soft and where it melts is very narrow.

The necessity for lead is usually restricted to filling up low spots if good repair practices have been followed, and even then the area to be filled

should be minor. However, this is not necessarily the case with customizing, where lead is usually used to cover a welded seam or as a filler to make a difficult reverse crown. No matter where the lead is used, the steps for application are similar.

There are certain basic steps involved in using body fillers, whether they be lead or plastic. In the case of lead, the area must be cleaned, tinned, filled, shaped and finished. With plastic, tinning is not involved. In the case of the beginner, nearly every one of these steps can lead to unsatisfactory results if these correct procedures are not followed. Remember, if the surface is not cleaned right, the lead may not stick. If the surface isn't tinned right, the lead won't stay in place. It is not easy to apply at first (especially on vertical panels), and shaping can be overdone. The entire job can be botched by careless finishing. Even so, leading is not difficult to master if the beginner is patient and willing to practice.

Paint, welding scale and rust are the foreign agents that are normally on any surface to be leaded. It is necessary to clean a larger area than will be covered with lead, since the filler must blend perfectly into the surrounding metal. An open-coat disc on the power sander will remove the initial paint, while a cup shaped wire brush on the same sander will make

short work of any weld scale or rust in the cavities. If this type of wire brush is not available, a smaller brush in an electric drill, or even a hand brush, can be used. The small abrasions left in the metal from the disc sander make an ideal surface for the lead to adhere to.

Acids have been used as cleaning agents, but they are more trouble than they're worth. Muriatic acid can remove weld scale and rust; paint stripper will take off paint, but these chemicals do seep down in hidden cracks and will come out and haunt you later after the finish paint is on.

After the surface has been cleaned of all foreign materials—that is, the surface is all bright and shiny (this is difficult if a welded seam is to be leaded, but it's essential)—the entire area must be thoroughly tinned. Lead will have difficulty sticking to the metal unless it has been properly tinned.

TINNING FLUX

Some kind of tinning flux is necessary, as the flux is a chemical cleaner of the steel. Since this is usually a two-step operation in bodywork, the flux will leave a burned residue after tinning and must be wiped away before lead is added. Tinning flux comes in a variety of types, but the kind normally associated with other forms of soldering is not acceptable in bodywork. Auto supply stores carry a wide range of tinning agents, in-

The Cheaters

cluding the pure-liquid type and the popular compounds, composed of flux and powdered lead. The compound has the advantage of applying the tinning lead at the same time the cleaner is being applied.

When tinning with the compounds, some method must be devised to get the compound onto the heated surface. This can be nothing more than a wadded rag, but the best is a piece of tightly wound steel wool gripped in pliers. The steel wool is pushed around in the tinning powder then applied directly to the heated panel.

When a liquid flux is used, the area to be tinned is first lightly heated then the flux brushed on. *Remember: heat applied during leading must be very closely controlled since it can distort panels, particularly those of the low-crown variety.* After the area is brushed with tinning liquid, heat the metal with brief passes of the torch until it is hot enough to melt the lead pressed against the surface. When pressing the lead bar, just a small mound will melt; then as the metal becomes too cold, the bar crumbles. A slight twisting motion of the bar will help get the correct amount. Repeat this brief heat and solder treatment to about one-third the area to be covered with lead.

At all times, the heat is applied in very brief brushing strokes, then removed. This controls the heat of the panel and the lead at a fairly constant level, somewhere between initial lead softening and actual melting. Of course, during tinning, the lead is actually melted.

To spread the lead over the surface and thereby gain the full tinning advantage, heat an area around a lead mound or two. As the lead changes appearance from the solid, grainy look to a shiny look (careful here because the change is rapid), wipe it across the panel with a wadded clean rag. Make all the wipes in the same direction, and make sure the entire area is tinned. There will be a series of overlapping wipe strokes, and when slightly cooled the tinned area will appear dull in contrast with the freshly sanded steel. While the lead is being wiped over the surface to get a good tin, the flux residue is being wiped away. It's obvious that tinning is an alternate heat-and-wipe situation. Compounds are best wiped with a rag after application, also.

Be careful when using heat and the rag on a tinned area. If too much pressure is applied to the rag, the tinning film can be completely wiped away. If too much heat is used over a tinned surface, the film can burn

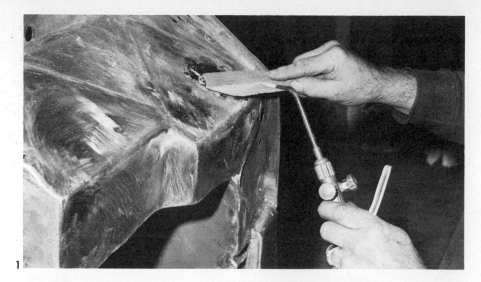

1

2

1. While lead remains in near-molten state, paddle is used to push lead around. Flame is repeatedly applied to keep lead nearly molten.

2. Vertical areas are difficult to do since lead melts and falls away, but practice will make such jobs easier. Lead is allowed to build up higher than surrounding surface; since second coat cannot be applied.

3. The #24-grit disc may be used for grinding lead, but a finer abrasive grit is better for the beginner as lead tends to cut rapidly away and it's easy to grind too deep and ruin the job. Grinding is primarily to clean surface crust off lead, knock down the high spots, until surface is shiny wherever lead was used.

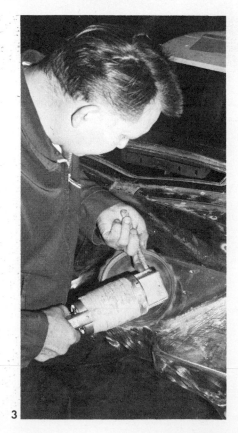

away. If a surface will not take a complete tinning, that is, if there are some small spots of bare metal that continue to show, it means the metal is not completely clean. Don't leave small, uncleaned and untinned spots and hope to bridge over with lead, such as craters in a welded seam. Get the metal as clean as you possibly can!

CONTROLLED HEAT

Up to this point, it is possible the   3

lead procedure could have been accomplished with a welding torch, or a blow torch, or even a cutting torch. Practically any kind of heating flame could have been used, provided the heat was used sparingly. But from now on the heat must be controlled more carefully, so properly adjusting the torch is of utmost importance.

Unlike all phases of welding, leading only requires a soft flame, a flame that is spread over a wide area. Generally, a medium-size tip is selected, one that might be used for welding slightly heavier steel gauge then sheetmetal. The acetylene is turned on as with welding and the torch is lit. Next the oxygen valve is opened slightly. The idea is to get a long, fuzzy flame, which is usually made up of a long, irregular blue cone with touches of yellow at the extreme tip. Even if the flame is toward the yellow side, it will still work.

When applying this flame to the metal, keep the tip well back and use just the end of the flame. Let it "lick" at the work. This will get the temperature up near where you want it and keep it there without undue heat concentration in a single, small area. Use the flame on the lead similar to the way it is used with brazing; flick the flame tip onto the metal, pass it across the lead, then flick it away. Now repeat this process until the desired results are achieved.

It is important to learn good torch control before the application of lead can even be considered, since merely keeping the unfinished lead on the panel will seem almost impossible at first. The secret is in keeping the lead at that particular temperature between first softening and melting.

The beginner is advised to work on horizontal, flat panels at first, until some experience has been gained in learning to recognize when lead is beginning to soften and how to control the torch flame. The beginner trying to lead a vertical panel, such as a door, will find most of the material on the ground. At the same time, using a relatively flat practice panel, such as a hood, will encourage good heating habits. Remember again, too much heat and the panel will distort.

APPLYING LEAD

Lead can be applied in one of two basic methods: from the bar or from a mush pot. The former is the most common for smaller areas, the latter is better for large areas or for beginners who have trouble keeping the bar at the right application temperature. The mush pot is nothing more than a melting container in which lead bar(s) have been melted. The torch is kept directed toward the pot when not being played over the metal surface to keep the lead plastic, but not at the runny, melted state. The lead is then scooped out of the pot on a leading paddle and applied to the metal surface, like stucco on a building wall. The metal surface must be kept at the right temperature, too, but since the large mass of lead is well heated, it can be spread with the paddle (a kind of wooden trowel) over a relatively large area. A mush pot can be anything, even an old hubcap. However, such a large amount of lead would mean either poor metalwork, or a very large welded seam. The latter is common to many customizing projects, such as top chopping and body sectioning. In these cases, it is best to hammer weld the seam, but if this isn't possible, the leading practice must be accepted. Even so, the lead is applied over a relatively narrow band.

More common is the application of the lead directly from the solid-bar state. If the panel is horizontal, this isn't too difficult since the melted

4

5

4. Final step in leading is to use a fine-toothed body file to bring the leaded areas down to height of adjoining original metal. If low spots or cavities show up from cross-filing, more lead cannot be added, as it will ruin previous work. Solution is to leave necessary filling to heavy priming and lots of block sanding.

5. The advent of plastic fillers that do not need heat to harden, have made it easy for sheer novices to become "body men." Plastic should never be applied over metal more than ¼-inch deep. This cross section piece was obviously "fixed" by a hair-brain.

6. Plastic fillers rely on a catalyst for hardening. There are many types available today, but in all cases go strictly by the manufacturers' instructions when mixing in the hardener. If not, you may have to wait a month for the stuff to set up, or just a few seconds. Thirty minutes is ideal hardening time, for it allows you to carefully apply the stuff, then take a breather before filing begins.

6

The Cheaters

lead will run onto the metal and puddle. Anywhere else, however, the puddle will continue to run onto the ground. When applying lead in this manner, heat the panel until the right temperature is reached, then the flame is played over the tip of the lead bar, usually about one inch of the tip. As the bar tip softens it is pressed onto the panel and the bar will break off right where it is too cold to stick. This can be accentuated by twisting the bar slightly as it is being pressed onto the panel. This procedure is repeated over the panel until enough lead has been applied. It is better to get too much than too little but more lead can be added as needed. Until experience is gained, keep pressure on the lead stick and make it crumple onto the panel.

The appearance of the lead is the key of successful working. When the solid bar begins to get shiny on one of the exposed edges, the temperature is about right for the plastic state. If the torch flame is kept on the lead, the shiny appearance will spread throughout the bar, which usually means the temperature is too high. When this happens, the lead will suddenly become liquid and run off the panel. Keeping pressure on the bar as it is heated will cause the bar to fold into the metal when it is hot enough, yet well before it becomes liquid. As a rule, apply the rough-lead buildup in the center of the working area.

Lead paddles are rather peculiar things in that any specific paddle probably will not feel exactly ''right'' when new, but even the beginner may find that an older, used paddle feels perfect the first time. Generally, new paddles seem large, sometimes unwieldy. There are good arguments for all sizes of paddles, but one about 4 inches long, excluding the curved

1. Never mix more plastic filler than you're going to use at a given time. The stuff left over will harden just as fast as that applied to the car. Although cardboard may be used as a mixing surface, as in previous photo, sheetmetal or glass is better, since foreign matter must not get mixed into plastic. After catalyst is added, the goo is thoroughly mixed.

2. This quarter panel had really taken a beating. Because the owner couldn't afford new sheetmetal, body man Lennie Morris repaired the damaged quarter panel.

3. Attempt at reaching the lower portion of the panel by crimping the trunk floorpan failed.

4. Attacking from the outside, Morris pokes holes through the quarter panel. A Morgan knocker is then inserted to pull the bow out of the metal.

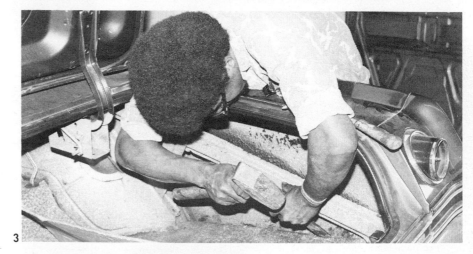

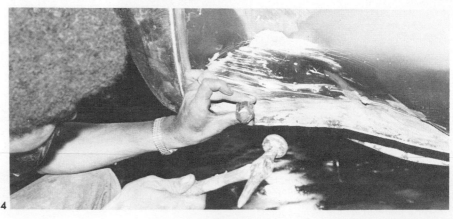

handle, is good for beginners. Paddles are made of quality hardwood, with a variety of face shapes ranging from flat to very high crowns. At least one flat and one half-round design should be in every toolbox.

The hardwood paddle can be burned by the flame, as most well-used paddles invariably are. This is bound to happen with so much alternation between flame and paddle on the lead surface, but burning will be reduced to a minimum as more experience with flame control is gained. Also, lead will tend to stick to the plain paddle. To counteract this tendency, the paddle face must be treated with a thin film of oil or beeswax. An ideal paddle lubricator can be made by cutting the side from a polish tin, then folding an oil soaked rag therein. Very lightly heat the paddle face and rub it on the rag, repeating as found necessary during the paddle process. Some body men feel beeswax has a better lubricating quality than oil. The minute the lead seems to drag or stick to the paddle, it should be lubricated as soon as possible.

PADDLING LEAD

Getting the lead onto the panel initially will seem extremely simple compared to paddling the lead out, simply because there is a certain amount of manual dexterity required in coordinating the flame and paddle. Still,

paddling lead is not unlike plastering a wall. Imagine yourself standing at a wall. The plaster trowel is usually held in the right hand, and the mortar board in the left. As a glob of plaster is stuck to the wall, it is immediately troweled out, otherwise the glob would fall. This alternating between left and right hands becomes a smooth movement with practice.

The same goes for paddling lead. The paddle is held in the prime working hand (left or right, as the case may be) and the torch in the opposite hand. The beginner will have a tendency to overheat the area at first, which may cause the lead alloy to separate into lumps of lead and tin. If this happens, more lead must be applied. The direct reaction to this overheat is an underheat, where the beginner then tries to work lead that is too cold to be spread.

Getting the lead and the surrounding metal up to the right temperature is done by holding the flame well away from the panel, with the tip of the soft flame just licking the surface. Move the flame over the area to be worked, which includes the metal and the lead, never stopping in any one spot. The idea is to heat everything uniformly, but it does not mean heating an area bigger than can be worked with a few paddle strokes.

Watch the sharp edges of the lead during this heating; mash down on the lead buildup often, as a test. The minute one little edge of lead starts to

brighten, the entire area of lead being heated is close to the plastic working state. Move the torch rapidly from this point on, flicking back to the lead only momentarily to keep the heat up.

The beginner will keep the lead in place by mashing down on it at first, which will show how soft and workable it really is. The torch plays across the lead and the paddle is used to push the lead around where it is needed. Rather than scrape the lead across the panel, it should be pulled. That is, do not lower the leading edge of the paddle and scrape, but raise the leading edge and pull the softened lead along. If the lead starts to get too hot, it will get brighter, so skip a couple of passes with the torch. If the lead is getting too cold, it will be harder to spread, or won't spread at all. Paddling lead across a metal surface is like buttering bread. If the butter is too warm, it flows too thin; if it is too cold, it doesn't spread at all.

Be careful not to keep heat on a lead area too long, as heat will cause

5. *Morgan knocker has a screw tip at one end which threads into the punched holes. The knocker uses the inertia of a 3 to 5-lb. sliding weight (arrow) to remove dents.*

6. *Starting at the lower left corner, Morris works progressively across and up the dented area. Opposite end of knocker is L-shaped to allow it to be used to straighten flat areas such as the lower lip of the quarter panel.*

5

6

The Cheaters

the lead's grain structure to become coarse. Heating an area several times and repaddling it may cause this structure change, which leaves pit holes in the finished job.

At the same time, do not get the surrounding metal too hot, as this will raise the temperature in the lead and cause it to run off. Too high a temperature will also encourage metal distortion. If some distortion is apparent the leaded area can be quenched with water after the paddling is finished but before the lead has become too cold. Throw water on the leaded surface with a rag or sponge, then as soon as the lead is cooled, rub the sponge or rag over the surface. Don't attempt this water quenching while the lead is still very hot (after paddling is the correct time, with no additional heat applied) as it will ruin the lead job. If the lead is too cold, the distortion will not be pulled out.

The beginner will find that not having enough lead to work will be his major trouble once the paddling technique is mastered. It is difficult to go back and add lead, since the temperature must be brought up carefully. The new lead must be applied and worked without overheating the already paddled lead film, and the two areas of lead must be heated enough to flow together at the mating point. If there is too much lead for a particular spot, it can be removed with the paddle while it is still in its plastic state. Ideally, the lead surface should be reasonably smooth and only slightly higher than the surrounding metal.

When lead is being used to create a specific surface, as in customizing, the amount used should be as little as possible. In past years, lead was often used as a substitute for good

metal shaping, a chore now often taken by plastic fillers. The term "lead-sled" came to mean any poorly done custom car. Thanks to better trained customizers, plastic filler or lead is used sparingly when it comes to major modifications.

FILING FILLERS

Both lead and plastic fillers file and grind away faster than the surrounding metal, so care must be taken not to cut the filler too much, nor to make gouges and scratches in the filler's surface. The beginner is cautioned to use the file for final finish work on either lead or plastic, as it will cut slower than a disc sander, and the long surface of the file will level the filler with the area of the surrounding metal.

The file will cut deep gouges if allowed to run uncontrolled over the lead. If the file is not held firmly, it may skip up on one edge, which will make a very bad cut, a cut that may not file out. It is possible to learn a lighter filing touch for filler by pulling the file rather than pushing it.

Another common mistake beginners fall heir to is cutting away too much of the filler, whether lead or plastic. There is almost always a crown to the surface being filed. If the file or sander is run across the filler only, until the edges are feathered, chances are the filler will be flatter than the crown. The correct procedure is to start on the edges and work to the middle, running the file lengthwise to the crown. This keeps the file cutting the minimum amount of filler to reach the level of the surrounding metal, gradually forming the correct crown in the filled area. The filler in the middle of the repaired depression is the last to be filed.

When the area is finished with the

file, all the edges should blend smoothly into the metal. If there is a tiny, low spot at the edge that does not smooth out, it may be picked up slightly or filled with putty later. A large, unfilled area indicates the lead was not run into the surrounding metal far enough, or the metal has distorted. Additional lead is the usual remedy if the panel cannot be picked up.

After the initial filing, the area should be block-sanded with #80 grit production paper. This paper is coarse enough to cut the file marks from the filler without loading up. It is only intended to finish off the filler and not to shape it, although such paper can be hand-held to finish off difficult areas, like reverse crowns. The disc sander should be used on a filler only by a professional. Of course, the beginner is not going to know the disadvantages of improper sander use unless he tries it, but the trial should be only on a practice panel. Generally, the sander cuts so rapidly that the beginner finds the filled area cut too low and flat. There is a certain health hazard associated with using a disc sander on lead also, in that the sander causes a fine lead dust that can be absorbed into the skin and/or breathed into the lungs. This can cause lead poisoning if kept up over a long period of time.

In summary, lead is an invaluable aid to the body man and customizer,

1. Morgan knocker was only partially successful. This panel had been banged before and the metal has work hardened.

2. Morris uses an air chisel to break the spot welds between the inner and outer portions of the quarter panel. Lip was rewelded after it was straightened. Pop rivets will work if you don't have access to welding equipment.

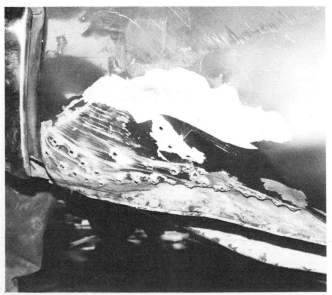

3. *The lower edge of the panel is backed up with a bodywork dolly as Morris works the metal with a body hammer. Keep the dolly firmly against the underside of the panel to prevent rebound. The panel was worked in this manner up to the crease line.*

4. *After grinding down to bare metal, the first layer of filler is applied. Use a wide blade putty knife or a plastic squeegee. Apply plastic with a firm sliding motion to ensure bond and force out air bubbles.*

5. *Cheese grater is used to eliminate high and low spots before the filler gets hard. Use a light touch. Plastic is just right to work when it peels through the grater openings in long strings.*

Because the metal cannot be worked after a plastic filler has been used, it is imperative that all high spots be driven down before the application of plastics. The area to be filled must be cleaned of rust, paint and welding scale, as with lead. Grind the metal with a $\#24$ open-coat disc to give a rough metal surface for good plastic ''bite,'' then wipe away any oil or waxes that might prevent a good bond. Clean an area larger than that to be repaired with surrounding paint feather-edged before the repair is started. This will allow the filler be spread into the surrounding metal to ensure the necessary buildup. Do not spread the filler over any paint, as it will probably peel later on. To cut down on the labor involved, do not fill more than is absolutely necessary.

Plastic fillers of this nature include a resin base and a catalyst. Unmixed, the two agents remain pliable over a long period of time, but once the catalyst is added to the resin, it will harden in a matter of minutes. It is possible to control the hardening time somewhat by the amount of catalyst (hardener) added, but the best course is to follow mixing instructions on the containers.

The most common type of plastic filler kit includes a specific amount of

but it must be used properly. Never use lead where the spot can better be repaired or shaped; only use lead if it is an economical and fast method of repair or modification.

PLASTIC FILLERS

Plastic and fiberglass repair procedures are often mistaken for one and the same thing, but they are not. The so-called plastic filler is basically a substitute for lead, while the fiberglass repair is primarily for fiberglass surfaces, but may be used on sheetmetal. In this respect, the latter is almost always used only as a repair of a rust-rotted area that could only be repaired by panel replacement or patching. This type of fiberglass repair is fully discussed in the chapter on fiberglass.

A tremendous amount of energy has been expended during the past two decades in plastic filler research, in an effort to create a true no-heat filler that will work as well as lead. While a perfect plastic filler has yet to

be found, the product of today is vastly improved over that of a few short years ago. Today, plastic can be relied upon to give a good, hard finish that will not shrink or crack with age, yet will adhere to the metal even under the most extreme temperature conditions.

There are many companies making plastic fillers, since the composition lends itself to small, local production as well as major company manufacture. Prices for such fillers range from very low to quite high, and about the only guideline for the beginner is to use the filler that the majority of local body men use. A plastic filler usually takes about 30 minutes to harden, which means that where time is an important cost factor, the use of lead may be faster. It takes less skill to apply a plastic filler, but the dust created from grinding some plastics can injure the lungs. By and large, the plastic filler has a definite place in auto body repair and customizing techniques.

The Cheaters

resin (usually contained in quart cans) and a small tube of liquid hardener. Normally, no more than two small drops of hardener are required for a golf-ball size hunk of resin. Any type of plastic filler must be thoroughly mixed. Since the mixture should be kept free of any contaminants, a piece of safety glass is the best mixing "board" available. It is easy to clean and store. Cardboard will work in a pinch.

Never mix more plastic than immediately needed, even if the fill will require several coats. The filler on the panel and that on the mixing board will harden at the same rate, so the unused portion is useless once it has been mixed.

Plastics can be applied with a wide putty knife, a rubber squeegee, or practically any kind of flexible straight edge. The rubber squeegee is perhaps the easiest to use, since it will tend to follow body contours and leave a smoother finish than the others.

As soon as the plastic is completely mixed, it should be applied to the work area. Apply the mixture onto the area with a downward-sideways motion to force out any air bubbles. These bubbles must not be left in the work, as they will shrink or burst later after the paint is applied. At the same time, this pressure will cause the plastic to gain maximum bond with the roughened metal.

If the area to be filled is more than ¼-inch deep, successive filling is necessary, with each coat allowed to dry before the next is applied. Such a deep fill might be a gouge, in which case the deepest part of the fill would receive the plastic first. No plastic would be feathered to the edges, instead this would be kept for the last coat.

If too much hardener is used, or if the material stands too long before it is applied, it will tend to roll up and pull loose from the metal. Don't both-

1. A second layer of filler was added after the first had hardened completely. Filler should never be applied more than ¼-inch deep.

2. Lower edge of panel is filled and high and low spots leveled out. Top portion of panel has been pulled back into shape and ground down to bare metal. Next, plastic will be applied.

3. After plastic filler has hardened, it is filed as described in text. If severe low spots show up, more filler can be added—unlike lead. When the surface has been built up properly, minor low spots or chips in plastic are wiped with glazing putty. Then an open-coat grinding disc backed with soft rubber backup pad, is used to featheredge filler to metal.

4

5

a very light touch, shaping carefully until the filler is almost down to the desired height. Let the plastic harden for a while longer, then finish it off with a long, flat block and #180 grit sandpaper. Coarser paper will tend to leave scratches. The long sandpaper "file" will smooth the filled spot into the surrounding area just as the lead file does. Air files, pneumatic tools having a long, narrow platen taking coarse sandpaper up to about 4-ins. by 16 ins., should be kept out of the hands of the novice. They cut too fast, at up to 3500 strokes per minute, and will eliminate a carefully formed crown of filler in short order. Used judiciously, though, and with experience, they have made the use of plastic fillers populars due to the speed (thus, time-saving) at which they operate. Finally, finish the area for painting with a regular rubber sanding block and #220 grit sandpaper or garnet paper.

If the plastic is allowed to become too hard, it must be worked out just as lead with a regular metal file and/or a disc sander. The beginner will find the file as necessary here as with lead since the filler can be cut down too low. If the sander is used, a respirator or some kind of nose protection should be used to protect the lungs against the plastic dust.

Plastic fillers should not be used as a substitute for poor body repair or sloppy customizing, no matter how easy they are to apply. Just as the lead-sled name was often attached to custom cars of old, the "putty-car" is common today. Using too much plastic filler is just asking for trouble. Plastic should never be used where the body is liable to flex or where strength is required, just as lead should never be used to bridge a gap that should have been welded. Nor is plastic acceptable as an edge. If an area must be filled out to an exposed edge or lip, lead should be used at the edge, then the plastic added. The lead won't be as strong as sheetmetal, but it won't chip like plastic.

In areas where there are extreme temperature fluctuations during short periods of time, plastic fillers have been known to give problems. If this is the case, local body men will have found which plastics should be utilized.

Apply a primer-surfacer that is recommended over plastic, as some paint compounds have a bad effect on fillers. The auto parts store specializing in paints will know what compounds will work. Should problems occur after the paint is applied, it will be only because of poor filler application (surface not clean, etc.) or because the paint is reacting to the filler. 🦅

4. Upper portion of fender has been ground down, as compared to lower part which has yet to be featheredged.

5. Final step before preparing for paint is running tape where original fender had a contour line, to be sure the line is straight. Disc grinder is used to "sharpen" up the edge of the stock crease line.

er going further; mix a new batch and start again.

Finishing plastic can be either very easy or extremely difficult, depending upon how long it is allowed to set before the finishing process is started. It is not uncommon to see a gouge obviously filled by the car's owner with plastic. Usually the owner has applied the filler rather roughly and apparently waited until the plastic has become very hard before attempting to file or sand it smooth. By then, it required a very sharp file, a disc sander, and lots of elbow grease. He had none of these.

A regular body file is not used to work plastic. The type of file used is referred to as a cheese grater, the kind of file often found in wood working. Blades for these files are available in a variety of sizes, as with normal lead files, for unusual contours. Special holders are also available, although the blade can be used without a holder.

Plastic fillers set up hard because of chemical interaction, thus they do not "dry" in the normal sense of the word. However, they are affected by high temperatures, so they will harden faster on a very hot day. To speed this hardening, lamps used for paint drying can be directed on the mixture. At any rate, it is best to begin working the material while it is still "soft." This can be determined by touching the surface lightly with the grater. When it is just right to work, the plastic will peel through the grater openings in long strings.

Work the area with the grater and

Tin Bending Tips

Picks, dollies, hammers and jacks. Here's how to use the tools of the bodyman's kit.

One of the important parts of learning how to do bodywork is the experience of working on many different types of dents, bumps and gashes. A good body man can do a job fast and well, simply because there isn't any type of collision damage that he hasn't seen at least once before. And if he's really experienced, he's not only seen it on *one* make of car, but probably on *every* make that's on the road today.

To photograph work in progress on several different kinds of collision damage, we went to Santa Monica College, where we talked to Eddie Kile, the body shop instructor. Eddie had lent us a hand on the Pound-Out Parade chapter in our last edition and we know that if there is one person in the bodywork business who knows where it's at, Eddie fits the bill—he's been in the body repair business for so many years that he automatically examines your car for signs of previous damage.

Because he was in the business long before all of the quick-fix plastics came on the market, Eddie Kile knows that a good body repair man is one who can work metal, not just

HOW-TO: Malibu Rear Door

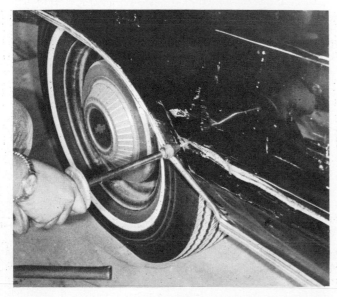

1. The nasty gash in the side of this Malibu rear door was accompanied by a healthy dent in the panel and is typical of the damage that occurs if you cut a pole too sharply.

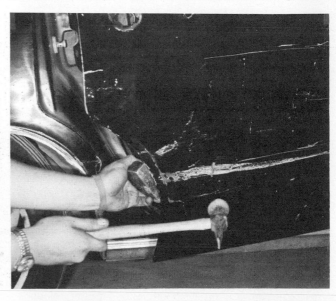

2. After using the Porto-Power with a wedgie inside the door to restore panel configuration as much as possible, a hammer and block of wood are used to knock out the smaller gashes.

3. A series of holes are drilled in the gash and a knocker is used to pull out the metal. Small damage to a panel can often be corrected by this step alone.

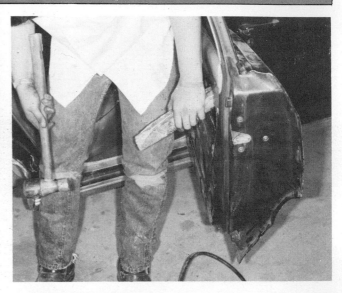

4. A hammer and dolly are used to bring the door edge back to shape. This step is important in lining up the door so that it'll close correctly.

slap some filler into the hole and smooth it out with a board. "We use filler, meaning lead or plastic, only when the metal itself cannot be repaired," Eddie said, "but because of auto styling and the types of damage that occur today, pure metal working is becoming harder and harder to do without at least a bit of filler."

The following series of photos show Eddie's students at work on several different types of common collision damage, which run the gamut from those types you can work on in the backyard to those that require equipment only a professional body man would have access to.

5. Judiciously applied, the spoon and hammer will contour the door panel, taking out most of the high spots. Go easy to avoid knocking metal in too far.

6. A flexible disc sander and #16 grit paper takes the finish down to the bare metal fast. Although many body men don't wear them, goggles are recommended for safety.

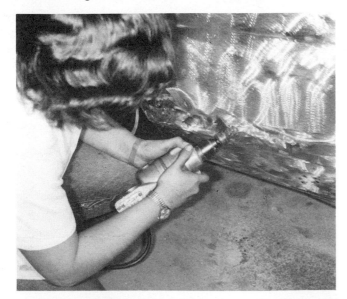

7. Finish is removed from low spots and crevices with a wire brush. Wear goggles here also, as a sliver of metal can end a bodyworking career.

8. A final working of the door edge with hammer and dolly assures a perfect fit and reduces the possibility that the untrained eye will be able to detect that damage.

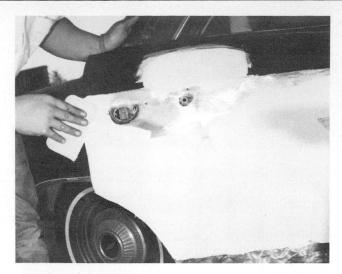

9. Body plastic is mixed and applied evenly above the lower crown line. You could do the entire panel at once, but shaping the crown line is more difficult that way.

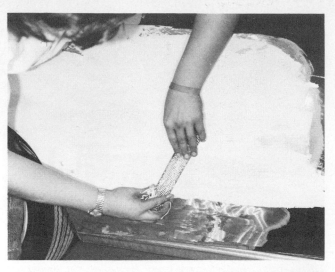

10. The cheese grater must be used at just the right moment. If the plastic is too wet, it drags and if too dry, it can't be filed. In this case, sand it down, and reapply.

11. A final sanding with the straight line sander will remove the cheese grater marks and show up any low spots that require another filling and featheredge prior to priming.

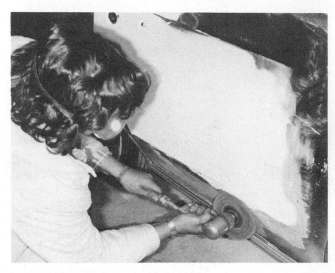

12. The small disc sander cuts the plastic along the crown line. Then apply plastic below the crown, file and sand. Use of filler here is unavoidable.

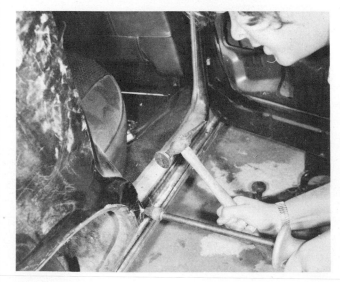

13. The leading edge of the rear quarter panel must be straightened. A knocker used with a hammer pulls the metal back out where it can be roughly shaped.

14. With the door handle back in place and a coat of primer on the metal, the crown line of the door is checked to match the quarter panel crown line repair.

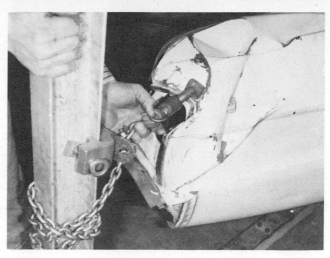

1. Crumpled rear fender on Chevy II is a tossup—to straighten or to replace? We're going to pull it back and do a bit of metal working, so off comes the bumper and trim.

2. The Blackhawk pulldozer is fastened to the damaged area after the spotlight has been removed. Using the pulldozer is sure a lot better than using the push jack inside.

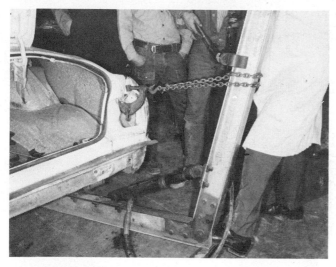

3. Instructor Eddie Kile supervises the pace of panel restoration as his class watches. The trick here is to not go too far, or not far enough—but just as far as necessary.

4. The placement of the pulldozer attachment unit is changed as the fender begins to assume its original shape. It's impossible to pull it out from one location.

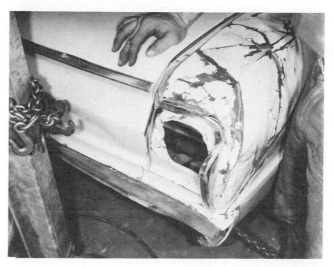

5. As the pulldozer is operated, the fender is hammered from inside to smooth out wrinkles and keep damaged area from tearing further which would just mean more work.

6. Damaged area has been restored to gross configuration by pulldozer, and now it's up to the body man and hand tools to do the rest. Job doesn't look so formidable now.

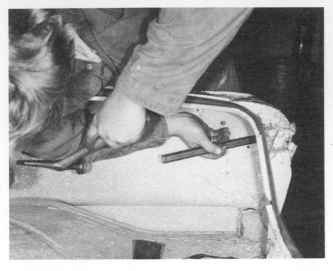

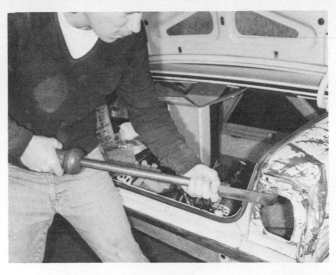

7. Hammer and punch used from inside applies local pressure to the edge of the stoplight opening. Some minor tearing of opening edge metal will be unavoidable.

8. A large knocker and claw pulls the fender in toward the trunk. This is fastest way to move the entire unit at once. Again, go slowly for obvious reasons.

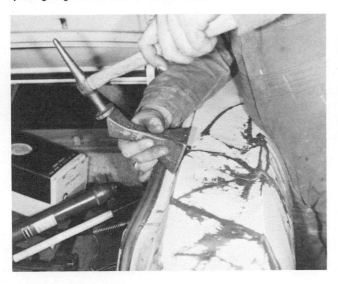

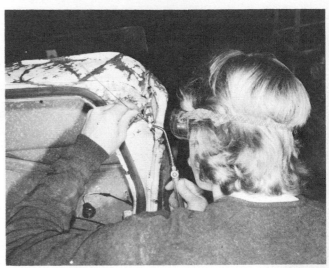

9. Fender line is reestablished with a hammer and dolly so that when the deck lid is closed, the gap between the panels will be very nearly uniform.

10. The tear in the metal along the panel line is welded with torch and steel rod. Adjoining edges of rip must be dollied into alignment before welding begins.

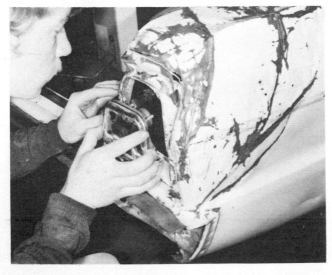

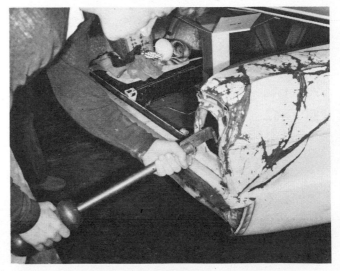

11. Stoplight unit is tried periodically to check on its fit and the progress of the repair. Several trial fits will probably be necessary before this job is finally completed.

12. Fender still has to move slightly toward the left, so the knocker and claw are used again. Go cautiously so that you will to avoid tearing the welds open.

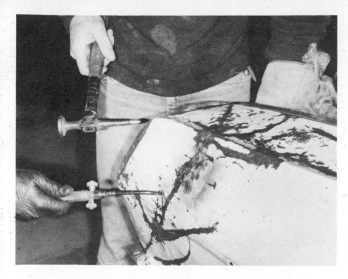

13. The metal bulge along the crease lines is removed by heat shrinking the fender. To get rid of the bulge, heated spots are hammered smartly while they still glow red.

14. A new trim moulding is used as a guide to fender repair progress. The stoplight fits correctly at this point, as does trim. It's looking good, but a lot of work remains.

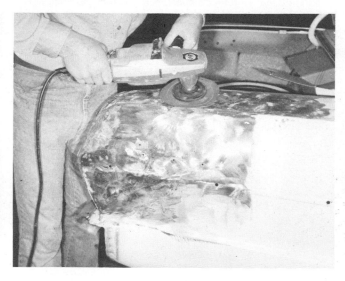

15. The entire area is ground to bare metal with high spots removed as much as practical. Where the grinder shows up severe low spots, they are tapped up, then grinding resumed.

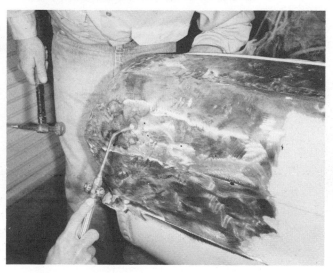

16. Remaining high spots are heat shrunk into place as fender assumes a considerably different appearance than at the beginning of the job. Fender can be saved after all.

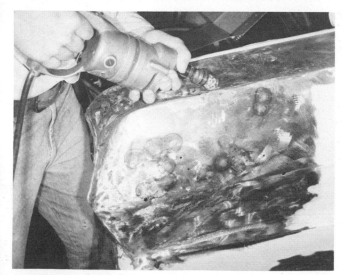

17. Low spots are ground with wire brush to remove all of the old finish and to clean out any scale from torch or other foreign matter that might be on the surface.

18. This is one of those jobs where the use of plastics is almost unavoidable for a fast, smooth finish. When Pat Nolind finishes, this fender will be ready for painting.

HOW-TO: Comet Engine Compartment

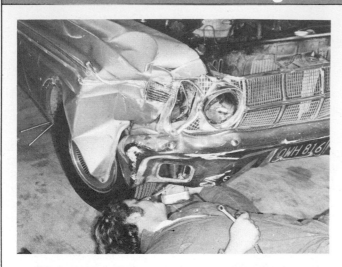

1. Comet front end was struck at 135° angle, completely ruining this front fender and grille. All this will be removed and replaced with new metal.

2. Comet is unit-body construction and measuring the two diagonals of the engine compartment reveals that impact moved front of compartment ¾-inch to the right.

3. Blackhawk pulldozer has 3-ton capacity and is connected to radiator shield panel at one end and to frame at the other, giving it something to pull against.

4. Note that pulldozer is secured to radiator shield panel in two places before pressure is applied. This prevents attachment bolt from being pulled through lighter metal.

5. Additional pressure is applied by angling a Porto-Power unit with its ram pushing from the lower left frame member to the upper right corner of engine compartment.

6. With both units in operation, compartment begins to move into line. Porto-Power and pulldozer are more arms for body man. New sheetmetal can now be fitted.

1. Deck lid damage is typical hazard of stop-go driving in heavy traffic. Trim removal is always the first step in gaining access to damaged area.

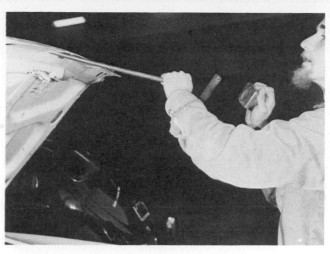

2. Difficulty in repair is compounded by double panel. Picking bar is inserted through holes in inside panel and struck with dolly to help spring outside panel back to shape.

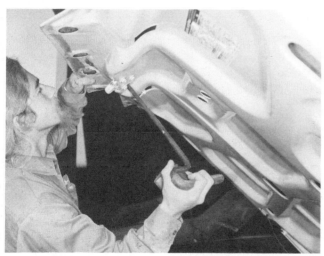

3. If sufficient leverage to move deck lid panel can't be obtained from one angle, try another. Bar is used wherever it can be inserted and pressure applied.

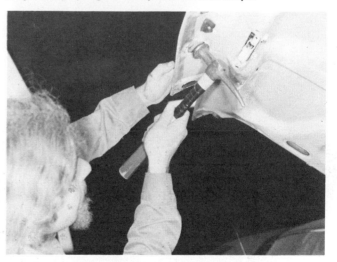

4. Deck lid line is straightened with hammer for perfect fit once trim is replaced. Inner panel access holes make it possible for a pry to be inserted.

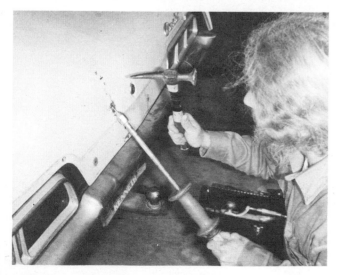

5. Knocker and hammer are used to pull out remainder of crease in outer panel. As outward pull is exerted on knocker, pick hammer "unlocks" stresses in metal.

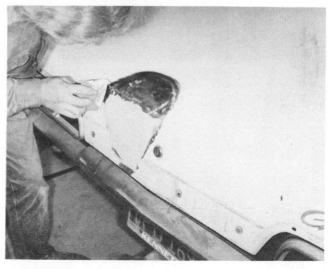

6. Repair area is ground to bare metal and plastic applied. Once sanded and primed, the trim is replaced and the car is ready for the customer.

HOW-TO: Mustang Quarter Panel

1. Mustang rear quarter panel damage is common but complicated by the lower sculpture panel line at point of impact. Interior trim panel is removed as the first step.

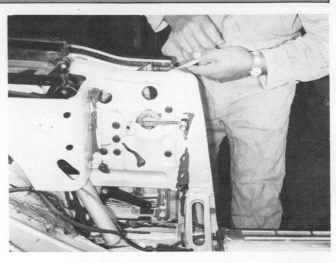

2. Window and mechanism must all come out before repair can be effected. This is slow and tricky procedure, and location; relationship of parts must be remembered.

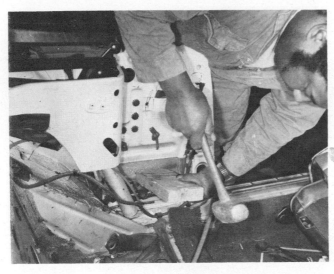

3. Once window mechanism is out, some of the panel contour can be restored with a hammer and block of wood. This should be done before bringing jack into play.

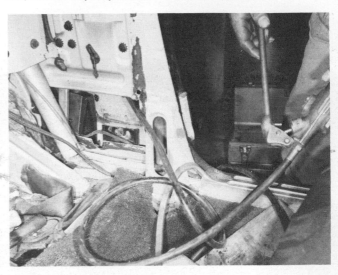

4. But for most of the damage, the 4-ton Porto-Power unit with wedgie attachment is necessary. In some cases inner panel would have to be cut to get jack in.

5. Once the attachment is set in place, watch outside of panel as Porto-Power is operated. As panel portion regains original shape somewhat, move wedgie to another area.

6. It is virtually guaranteed that some parts of panel will spring back too high. Equalize with a body hammer to keep repair process progressing evenly.

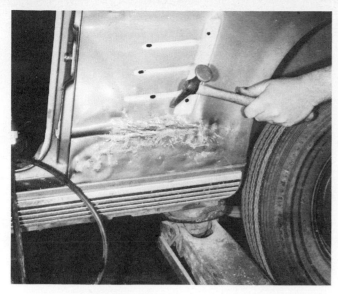

7. Here's another tricky step—restoring the sculpture line by working the metal with a hammer. Remember, lots of light hits are better than a few hard ones.

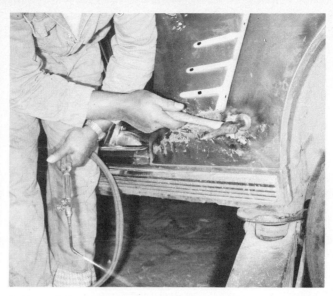

8. Heat shrinking the bulge behind the panel sculpture helps to bring the sculpture line back to normal. Spots are heated cherry red, then rapped with hammer while still hot.

9. Grinding is the next step and care is required to avoid cutting through the metal as the disc is tilted. If disc edge is trimmed to sawtooth edge, it'll lessen digging tendency.

10. The upper sculpture line is also worked with the grinder. Once these two areas are completed, the rest of the repair area is sanded down to the bare metal.

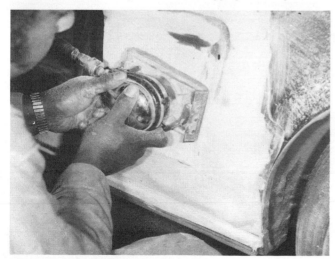

11. Plastic is applied and sanded to finish a perfect restoration of the sculpture lines. Finishing crevices isn't necessary because the trim will hide any crevices that remain.

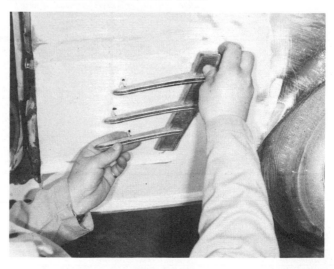

12. Before priming, the trim is temporarily refitted to the panel as a double check on sculpture line and panel contour and any adjustments that were made during repair work.

HOW-TO: Chevrolet Hood

1. Hood and grille were damaged in two places. Bumper, grille and trim are not salvageable so will all come off and be replaced with Chevy agency parts.

2. Porto-Power unit is placed between hood hinge and grip wrench. Any hydraulic ram like this pushes at both ends and has to be placed with care or you'll bend something.

3. After using the Porto-Power, Eddie Kile brings the hood down on a 2x4 with a sharp blow to help spring damaged area out as much as possible, repeating if necessary.

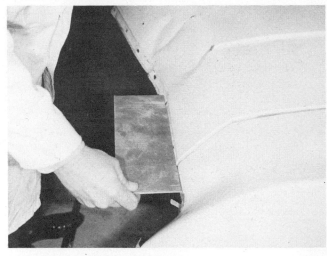

4. Eddie uses a piece of aluminum to check panel edge line for correct fit. Eyeballing it isn't good enough here, as gaps are often deceiving.

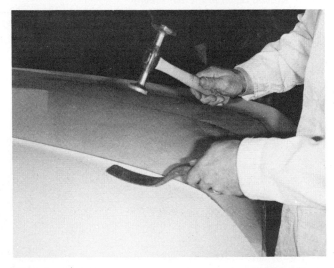

5. Spoon and hammer are also of help in spring-hammering the damaged area back into place. Spoon is lightly but repeatedly tapped as it's moved over the area.

6. New trim is now fitted to hood line to check progress and to determine further steps to be taken in repair. Eyeballing, or rubbing with palm may turn up more damage.

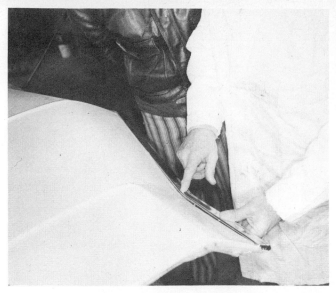

7. Edge line is almost restored on this side. Working a hood like this one without the new trim as a guide is almost impossible, since you can't eyeball a crooked line.

8. Hood is held and hammer used from underside. Double panel construction of hood makes this a slow and tedious stage. Sometimes a pry can be inserted between panels.

9. Reversing the direction of the hammer blows helps to keep the repair uniform instead of turning the creases into a large bulge; go back and forth over area.

10. Grinder and #16 grit paper are used to cut the high spots and to remove the finish to the bare metal. Keep disc nearly flat to panel so metal won't be cut clear through.

11. Low spots can be cleaned with a wire brush though this will take a lot of elbow grease to get them absolutely clean. There is a better way to do this.

12. Using a power drill and wire brush is much faster. Once this is finished, plastic is applied and sanded to restore panel configuration completely.

HOW-TO: Dodge Front End

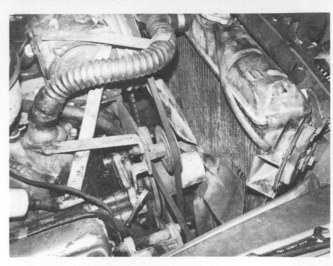

1. This Dodge suffered a square hit on the front end, and while it would be normal to replace sheetmetal with junkyard parts, none were available for this model.

2. Radiator was knocked into fan, so it too must be replaced. All the parts damaged beyond repair had to be purchased new; expensive but necessary.

3. A problem always encountered with damage this severe is getting at the nuts and bolts to remove the pieces. Sometimes a torch is needed, though pry worked here.

4. Left fender could have been repaired, but the time it would take would necessitate a cost greater than a replacement fender, so it will be junked out.

5. Though both fenders will be replaced, they are left in place temporarily. With damaged grille and related pieces off, jacks will be used to pull the fenders out.

6. As fenders are jacked out to approximate shape, they'll bring adjoining panels and related bracing with them which will simplify attachment of new fenders.

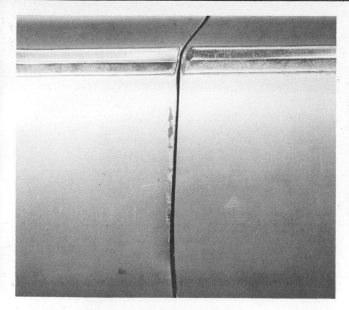

7. Fenders were hit hard enough that the gap between the doors was closed. Jacking old fenders back to the proper position restores gap so new fenders will align.

8. Everything that will be replaced has by now been removed. Frame horns were knocked out of alignment so next step will be jacking them back into alignment.

9. Next, inner fender panels are jacked out with a bulldozer jack. Measurements from new fender bolt holes are checked on panels so they won't be stretched too far.

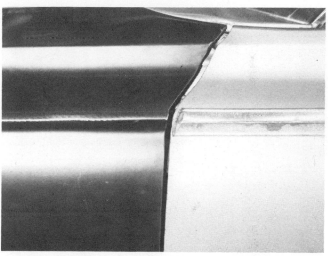

10. Because old fenders had been roughly aligned before removal, new fender bolts on in pretty good alignment and needs only minor adjustment to get the gap even.

11. Hood gap is also checked between cowl, to see if hood had been shifted in accident, and between fender as reassurance that fender is located where it should be.

12. From here, it's a matter of bolting on new pieces, then paint preparation. Obviously, sheetmetal from a wrecking yard would have eased the job considerably.

HOW-TO: Ford Quarter Panel

1. Two-inch depression in rear quarter panel of '70 LTD is deceptive. Regular body shop would fill with plastic. We're going to work sheetmetal first to near perfect contours.

2. Safety light on side of fender is easy to remove by going through trunk. On this car, rear fender panel is also inside wall of trunk. Loose objects in trunk can dent fender.

3. The worst of the dent can be removed with a hard rubber hammer. This brings panel closer to its original shape; be sure you don't make the dent worse.

4. Rubber hammer is exchanged for the flat surface of a picking hammer. Smaller and harder head will flatten wrinkles when backed up with a flat dolly.

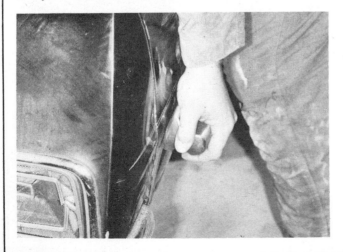

5. This operation is done with a dolly pressed firmly against the exterior of the panel, exactly opposite the area struck with the hammer. Light raps will help shrink metal.

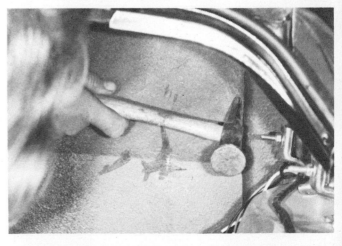

6. Sharp end of picking hammer is used in tight spots that are close to panel corners and hard to reach with flat side. Use care with pointed end, don't use flat dolly here.

7. Hand is used instead of dolly for this hammering operation, because sense of touch avoids creation of high spots that will have to be ground out later.

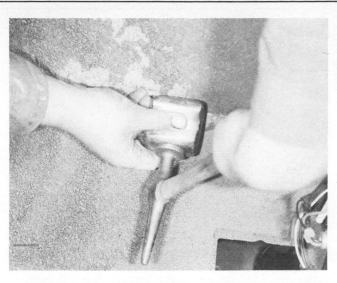

8. Panel is fairly smooth, but it's still a bit low. Work entire area slowly and evenly with hammer and dolly to bring damaged area back to original shape.

9. Body file is pressed into service to remove high spots (and paint). This part of the job requires plenty of muscle and a good eye. Different files will help here.

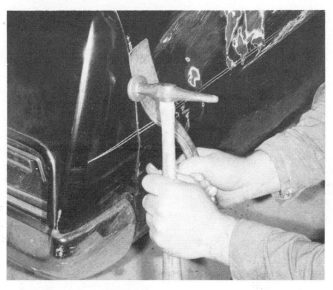

10. Match the end of the panel with the fender cap with a spoon and hammer. Always ease into hammering steps gradually to avoid overworking the metal.

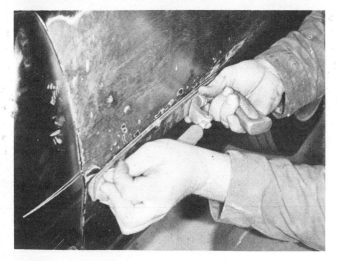

11. Most fender panels have a sculpture line which must be redefined when the fender is dented. Here, a contour file is used above and below the line. Don't file peak thin.

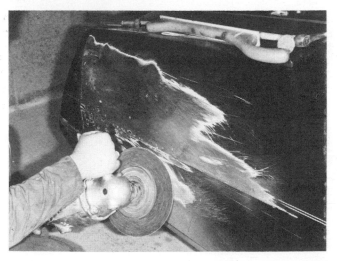

12. After hammering and contouring is nearly complete, body grinder is used to remove all paint in the area. Expose bare metal to prepare for plastic, or filler will not stay.

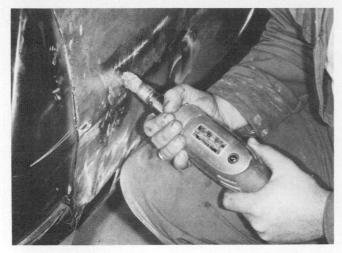

13. Low spots will appear quickly because they will contain old paint. Clean them out thoroughly with rotary brush, or filler will fall out eventually. Surface must be clean.

14. Because the metal was worked very close to perfection, only a very thin coat of plastic filler is needed. Plastic should be used in thin layers in finish coats.

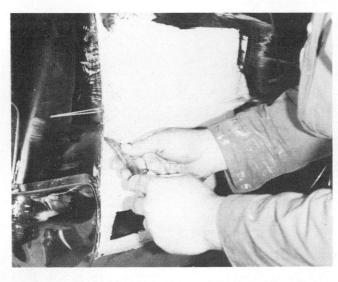

15. Remove excess filler from between the two adjacent panels with a sharp instrument. Do it while the filler is still wet, as it is much easier. Plastic will set in 3-10 minutes.

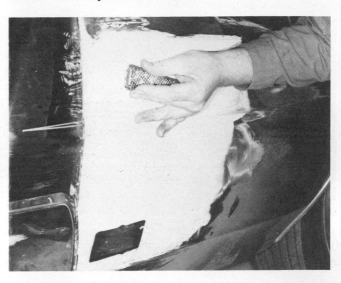

16. Use a cheese grater rather than a file when working thin applications of plastic filler. Begin work just after filler begins to set to remove excess. Use hands to check shape.

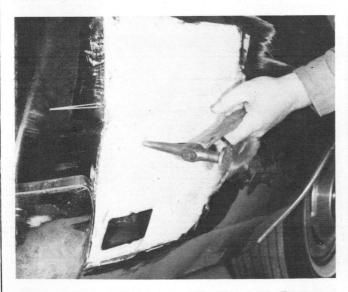

17. Use of the grater may expose some high spots. These may be hammered lightly into place, but use care when hammering on filler or you may crack it. Note hole for safety light.

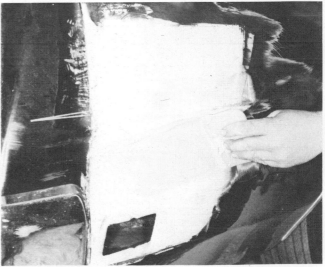

18. Final application of plastic is also thin. Cheese grater will be used once more, then repair spot is ready for final sanding and priming. "Green stuff" may be used to fill pits.

1. Rusted out seat wells in this '60 El Camino pose a common problem for drivers living in snow-bound or salt-air sections of the country. Salt attacks sheetmetal with vengeance.

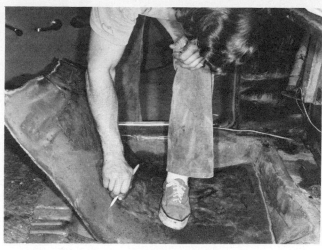

2. Short of replacing the entire floorpan, there's no way to halt effects of rusting. But years of life can be added by brazing in a new sheetmetal patch. Remove all damaged metal.

3. After measuring and cutting to the size of the patch area, sheetmetal should be trial-fitted to ensure that brazing is done to unrusted metal. Use heavy gauge metal for patch.

4. Further trial fitting and trimming will provide a tight, close fit that will conform well to the seat area. Note this floor was completely rotted out. Driver must have had wet feet.

5. Tack new floor every 4 to 6 inches with brazing rod and torch. Additional hands might help in pressing new piece down for tight contact with pan.

6. Once tack spots are made on all four sides and corners, entire seam is brazed. Seat can then be positioned and new bolt holes can be drilled for seat and seat belts.

The Why's and Wherefore's of Fiberglass

Strong stuff, and demanding skill, 'glass is nevertheless no mystery; it's merely knowing materials and techniques.

Those earlier fears associated with the repair of fiberglass panels used on many cars today have been largely overcome with recent developments in materials and technique. This is good news to the body man, who will be facing the ever-increasing use of this body panel construction material. But, as is the case with all areas of car repair, only practice will make the novice proficient in the use of fiberglass after the basics are understood.

Plastic cars were introduced to the automotive sport during the early 1950's, although fiberglass had been experimented with for many years previously. Henry Ford made the newspaper front pages by banging away at 'glass fenders on pre-WW II cars, but the product remained more an oddity than anything else. These earlier plastics required highly specialized manufacturing processes. This was all changed with the availability and introduction of low-cost fiber and polyester resins.

Fiberglass can easily be likened to concrete, a material well suited to molding but not exceptionally strong in itself. However, with the addition of steel reinforcements, concrete becomes the basis for fantastic architectural schemes. And that's the way it is with fiberglass.

By itself, resin is easily formed but has little strength. This is the job of 'glass fiber reinforcements, which are available as interwoven blankets or as matted blankets (the latter formed by pressing individual filaments together with a weak binder). There is no use working with fiberglass unless you understand what it is.

Synthetic resins come in a number of forms, including phenolics, acrylics, epoxies, ureas and polyesters. The entire enthusiast industry has chosen polyesters because they are easy to use and control—and are inexpensive as well. While the material for an aluminum car body may cost upwards of $500, the same body can be formed from fiberglass for less than one-fifth that figure.

Resins of polyester are a heavy liquid, weighing about 9 lbs. per gal. and ranging in viscosity between water thin and molasses thick (between 75 and 70,000cps). Enthusiasts use a cps of about 700, since this is the easiest to work with and easily saturates both fiberglass mat and cloth.

It is the possibility of resin curing itself, or hardening, that makes it so desirable as a binder with fiberglass filaments as the core strength material. For resin to harden, it must have a catalyst added, then be heated to 200°F. for approximately 2 hours. However, if the heat is not added, the combination of resin and catalyst can last for several days before the catalyst begins to cause internal heat and subsequent hardening. This chemical heat, called an exothermic reaction, will turn the liquid into a solid; a characteristic that hobbyists use to advantage in plastic crafts.

Exothermic heat cures the resin just as the external heat will, but at a much slower rate—far too slow for the auto body builder or repairman. Since a big heating oven is not available, and long natural curing time is unsatisfactory, an accelerator is added. This accelerator serves to "kick" the catalyst in a much shorter time, causing the exothermic heat to intensify. Thus the builder can vary the time resin will "kick" simply by the catalyst/accelerator combination he uses. However, the resin will harden much faster in a large mass (due to the exothermic heat involved) than when spread thin. That's why resin must be mixed in relatively small batches to avoid unnecessary waste.

The most common resin/catalyst/accelerator formula calls for about 2% catalyst and accelerator by weight. This percentage will hold true throughout numerous mixing sequences if good materials are used each time.

Room temperature has an effect on curing time, with the time speeding up on a hot day and slowing down on a cold day. If a bucket of pure resin is mixed with catalyst and accelerator at the 2% basis, it will start to set in about 40 mins. and cure completely in two hours at 70°F. ambient temperature. Using this as a base, the enthusiast can vary his formula to suit his own conditions.

SELECTING MATERIALS

It may be difficult to select materials without prior experience, but the best guide is always to go for quality. There are resins for all kinds of different uses, some that do not cure at

1

room temperatures, others that are inhibited by air and never surface cure. Tell the supplier what you have in mind and he will give you the correct materials.

Just as quality resin of the correct type for automobile bodies is necessary for any type of fiberglass work—whether molding an entire body or making a small patch—quality 'glass fibers for the reinforcement are necessary. A number of different reinforcements might be used, such as rayon, nylon, linen, cotton, etc., but none has proven as suitable as 'glass.

'Glass fibers are made by applying heat and pressure to 'glass which is in marble form, producing long filaments (called fibers or rovings) that can be bunched in various ways, much in the same manner as ordinary sewing thread. To make manufacture and subsequent handling easier, a binding is sometimes included at this stage of manufacture.

Two types of fiberglass are used in body manufacture and repair: woven cloth and mat. Woven cloth is practically the same as any other woven material, but the texture of the weave, which means the amount of 'glass contained in a particular square inch of cloth, has a direct bearing on cloth strength. For building a car, cloth from .010- to .015-in. thick and with a moderately open weave is recommended. This gives the strength of 'glass plus the texture for good resin penetration. Because fiberglass materials cost in proportion to amount, some manufacturers of specialty bodies try to control cost by using less material. This can only result in an inferior product, something many buyers find out the hard way. Always check the reputation of the builder first, and if possible inspect one of his products. It is possible to build up the strength of an inferior product, but this is merely raising the cost at least 50%.

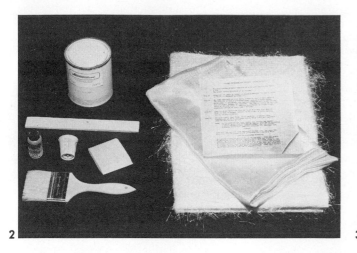

2

3

4

1. True testament to the claim that "you can build anything out of fiberglass" is this completely handbuilt street digger. Owner Mike Minette of Dallas had never done any 'glasswork before but built his own mold and body. The project took a full year.

2. Although you can't build a whole car with one, there are many 'glass repair kits on the market for repair of boats, cars, helmets; and anything else constructed of fiberglass.

3. You could realistically "build" a Corvette from the many custom and replacement pieces available for the 'glass sports cars, like these parts by Eckler's Corvette World, one of several Corvette specialty shops.

4. The range of automotive products available in fiberglass today is staggering. From dragster panels, campers, boats, custom seats, scoops, spoilers, fender flares, to complete reproductions of bodies for early Ford T's, A's and '32-'34 roadsters.

5. A new product from 3M that should be plenty handy to the 'glass worker is "Sunset" fiberglass repair, a 4x6-in. sheet of cloth impregnated with resin and ready to use. Peel the backing off, apply to the job, expose to direct sunlight and it hardens to a strong repair. At $1.39, Sunset is hard to beat.

6. When only a small area needs to be repaired, it can be filled with a good body filler, like Don Bailey's Corvette-Fill compound.

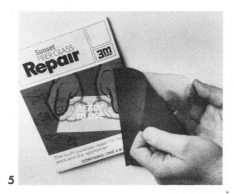

5

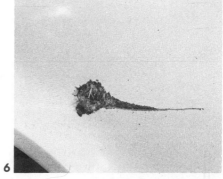

6

Why's of Fiberglass

Mat is designed to give thickness to a laminate, and consequent strength, at a reasonable price. It is not as strong as cloth, but is ideal for use as a thickness agent in conjunction with resin and cloth, reducing the cost over several layers of cloth. The 'glass fibers are laid so they run in one direction. A sheet is then laid against another with fibers running 90° opposite; thus a kind of laminated plywood effect is obtained, ensuring very good strength qualities.

DuPont Co. has long been producing a special treatment for fiberglass, but most companies have treatments to achieve the same results. DuPont calls their process the 114 treatment, which really consists of two steps—treatment 112 and treatment 114. In the former, the cloth is run through towers where it is subjected to blasts of heat to drive off oils necessary during weaving. The cleaned cloth is then given treatment 114, which is a light chroming of the surface. With any treatment, the objective is a 'glass product easier to laminate, again giving extra strength.

Check with any body shop and chances are you'll find only one or two metal men thoroughly familiar with fiberglass repairs. It is a profitable repair business, but because of the products involved, it is not integrated into the overall metal repair trade as it should be. Part of this problem stems from the fact that fiberglass can irritate the skin. This irritation can be circumvented by using a protective cream on the hands, or rubber gloves. Wear long sleeved shirts, button the collar, and use a respirator if necessary. Fiberglass dust kicked up by a disc grinder may irritate the nostrils.

Resin mixtures should be used in well ventilated areas, since toxic fumes are involved. These same resins will tend to accumulate on tools, shoes, clothing, practically everything—so the resin should be cleaned while it is still soft. Lacquer thinner is an excellent cleaning agent.

There are three general kinds of fiberglass parts to contend with: matched metal molds, spray lay-ups, and hand lay-ups. All will come into play if the repair shop specializes in custom jobs. With matched metal molds, chopped fiber and polyester resin are mixed, catalyst added, and the combination placed in a male/female mold. Heat and pressure are applied. The finished piece is ready in a few minutes, which means that the metal mold procedure is a fast and inexpensive way to produce fiberglass parts in quantity. However, the strength of the part may not be quite as great.

With spray lay-up, chopped 'glass roving is blown into a female mold along with catalyzed resin. The mixture is then rolled by hand and allowed to cure at ambient temperatures. This type of lay-up is popular with smaller manufacturers, although the builder must control the percentage of 'glass and resin to get correct strength.

Hand lay-up is the general method of the low-volume producer, or the one-off customizer. This includes laying 'glass mat, cloth or roving—or a combination of these—in the female mold and saturating the pieces with resin. The entire surface must be carefully rolled, to ensure the proper mixture and balance throughout and the removal of air bubbles. Pieces formed this way are usually very strong and thick, but the process is more costly than the others.

Repair of any of these fiberglass parts will follow the same general scheme (even a metal panel that is heavily rusted may be repaired much the same way). To repair large or small holes, first remove the damaged material and bevel the edges to about 20°. Grind off the paint and gel coat to reach the raw fiberglass. This should be done on both sides for maximum bond strength.

REPAIR KITS

Special fiberglass repair kits are available for this type of work, and may be used on either steel or fiberglass. In the case of steel, however, an epoxy resin must be used rather than polyester, as the latter will not adhere well to metal. The epoxy kit can be used for both metal and fiberglass.

Cut two pieces of mat so they will extend past the hole edges about 2 ins. Mix the resin and catalyst (hardener) per the container directions, then spread the resin through the fiberglass. A handy non-stick work area is made by a polyethylene sheet (suit bags from the cleaners work well). Coat both inner and outer surfaces of the hole with resin mixture; then when this mix is tacky, apply the saturated mat to both the inner and outer surfaces. Press the two patches together, working out any air bubbles, which should leave a saucer-like depression.

Allow the repair to cure, and since this is a chemical action, as soon as the surface is hard, it is hard clear through. The curing can be speeded up by raising the temperature, easy enough to do by placing heat lamps about 18 ins. from the work. After the spot is cured, grind the surface smooth and fill the remaining low spot(s) with plastic filler from the kit. If additional coats of resin are necessary, sand lightly between coats.

Closing a large hole is slightly different, in that larger, stronger patches are required. Place a piece of cloth on the polyethylene bag, cut larger than the hole, and saturate it with

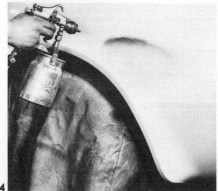

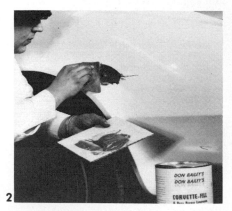

resin. Then place two pieces of mat on the cloth, both pieces cut larger than the hole and both thoroughly saturated with resin. Stick this thick patch to the underside of the hole after resin applied to the parent material is tacky, and remove air bubbles by pressing with the poly bag. The mat side is placed toward the body. Make a similar patch and apply it to the hole outside, then finish the piece as before.

Fiberglass mat and resin can be used very well to reinforce areas subject to excessive stress, and for tying in parts of fiberglass to wood, etc. Pure fiberglass is best for this work, as it hardens when spread over the damaged surface and is ideal when a mounting bracket is being replaced on a fiberglass piece.

To tie in a wooden piece, or a mounting bracket, coat the 'glass surface with the pure resin (Unican calls it Canned Fiberglass), push the tie-in piece into place, and apply more resin. Mat or cloth may be included if desired.

Repairing splits and cracks is very common with fiberglass bodies subjected to stress. Kits, such as those supplied by Fibreglass-Evercoat, are ideal for this purpose also. Remove the loose material and grind a broad "V" down the fissure. Clean the inside of the split also. Cut a piece of mat and apply to inner surface with the resin mix. Use two pieces of mat if there is excessive stress in the area. Cover the mat with a

piece of saturated cloth pressed firmly in place. Here the repair is much the same as with holes. The fiberglass structure is now reinforced and the crack may be filled with plastic filler. Sometimes small impact cracks may be repaired directly with pure resin and a filler, but the addition of a mat/cloth reinforcement is added insurance.

CANNED FIBERGLASS

Unlike metal, a fiberglass body does not crumple when damaged—with a blow to one part being transferred throughout the panel. Instead, the fiberglass will resist considerable force and then crack or shatter. It is possible to rebuild a shattered area from the various pieces, much like a jigsaw puzzle. Unican's canned fiberglass is ideal for this type of repair.

Working from the back side, remove all the dirt and broken pieces from the structure edge. Find a piece that mates to the main structure and clamp into place. Smear a coating of canned fiberglass on both pieces, building a bridge over the crack. Repeat this process with each of the pieces until all are glued into a rough, basically reconstructed piece.

At this point, check for rigidity, as more canned fiberglass may be required on the backside. All the raw edges will be exposed to the outside. With a rough disc, grind the whole outer surface to shape, removing all the high points and corners. This leaves a thin shell of the desired shape.

A complete rebuild is now possible by cutting 1 ft. pieces of fiberglass mat and laying them onto this thin shell form. Saturate the mat and roll it into place. As the edges of mat will taper out when rolled, shingle the area for consistent thickness.

When an entire panel must be replaced, it is possible to purchase the panels from specialty supply houses or direct from the manufacturer. Corvettes and Avantis are the most common production fiberglass cars. When a panel is being replaced, it is trimmed to fit the car body and attached with mat and cloth — as mentioned in hole or crack repair.

MAKING A MOLD

But it may be more economical to make up your own mold and repair the missing piece. Making a mold is easy, and can be done by either backing the missing area with formed wire and cardboard (as a base for repair mat and cloth, a kind of rough male inner mold), or by taking a female mold off a similar panel.

Consider the situation of a Corvette rear fender. Mark off a similar fender with masking tape slightly larger in area than the damaged area. Mask the surrounding area with paper so spilled 'glass and resin will not damage it. Using Johnson paste floor wax, liberally smear the unmasked section of the fender, leaving a wet coat of wax over the surface. In some instances it is possible to lay a piece of Saran Wrap over the area as a

5

6

7

8

1. *Corvette-Fill features a metallic base rather than the more common but hazardous asbestos. After roughing up the area with 80-grit paper, mix the hardener thoroughly into filler.*

2. *Corvette-Fill sets up hard in 15 minutes at 70° F, so apply it smooth the first time and don't keep trying to go over for a smoother application.*

3. *After curing, sand the filler with 80-grit paper, then 120-grit, and finish up with a 240-grit paper.*

4. *After heavy primering, sand again with 240-grit paper, clean with wax and grease remover and tack rag; you're ready to shoot a color coat.*

5. *When a large part of a 'Vette is damaged, you'll have to cut off the offending, crunched piece and 'glass on a replacement panel.*

6. *When a panel is replaced, the new panel is temporarily held in place with screws and metal tabs.*

7. *When the mating edges have been glassed together from the backside, the tabs are removed and the seams ground in a "trough" with a grinder.*

8. *The "trough" is filled in with glass matte and resin, and ground down when hard. All that's left is final sanding, priming, and paint.*

Why's of Fiberglass

mold base. This won't work with reverse curves, but the wrap will adhere to most other compound curves.

Thin layers of mat should be used, and Unican has a special mold-making veil just for the purpose. This matte is cut into small pieces ranging from 2 x 4 ins. to 4 x 6 ins.

Saturate the small pieces of mat with resin and lay on the waxed surface, with the smallest pieces used around the edges. Lay on pieces in an overlapping shingle manner until the entire surface has been covered. The small pieces will conform to the curves better than a single large piece. To force the mat into crevices and indentations, use a small paint brush wetted in resin. Push the material into place with the bristle ends; do not brush back and forth. After the whole surface has been covered with one layer, allow the mold to harden at least one hour.

After the mold has thoroughly cured, gently work the piece away from the original fender, remove the wax and polish the fender. The mold will be slightly larger than the original damaged area. Place it under the damaged fender and align with the panel. 'Glass the mold in place and then finish as with all other repairs, using mat to build up the area to the original fender thickness. This is slightly more complicated than making a backing of wire and/or cardboard, but it works much better in areas of many compound curves.

In the case of Corvettes, special molds are available for panel construction, but these would not be necessary unless considerable Corvette body repair were contemplated. When new panels are being installed, it is easiest to get alignment by securing the replacement panel to the body with a backup bonding strip of 'glass held in place with screws. When the beveled crack is filled, the screws are removed and the holes filled.

Repairing sheet metal with 'glass kits is slightly different but just as easy. First, clean the metal to bare surface with a No. 16 or No. 24-grind disc, to at least 6 ins. beyond the area being repaired. Indent the area to be repaired, making a sunken lip about 2 ins. wide beyond the damaged area. Cut a piece of matte the same size of the surface being repaired; then a piece of cloth the same size. Several pieces of matte may be needed to fill the indentation. Brush the resin mixture on the clean metal surface and saturate the matte and cloth, allowing all components to become tacky.

Apply the matte and cloth patches, pressing the laminations down tightly with a polyethylene bag to produce a tight bond (cloth to the outside).

After the material has cured, sand and file the surface and fill with plastic filler if necessary. If the hole being repaired is larger than 3 ins. in diameter, it must be repaired like large holes in fiberglass, although no inner patch is used.

Low spots, waves and irregularities in general that are common to fiberglass bodies are usually smoothed with filler and worked with a grater and sanding file. Because fiberglass is such a facile material, it is possible to customize bodies with a relatively low skill in bodywork. However, it is not advisable to use fiberglass in great content on a metal custom.

If a special fiberglass body is desired, it can be made up from a mold. This procedure is rather expensive, but is especially useful if more than one body is to be be made. Dune

1

2

3

4

5   6   7

buggy body builders have found fiberglass the perfect material, as have many custom and hot rod enthusiasts. *Perfecto!*

There must be some kind of basis for the mold, and this becomes the mockup. In the case of hot rodding, original metal bodies are usually used. The metal is carefully straightened to perfect condition, as with an old Model T body, and most of the hard work is already done. However, if a special design is called for, the mock-up must be built from scratch. It is possible to utilize a basic body as the mock-up foundation, changing the contours with various materials.

NEW DESIGNS

For a new design, a mock-up is

1. Another one of Eckler's Corvette goodies is this one-piece front end (rather than 11 in a stock one) with flares and flip-up feature.

2. Eckler's has four different kits for headlight modifications. This one is cute, but illegal in many states due to the plexiglass covers.

3. Corvette lovers can hide even 12-in.-wide tires under their cars with the fiberglass flares available from Eckler's, Bruno's, Don Bailey, Acme Fabricating Co., and others.

4. Handcrafted 'glass bodies need not be built in a mold, especially if the design is to be a one-off. This body on a Corvette chassis was made of individual pieces, then joined together with 'glass by Silva Engineering of Salem, Mass.

5. Another Silva creation, this time a modified production Corvette body. Only fiberglass can so easily be used creatively to form swooping fender lines and custom front ends.

6. Fender flares of 'glass are even available for many steel-bodied cars. These rear flares from Maier Racing are for the '65-'66 Mustangs.

7. The Gibbon Body Shop of Gibbon, Nebraska makes a number of fiberglass replica bodies for early Fords, like this '29 roadster-pickup body that wowed 'em at the Street Rod Nats in St. Paul. Gibbon also has coming a '30 Ford touring body and pickup bed.

made (as with aluminum) and covered with wire. The wire is fixed between the plywood bulkheads, about one inch below the proposed surface and is used to keep the plaster in place and thin. After the mock-up substructure is assembled, it should be sprayed with some kind of varnish or shellac to prevent the wood from extracting water from the plaster.

Short-time casting plaster is the most common material used (plaster of Paris). A thin solution is mixed, and small mattes of "shredded hemp," "shredded rope" or "long fiber" are dipped into the solution and applied about ¼-in. thick over the wire mesh. Allow to dry.

A thick plaster mix is applied over this plaster-hemp base to within about ⅛-in. of the finished surface. Apply this plaster to the entire model. Brush on a thin coat of orange shellac to prevent the bottom layer of plaster from drawing water from the final coats. A thin, flexible metal blade, called a spline, is used to apply the final plaster coats. This blade is about 1-in. wide by 2- to 3-ft. long, and is used to ensure flowing contours. A thin mixture of plaster is applied to the mold and smoothed by running the spline guide across the templates. It is easiest to work with two sections (three templates) at a time.

After this first coat of thin plaster has been applied, but not dried, a second coat is applied and a shorter spline is used. The amateur can usually only work about three square feet at a time. The plaster is allowed to dry and is then smoothed with graters, sander or file. An excellent grater can be made by wrapping expanded metal around a 2 x 4 piece of wood.

After the plaster is really dry, which takes about 2 weeks, it may be sanded. Spray or brush on thick coats of lacquer primer (this lacquer is important) and sand the mock-up as on any ordinary car. Paint the mock-up with a good gloss lacquer, and fill small imperfections with putty and filler as with a metal or fiberglass body.

Be careful when sanding a high spot, as any breakthrough to the plaster must be carefully featheredged and repainted.

A parting agent must be applied to the mock-up if a female mold is being made (and this is highly recommended, since use of the mock-up for a male mold will produce a rough outer body finish). Several parting agents are available, with lacquer-type cellulose acetate solution the most common. To 1 gal. of acetone add ½ lb. of cellulose acetate molding compound. Polyvinyl alcohol, which can be dissolved in hot water, makes a fine parting agent. Whatever type of parting agent is used, it must be coated with a good wax—a thick coat—and then the mock-up is highly-polished.

The female mold is made by spraying on a coat of polyester resin, followed by a second coat. This rather thick coat of pure resin is necessary if imperfections in the female mold are to be sanded out. Next add a layer of cloth to the entire mock-up, thoroughly saturated with resin. Work out all trapped air with a roller. Allow this layer of cloth to cure, then apply two or more layers of matte, followed by another layer of cloth.

The mold may need to separate, depending upon the "draw" of the mock-up. Most sports car-type bodies split cross-wise in the cockpit area, Model T's split down the middle, etc. Pieces of plywood may be constructed into a framework and laminated to the mold as further support, also forming a bench to hold the inverted mold. Making the actual body is then a matter of 'glass lamination, using a good parting agent and wax in the mold. The body is made from resin and layers of cloth/mat applied over a gel coat.

Fiberglass is indeed a wonder material, and is sure to find expanded use in automobile body making. Learning to work with all its many phases is absolutely essential for anyone contemplating a career in the business.

Why's of Fiberglass

'VETTE FENDER FLARES

There are a lot of flare kits on the market; however, we chose to do this story at Bruno's Corvette, a repair and custom shop located at 11055 Ventura Blvd., Studio City, Calif. Bruno has flares available ranging in width from 1 in. to 5 ins. wider than stock, and they'll cover anything up to and including drag slicks. This particular job will use the 5-in.-wide flares and will cost between $150 and $200 in labor to install the pair, less painting. The flares cost $35 each.

Installing flares is not beyond the ability of the average car buff who has even a small amount of tinkering prowess. Basically, it consists of bonding, filing and sanding.

For tools, as a bare minimum you'll need: a disc grinder—this can be a high-speed electric drill with a flexible grinding disc attachment—and a "cheese grater" type half-round file. The Stanley Tool Co. has a line of Surform files that are designed for this job. A screwdriver, a small square of soft rubber for a squeegee, a small roller and a batch of sandpaper and you're about ready. Don't forget an air filtering mask and goggles for self-protection.

Materials are another matter. First, you'll need about a half gallon of acetone to get the resin off you and your tools. Be very careful with this stuff. It is much more volatile and flammable than gasoline . . . keep it tightly covered at all times.

You will need at least a square yard each of 2-oz. cloth and mat, along with a half gallon of resin and

HOW-TO: 'Vette Fender Flares

1. Using locating tabs as a guide, mount flare on car body in desired location, paying close attention to the fit up front along the rear edge of the door opening.

2. Secure flare to car with sheetmetal screws in holes provided, and use a grease pencil to mark a line on the body along the edge of the flare. Line is a guide.

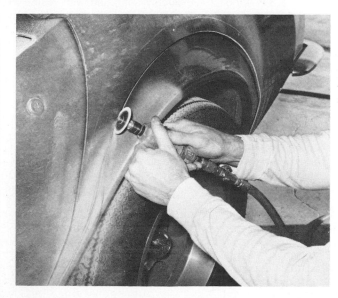

3. With a saber saw or small grinder, cut a new opening about an inch lower than the line you scribed; closer where you approach the edge of the doorpost section.

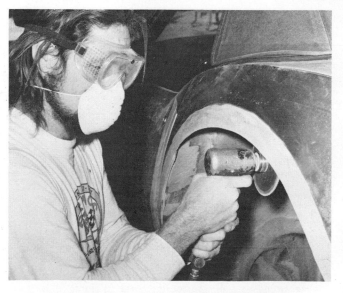

4. Wearing a protective mask, grind the back of the flare and both sides of the body around the wheelwell. Backside grinding is easy with the disc reversed.

a couple of ounces of catalyst. Bruno will supply his special-formula Fiberweld, a combination filler and bonding material, for $25 per gallon; you'll need at least a half gallon for two flares. If you plan on any additional repair and patch work, get a gallon; this stuff is the greatest. Don't forget the face mask, as Fiberweld contains asbestos. Finally, you will need a half gallon of commercial body filler; we used *Rez-zin*, which is available at most body shop suppliers. Oh, yes, get a tube of ''green stuff'' too.

For your own protection, cover yourself as completely as possible: long-sleeved shirt, mask, goggles, etc. Keep the car buttoned up too—if you get this stuff inside the car you'll *never* get it all out again.

Choose a moderate day—or a heated garage—to do your work; resin catalyst is temperature sensitive and reacts best around 70°F. The resin-to-catalyst ratio should be 1 oz. catalyst per gallon of resin. Too much catalyst and the mix goes off too soon and is unworkable; not enough and the job takes forever to cure. Mix only the quantity you're going to use immediately; it won't keep over about half an hour per batch. Don't soak the patches; a resin-rich patch makes a weak joint. Roll and squeegee out excess resin and all air bubbles, and get the mat down against the flare and body. Remember, air expands with heat and any trapped bubbles will surface the first time you park the car in the sun . . . and ruin your paint job. Use a cheap, semi-stiff bristle brush to apply the resin and work the glass patches into place.

Don't be afraid of this stuff! If you goof, just slap some more mat back on and fill in the goof—it's foolproof. Okay, now just follow the pictures and see how it's done.

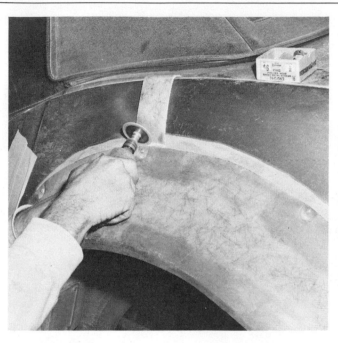

5. Reinstall the flare with the screws and cut off the locating tabs now. Be sure the flare fits the body well and at this time add extra screws at 5-in. intervals.

6. Mix up a small batch of Bruno's Fiberweld and catalyst; use about 20 drops of catalyst to a golf ball-sized blob of Fiberweld. Catalyst ratio is critical.

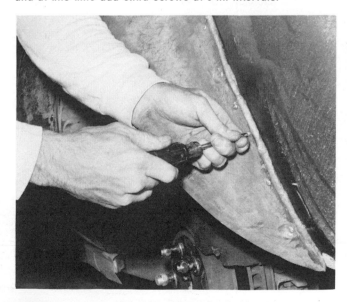

7. Back out the screws and pack fiberweld between the flare and the body. Then tighten flare firmly against the body and squeegee the excess off the seam.

8. Fill the inside gap between the flare and car body with Fiberweld. Pack it in solid and work out all air bubbles. Allow to cure until fairly hard: about 2 hours.

HOW-TO: 'Vette Fender Flares

9. Work resin/catalyst mix into small mat patches. Do not soak patch. Tear mat apart to give fuzzy edges for better overlapping. Cut glass cloth slightly wider.

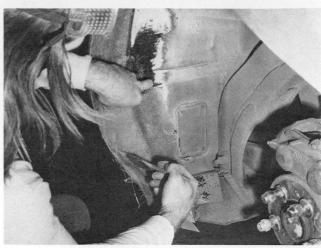

10. Mat patches should overlap Fiberweld used to fill space between flare and body. Work out all air bubbles. Apply wider glass-cloth patches over the matted area.

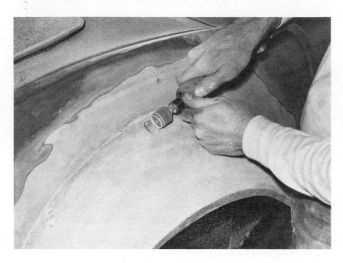

11. Grind out screw dimples, then sand entire surface with 80-grit paper to remove mold wax. Fill the screw dimples with Fiberweld and grind flush when semi-hard.

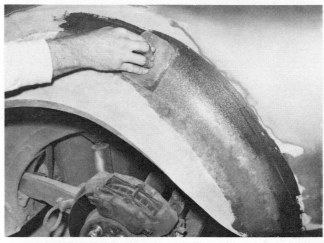

12. Thin commercial body filler slightly with resin after adding catalyst. Squeegee a thin coat over the seam area, fill all surface voids and allow to cure.

13. Cut curved strips of mat about 3 ins. wide, then tear into 6-in. lengths with fuzzy ends. Curved patch will fit fender without wrinkles. No cloth is used here.

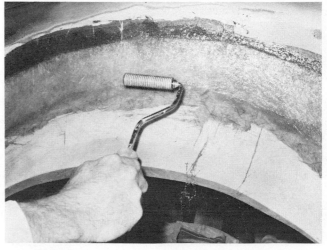

14. Using an old paintbrush, work wet patches down into seam area, then use special roller to roll out excess resin and get mat down against body and flare.

15. Use 24-grit paper with a very flexible backing pad. With short, overlapping vertical strokes, grind the area to the desired finished radius; then featheredge everything.

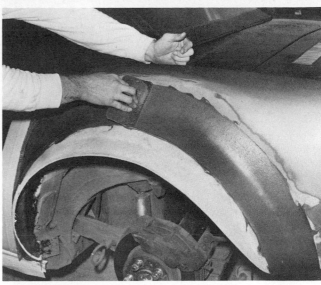

16. Squeegee on a fairly heavy coat of commerical body filler to fill any low spots. Wipe on in long, smooth passes—don't worry, it won't stick to the paint job.

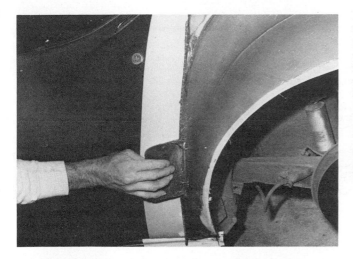

17. Using cardboard in the door opening keeps the edge straight. Work body filler in against lower edge, shaping carefully at lower tip of flare. Let cure to semi-soft.

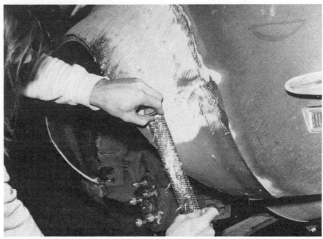

18. Work the entire area with the cheese-grater type file, removing and shaping the body filler while it's still soft; this stuff is impossible to file when hard.

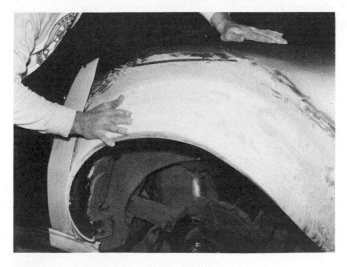

19. Using 40-grit paper and hand pressure, sand the entire flare and fillet; your hand will feel uneven areas that your eye can't see. Re-bondo any low spots.

20. Before priming, flare is sanded with 80-grit paper, 100-grit, then 220-wet and 320-wet to obtain a glass-smooth finish—now you can shoot primer and final paint.

Rear Fender Flaring

A sensible bodyworking beginner's project to make those fat tires legal.

There's no doubt that "mag" wheels and wide tires have become trademarks of the street machine movement. They're so popular that today you find new car dealers selling them as options, and on the road you can find them on old cars, new cars, tiny import cars, big luxury cars, and even on pickups, vans and semis. Everybody likes them, but they do have their drawbacks. The drawback we're concerned with here is the tire-to-fender clearance problem. Although in recent years the Detroit manufacturers have taken this into consideration in the styling and design of a few models, installation of wheels and tires that are wider than stock, especially on the rear, still creates a clearance problem on most street machines. Oh sure, you may be able to bolt them on the car, but what about when you hit a bump at speed, even low speed? Scraaape goes the fender on your nice new tire that you paid top dollar for!

In some cases, where the clearance problem is a small one, the solution can be as easy as simply notching the *inner* lip of the fender edge with a hacksaw cut every inch or so, and then bending the lip up inside the wheelwell to gain maybe a ½-in. of clearance between this lip and the sidewall of the tire. We tried that on a '66 Mustang with limited success; it would only scrape the tires on big bumps.

The best solution to the problem, in fact the *only* solution in cases of extreme interference, is to re-radius the wheelwell opening. On a lot of cars you might want to do this even if there isn't a clearance problem, just to make the car *look* better. Flared wheelwells generally look sharp, but the style is up to you as long as it suits your purposes. Depending on the tire and wheel size, the flare can be mild or wild, 1 in. or several, and the shape can be rearranged to suit you also, from square to round or vice-versa. This is customizing, so use your own imagination.

We wanted just a simple flare job at the rear to save wear and tear on tires and make the car distinctive. Customizer Carl Green has performed dozens of these transformations and agreed to do it for our camera. Carl has done paint and body work in three of the top custom shops in the nation, Darryl Starbird's in Wichita,

Kans., Dean Jeffries' here in Hollywood, and Dave Puhl's House of Customs in Chicago, so he's eminently qualified to show you how this job can be done.

You start by buying some e.m.t. tubing, otherwise known as electrical-mechanical tubing or simply conduit. It's light and inexpensive; we bought a 10-ft. length of ½-in. tubing for $1.29, and that's generally enough to do two wheelwells. There's no real "trick" to the procedure, just go carefully, think, and don't rush it. Basically, you hammer and dolly the fender from flat to an outward flare or curve around the opening, braze the tubing to the edge all around the opening to form a smooth, new lip, grind it down and follow normal filler and sanding procedures to smooth it out. You can make the flare large or small, depending on where you braze the tubing onto the fender. You can dolly the fender until it flares out several inches, or even add new metal if you need to. The conduit also strengthens the fender greatly, and you can make the opening larger in

diameter if you want, just by bending a larger radius in the conduit before you start. For a simple, same-diameter opening, just shape the tubing around the tire you plan to use. How you make it meet the body at the front and rear of the opening is up to you also. On ours, the body was cut so the tubing could fit in it ahead of the wheel, and blend gradually outward as it went around the opening, while at the rear it was bent into an extra outward flare at the bottom to form a small "splash guard." The use of this lightweight tubing allows a lot of creative freedom in this kind of customizing, and varied effects can be gained with different shapes, and even different diameter tubing. And when you've found the design you want, and you've done it, not only will the car be more individual but in states (like California) where you can't have the tire stick out of the wheelwell, it'll be legal, too. All this and custom wheelwells have the practical benefit of allowing those big tires to clear the body on bumps and drive-in ramps!

Stock wheelwell on '66 Mustang is a good starting point, as it's round in stock form, but wide mag wheels brought tires out where fender lip scraped sidewalls.

1. The new "bead" for the reshaped opening will be made from light electrical tubing. It is easily shaped by bending it carefully over a tire or similar object.

2. After bending, trial fitting, and even bending the tubing over other objects, the tubing can be curved into the shape and the radius size desired.

3. The fender's inner lip must be bent outward to form the flare. In the case illustrated, the lip had previously been notched and hammered flat on the inside.

4. Once the kinks are out, the inner and outer lips are separated with a pry bar, and the metal at the front of the wheel-well notched to receive end of the conduit.

5. Body man Carl Green deftly uses a body hammer and dolly to make the now-flat fender edge flare outward instead of in. He works slowly, carefully around radius.

6. Bird's eye view after fender metal has been brought out to new shape. If the job is done with proper care, as little distortion as possible will make finishing easier.

HOW-TO

7. When amount of flare is determined, the conduit is clamped in place to show the excess metal to be trimmed. Tube would be brazed outside for larger lip.

8. With the outside edge trimmed to fit snugly against the conduit all the way around the new opening, Carl next trims back the metal edge of the inner panel.

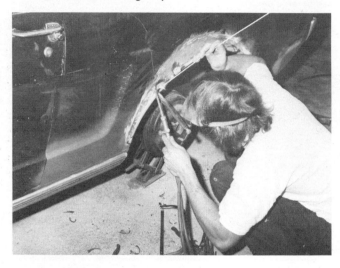

9. The conduit is carefully tack welded in place at widely spaced intervals to reduce heat buildup and resulting warpage. Inch-long tacks will suffice for now.

10. It's a good idea at this point to bounce the car as hard as you can to make certain that the fender and its new lip will clear the tires on a hard bump.

11. With the conduit fully brazed along the fender, the extreme back end of it is now heated and slowly bent to follow the contours of the fender at this point.

12. When conduit is cut and brazed, fender lip (arrow) sheet-metal at corner is pried out to form an extra bit of flare, making a small, built-in splash guard.

13. Most of the hard work is out of the way now. The last metalworking step is to beat the edge of the inner panel down to the conduit and braze the inside seam for strength.

14. With brazing completed, the whole fenderwell area is ground down and the old paint sanded off the body around the opening in preparation for the final bodywork.

15. A thin coat of body filler is spread over flare to smooth it into the fender. If work has been done right, little filler is needed, and much will be sanded off.

16. Before the filler has completely hardened, a special "cheese grater" hand file is used to carefully remove excess filler and form the basic blending contours.

17. A combination of sander, files, and hand-sanding gets everything smooth enough for paint. Another small batch of filler may have to be mixed to fill minor low spots.

18. Although light colored primer doesn't show off the amount of flare, you can see how it smoothly blends to body at front, and the splash guard width at rear.

The Technique of Hammer Welding

Often compromised in a large shop, that "certain feel" will never come from a blacksmith's bludgeon.

Late-night TV watchers have probably seen blacksmiths in old Western movies heat two pieces of iron in a forge, then join them by pounding them on an anvil. This is *not* hammer welding by today's bodyworking standards. Hammer welding as it's done in the bodyworking trade is ordinary gas welding followed by some tricky hammer and dolly work on the welded joint to provide as smooth and distortion-free a seam as possible.

Among the several facets of bodywork and painting that require a certain finesse and "feel," hammer welding is perhaps the most prominent. It isn't difficult, but because several basic tenets of metalworking are involved, very few metal men practice the art. While it may be easier for a quick repair to use a filler, the workman who strives for quality will take a moment longer and do the best job possible.

Customizers particularly find hammer welding advantageous, usually in situations calling for maximum strength and minimum filler. This might be a front end modification or a top chop, but the finished job is far superior to the use of lead or plastic. It also allows the metal man to gain better control over the panel, to shape and mold it the way he wants it with stress in the right place.

Hammer welding is normally involved in only three bodywork situations: repair of a tear, replacement of a panel and modification of a panel. In all three, the emphasis is upon quality and metal control, not economy. A commercial body shop cannot expect to include hammer welding on a large scale, simply because every minute spent in labor reduces its profit margin. Where quality is stressed, as in a custom or restoration operation, the customer demands premium work and is willing to bear the extra cost.

Consider a metal tear in a quarter panel. It is easy to rough the panel into shape and then weld the tear quickly: The bead is then ground off and beaten down so filler will cover the depression. Most modern body shops rely solely on plastics for this repair job. Obviously, there is some unusual stress buildup around the welded area, which may cause problems elsewhere in the panel.

It is also possible to rough the panel back into shape until the torn metal edges can be aligned carefully, then hammer weld the rip closed. With such a situation, the area adjacent to the tear will probably be stretched, but when the metal is welded and hammered, a natural shrinking force is introduced that tends to pull the stretch out. After the initial hammer welding, the area may be treated as a gouge—keep on shrinking and working the panel until it assumes its original shape.

It is in panel replacement and modification (especially by the customizer) that hammer welding takes on such importance. Unless the panel is preshaped to the new contour it is entering (with seams hammer welded), there will be a need for an excessive amount of filler material. In some radical cases, the entire panel will end up with a filler coat to varying degrees. It was from a situation like this that early custom cars earned the nickname "Lead Sleds." Anyone can sling lead and plastic, but it takes a craftsman to work metal. That's what counts.

This is not to say that every seam should be hammer welded; far from it. When a panel can be replaced and the joint made by spot welding, riveting or even ordinary fusion welding—and the joint will not show—fine. But if the seam is in the open and affects the panel's strength, hammer welding must be considered.

Take the situation where the bottom edge of an exterior panel has rusted away. Only about 2 ins. of the metal is really cancerous, but the replacement strip will be from 3 to 4 ins. wide. This strip will usually have very little (or no) crown and will gen-

1

2

erally include a folded lip of 90° or more. Whether the panel is on a door, cowl or quarter area, it does not matter. The metal man will be working directly in the middle of a nearly flat surface with heat. That means a high distortion possibility, which requires torch control.

AN IMPERATIVE

It is absolutely imperative that all hammer welding include the smallest possible weld bead. To accomplish this, the panels to be mated must fit as closely as they can. The replacement panel should be shaped and trimmed first, then held over the area to be replaced and well marked. It is wise to cut away the bad metal with as little distortion as possible, so this rules out the ''hot wrench'' immediately. A manual or air-operated chisel can be used, but there is a rather rough edge left which must be worked. Better yet, use a saber saw or nibbler.

After the initial rough cut, try the replacement panel on for size. It will generally be off just a whisker, because there is usually too much metal

3

1. Hammer welding is a time-consuming technique not often seen in regular bodywork, but necessary for show-quality work when butting two pieces of sheetmetal together. One of the prime tools needed is a (homemade) torch rest like this one, which has a shield to keep the lighted torch from scorching the floor; a tray for tips, and tubes to hold welding rod.

2. Here's a typical butt-joint of two pieces of sheetmetal which has been hammer welded. A few passes of the grinder and this undistorted seam is almost ready for primer and a few dabs of glaze. Normal overlap seam would have been quicker, but would have required lots of filler.

3. Here's a typical problem (for the early car restorer/rodder) that took good hammer welding to solve. A '32 Ford roadster had badly damaged rear corners, so this coupe rear section was purchased for needed parts.

4. Unfortunately, our sources were wrong when they said a coupe section was the same as a roadster; so this would be no cut-and-weld easy task. The bead lines didn't line up.

5. Bodyman Carl Green saved as much of the original metal as possible, cutting off the part to be replaced.

6. With the coupe section held up in place, the fit looks good except for the outside two bead lines.

7. Carl carefully made a sectioning cut through the middle of the body's depressed area, using masking tape as a guide. If the cut had not been made through the middle, the bottom raised areas would not match up.

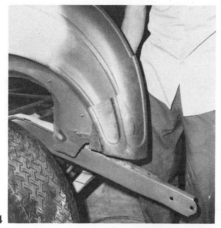

4

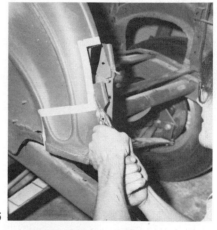

5

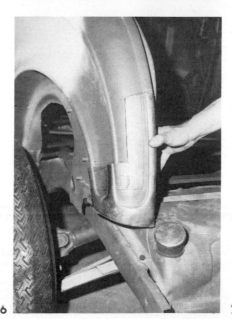

6

7

Hammer Welding

remaining on the parent panel. This thin strip may be trimmed off with a good pair of aviation tin snips, although such snips have a tendency to roll the tiny edge rather than make a clean cut, while the body grinder will make the ultimate fitting easier. The two panel edges should fit flush along the full length, with no more than 1/16-in. gap at any part. If the edges touch, all the better. A gap requires too much filler rod, resulting in a larger bead, and as the bead size gets larger, the hammer weld becomes increasingly poorer.

Clamp the pieces together and tack weld the edges. Use very little or no filler rod and make the tack tiny. Speed is important here, as well as a very small flame. Often too large a tip will be used, resulting in too much heat immediately adjacent to the edge. This causes the metal to crawl excessively and makes a perfect fusion weld almost impossible. A correct hammer weld cannot be made if the metal edges lap.

Make sure the edges are level during and after the tack weld. If not, heat the tack in a restricted area and use the hammer and dolly to level the edges. This means a few light taps, not heavy blows, as the metal is hot.

After the panels are tacked, start at one end with the hammer welding process. Be prepared to travel rapidly, not so much with the torch as with the hammer and dolly. The railroad dolly is well suited to hammer welding, since it has a number of convenient crowns and is easy to hold. The hammer face should be nearly flat.

Hammer welding calls for an alternate use of torch and hammer/dolly, so some sort of torch stand is required. This will allow the torch to be hung out of the way and remain lit, yet close at hand. A bucket of water will be useful if an extensive weld is involved, as the dolly will become hot after awhile and can be cooled by dipping it into the water. It is also wise to wear a glove on the dolly hand, to protect against a burn from either the dolly or slag falling from the welded surface's underside. Remember, every tool must be close at hand to ensure speed.

There are two ways to make a hammer weld. The simplest method is to weld the entire seam at once, then follow with spot heat and the hammer/dolly. A better way is to weld a short 2-in. section, then use the hammer, then weld again. This way the area is still hot from welding and does not need reheating, allowing better control of the metal.

Lay the torch tip flatter to the plane of travel than with normal fusion

1

3

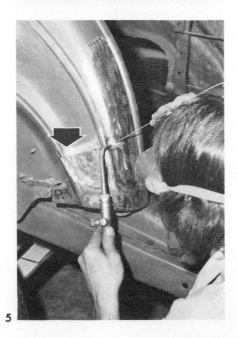

5

2

4

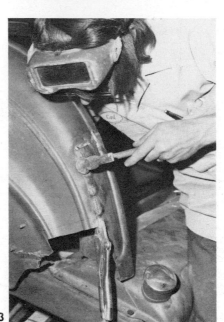

6

1. With the body and the new piece cleaned of paint along the cut edges, Carl clamped the pieces together with vise-grips. Arrow shows portion that was rotted out originally.

2. Carl places short tack-welds at about three-inch intervals, applying as little heat as possible.

3. Now the hammer welding starts! With the tacks completed, but with the visegrips still in place, Carl starts the full weld. After each length of about two inches of bead, he quickly stops welding; lays torch in his rack, and starts with hammer and dolly. Since welded panel usually shrinks along weld, he uses the dolly from behind to slap up the low area, then hammers bead flat.

4. Where the beads meet body, Carl creases the hammer weld with the wedge end of a finishing hammer. His shop (Carl Green Enterprises, 7749 Densmore #7, Van Nuys, Calif.) does a lot of antique and custom car work, so hammer welding is an everyday job.

5. A thin strip was trimmed from the left-corner piece so that the center bead would line up on the body, and this was hammer-welded in place. Fit of the fenderwell bead (arrow) was accomplished by using again the wedge end of the finishing hammer. Corner finally takes shape.

6. After grinding down the seams, a little primer and putty brings this part of our roadster project that much closer to completion. No one will ever know (except you) what went into these stock-looking corners.

7. Another typical problem that is best solved with hammer welding is replacing a lower, rusted-out area on an early car's cowl or quarter. Here the rusted section is cut off and the trim line ground straight. Flush fit of the panels to be welded is critical to a good hammer weld.

8. Vise-grips will keep the panel in place during tack welding; mating surfaces should be hammered up or down to flush exactly during tacking.

9. Anytime a butt weld is being made it can distort nearby low-crown panels. The torch should have a very small flame; the tip may be laid flatter to direct flame at area just welded.

10. Hammer each tack immediately, as this will tend to shrink the area and eliminate any distortion caused by the heat. It also keeps the edges flush. Don't worry about distortion in larger panel at this time.

11. This is how a good fusion weld will look, with little bead buildup. Such a weld is possible as panels grow together when heated edges melt and form bond without filler rod drops.

12. Continue the alternate welding, hammering schedule until the entire joint is closed. Keep the dolly firmly against underside of panel to reduce rebound; use hammer smartly.

7

8

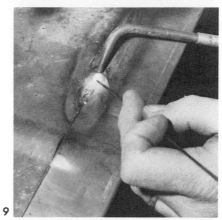

9

10

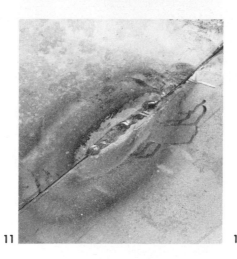

11

12

welding, thus reducing the heat to the metal. The filler rod can also be held at an opposite low angle to shield the edges. Although the two metal pieces touch, they will tend to grow toward each other even more when the heat is applied, allowing the edges to melt and flow together without the necessity of the filler rod. Such flowing may be difficult at first, but can be accomplished easily as experience is gained. An occasional hole will develop which must be filled by a drop from the rod, but the idea is to make the weld rapidly and with as little heat and rod as possible. At the same time, the edges should be kept level.

Immediately upon setting the torch aside, place the dolly against the underside and hold it firmly to the weld. Slap the bead rapidly with the dinging hammer—working back and forth from one end of the seam to the other. This will cause the bead to flatten out and have a shrinking effect on the panel, which has tried to grow with the heat. If one panel has not stayed level, that area must be reheated and hammered until it is level across the bead. The objective here is to flatten the mating joint so as to minimize follow-up work.

Continue across the entire joint in this way, alternating between torch and hammer/dolly. It is possible to feel the area with a palm, but remember that the metal stays hot. Wipe the

Hammer Welding

hand quickly across the surface to detect stretched spots and to determine how the panel contour is being affected.

STRETCH MARKS

After the seam has been hammer welded, check for a stretched area. Wherever one is found, shrink the panel as necessary. The welded seam should look almost flush with the surrounding panel, or even be in a very slight valley. If the bead has been too big, it will have been flattened on top and bottom by the hammer and dolly, but will still stick up from the surface slightly.

Grind the weld with a disc sander, using a flexible disc pad which will allow the disc to follow the contour rather than cut into it. This grinding should cut down the bead ridges and will show up the low spots along the bead that must be picked up. Use a picking hammer from the bottom and a picking dolly on top (an ordinary dolly will substitute) and raise only those low craters that remain. At this stage, hammer welding is very similar to crease repair and requires a good deal of patience, particularly from the beginner.

Resort to the file and grinder often during this picking operation, as no filler will be used since the two panels have become one. As the small craters are raised—and the high spots taken down with normal hammer/dolly technique—keep running the hand across the entire panel. Look across the panel from several different angles, trying to find a break in the contour. For the most part, the problems will be confined to the immediate seam area.

After as many of the craters and tiny low spots have been removed as practical, wash the surface thoroughly with a good metal prep, using a wire brush to clean out the minute depressions that remain. Finish off the surface with the smoother grinder discs, followed by a "jitterbug" oscillating air sander. Prime the bare metal and allow the primer to set completely before going over the seam with a thin coat of glazing compound. This glaze will get down into the small pockmarks that remain, resulting in a perfectly smooth job.

There is no substitute for hammer welding on a panel that's being repaired or patched, if *both* sides of the panel will be visible. Though this is not common in ordinary bodyworking, it's becoming more prevalent on restored cars slated for display, where onlookers or show judges may inspect the underside of a fender as closely as the top side. An example

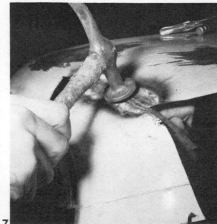

of this, with step-by-step photos, is included in another chapter.

For a number of years now, it has been common for the more experienced automotive enthusiasts to extol the virtues of this or that custom job by claiming hammer welding. There are a number of customizers famous for this type of work, and their products show the quality. Obviously, any car that has been modified will stand a better chance of lasting indefinitely (the sheetmetal, that is) if it has been hammer welded. This kind of technique requires practice, no doubt about it, but the results are immediately apparent. Fortunately, the student need make only a few short hammer welds to get the idea. From there on it's a matter of using his new-found secret.

1. Pick hammer is used to raise the low spots, but dolly is kept on top to keep from raising spots too high. This is where experience with the hammer will begin to pay off.

2. After the new section is hammer welded, the surrounding panel may be worked as necessary since "growth" through heat of welding may cause distortion. In this case, original part of weld needed several shrinks to remove "oil-canning."

3. Although it usually isn't to be found in the average body man's kit of tools, the shrinking dolly is a handy item. It is grooved to "grip" metal and is used in conjuction with an aluminum hammer.

4. This is the panel as it appears in nearly finished condition. Some tiny low areas remain to be picked up and filed, then panel will be primed. Remaining imperfections are glazed.

5. Then there are the more ambitious hammer welding jobs, such as this top chop on a 1954 Ford pickup truck. Long section of metal was roughed into shape, then hammer welded.

6. Because so very much hammer welding was necessary, convenient hook was made from handy sheetmetal for torch. Forming metal in this fashion may be time consuming, but it means excellent result.

7. With most top chops, strips of metal must be added. These should be formed before tack welding to top, but edges should mate as closely as on panel previously discussed.

8. This gap is much too big for a hammer weld bead, although it can be filled with large rod. Such cuts are necessary in many customizing jobs to get proper contour relationship.

9. For such gaps, insert small strips of metal, weld short beads on either side and hammer weld away!

10. Norm Grabowski's finished '54 Ford pickup is so well executed, that few people realize extent of work done. Thanks to hammer welding, Norm's pickup is a real winner.

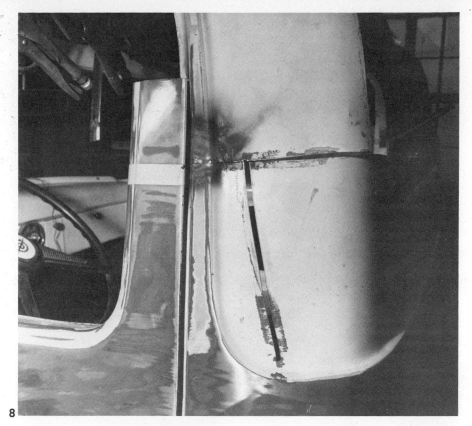

8

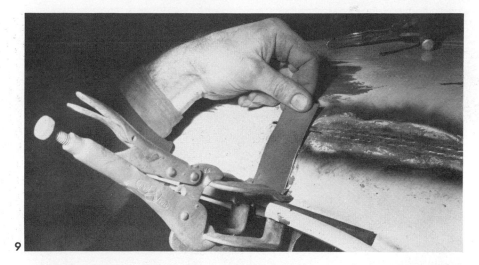

9

10

Vintage Bodywork

You won't surrender to maximum frustration, but will learn that patience is the name of the only game in "Vintage-town."

Old-timers to the hot rod sport have a favorite saying about the quality of body and fender work. "If it's flawless, paint it black." Indeed, black is the most unforgiving color that can be sprayed on a surface. The slightest imperfection, something the eye could never discern otherwise, will stand out like a sore thumb when painted a shiny black on black.

Yet black is the standard by which the really good custom jobs are judged. The car doesn't have to be painted that color, but would it stand up if it were? It is this subtle reality that prompts customizers to paint their personal cars black, or a similar dark tone.

A person doesn't have to be an accomplished body and fender man to give his vehicle a thorough detail-ing, or as it's called in the enthusiast world, "super sanitary." He does have to pay strict attention to the small things.

Nothing detracts from a beautiful custom or hot rod as much as poor panel preparation. This doesn't mean the paint, because a good paint job over a wavy panel indicates either a lack of talent or a lack of interest in preparation. Since patience is 90% of talent, the answer is lack of interest.

In preparing the metal and fiber-glass panels of a vehicle, it is easy to overlook the tiny dings and waves that will show so blatantly later on. It is very easy to throw a prime coat on the car and follow immediately with color, impatience being what it is. Generally speaking, this special attention to detail of metal work breaks up into three categories: cars produced before 1948, cars made after 1948 and fiberglass cars. Each category includes some peculiar problems.

OLDER CAR PROBLEMS

Take the early cars, for instance. When a 1947 Ford tudor sedan is being restored to original condition, even down to the dark maroon paint job, there are plenty of things to consider—not the least of which is replacement of a few bent chrome

Whether hot rod or restoration, backyard or farmed out, every owner and prospective owner of an early car should learn about the special body techniques employed in renewing them.

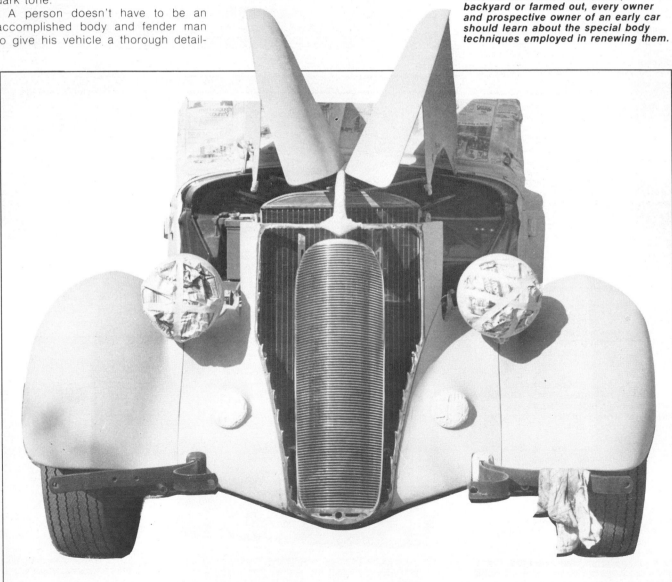

1. Here is a good example of a panel that could be fixed up haphazardly. Rust has begun to eat away at bottom of '29 Model A roadster cowl.

2. The best way is to cut off the offending area and add a new panel. This is much more work, but renewed panel will last a long time.

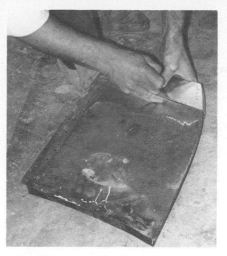

3. Hold new section over original panel and mark mating line, then trim the original panel to get a good fit between each of the mating pieces.

4. Clamp the two pieces together and tack weld, using the hammer/dolly technique; this is important to all phases of metal body repair.

5. If the new panel is rather thin and the entire weld is not too long, hammer welding may not be necessary; fillers may be used.

6. Grind the welded area to check for high and low spots and to cut down ridge left from welding. Low spots must be picked up next to bead.

7. The finished panel looks like it is flat; in reality it has slight compound curve which can be made by further hammer and dolly work.

8. The bare metal should be smoothed with #220- or a #340-grit sandpaper, clean with a caustic like MetalPrep. Primer/surfacer will fill sand marks.

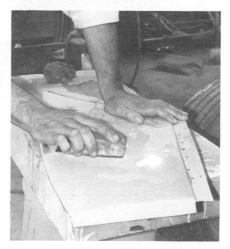

9. Sand and prime several times until smooth. The final panel looks as good as new. Holes drilled in leading flange connect cowl to firewall.

Vintage Bodywork

strips and replating of all the other chrome. Obviously, the car would not be as perfect if this chrome were overlooked. But what about the waves in the hood? These older cars were prone to develop hood waves, an imperfection that shows up almost immediately.

Such a problem usually does not stem from damage, it's just old age and quite difficult to cure. Yet a weekend spent on making the panel perfect is invaluable. More of a problem is the damaged area that has been straightened poorly. This is not uncommon on older cars, and will usually include a fender or door panel. If possible, replace the panel. If not, straighten what is there.

On pre-1935 cars, the experts look for imperfections in a number of significant places. First of all, has there been a repair of rusted areas? This would be the base of the cowl and quarter panels, bottom of the doors, and around the panel beneath the

deck lid. If there has been no repair, the rusted surface is obvious. But more important, has there been a poor repair? There is a 1929 roadster that runs in a West Coast club. Its quarter panel base on one side has been repaired, but without the original body roll. The other side is stock with the roll.

The point here is to keep everything the way it is supposed to be, not half way. When the real enthusiasts begin picking a particular early car apart, they look for bad metal in the deck lid (flat spots that run across the lid, very common), high and low spots in the metal panels directly above and below the deck lid, short vertical waves in the quarter panels above the rear fenders (also quite common), flat spots in the hood, and irregular fender edges.

SPECIAL PANEL PROBLEMS

Fixing up an early car deck lid can be a study in maximum frustration. This is a relatively low-crowned panel, but it normally has a curve in both

directions. When it gets flat spots, they usually appear almost as bands, about 4 ins. wide, from one side to the other. How they get there is anybody's guess—by people leaning on the lid, things piled on it, etc. Whatever the cause, it should be cured. In some cases where a rumble seat is installed, the body stops have been damaged, allowing the lid to contact the lower body panel. But in this instance, the spot will be a definite crease and not a wide band. Another cause of deck lid banding (also applicable to doors, tops and hoods) is sandblasting. Very few sandblasting operators will take the extra effort and care necessary to keep blast distortion to a minimum. This requires a lower air pressure and finer (older) grit sand, which means more labor time per piece. Avoid sandblasting sheetmetal if at all possible! There are other types of cleaners available; in larger cities chemical vats are used to strip paints and work wonders on old car bodies.

The quick and dirty way to repair a

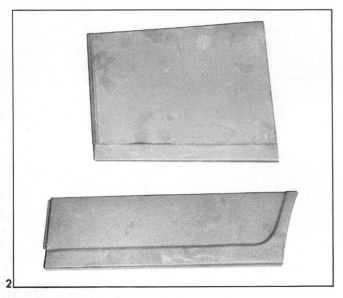

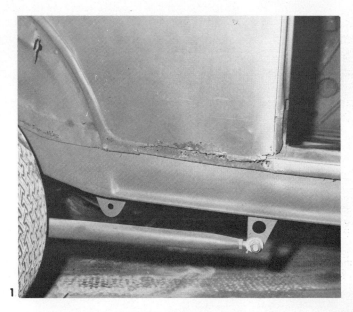

1. The most common problem with the older car is rust, which even in the the drier parts of the country has usually taken its toll on at least the lower parts of a vintage car. This section is to be cut out and replaced.

2. In the case of the early Ford we pictured, we were in luck because reproduction patch panels are sold by several antique parts suppliers. If none are available for your car, you'll have to have some made at a sheetmetal shop. A patch for the lower part of a panel shouldn't be hard to duplicate, because few curves are involved in these areas.

3. The new panel has been trimmed to fit where the rust was cut out, and it is hammer-welded in place. The corners though, must be brazed to the car because the bodyman can't reach the backside with his dolly to do a proper hammer-weld in the corners.

"banded" deck lid is with large amounts of plastic filler, but this isn't the best way. The metal should be worked. Raising all the low bands can be accomplished by either picking and prying, or by cutting the inner panel away and working with a dolly and hammer. The latter is preferable. When the inner panel is cut out, use tin snips or a panel cutter. Do not use the torch, as it tends to cause distortion unless handled by a professional in the business.

With the inner panel removed (same goes for doors) work up all the low spots as shown in Chapter 1. Since the metal will tend to work-

harden during this process, the panel will hold shape better after working. Always check the progress with an adjustable body file. Since the flattened spots will have displaced the panel elsewhere, the edges of the bands will tend to be high. After the panel is perfect, the inner panel is spot-brazed back in place (do not localize heat which will cause external panel distortion).

The body panels directly above the deck lid on older cars are not as large as the deck lid, but often cause as much trouble. The upper panel normally requires work to smooth out low spots. Again, these spots can be

filled with plastic, but since the panel is easy to reach it is better worked out in the traditional manner. The lower panel is not so easy. This particular piece of sheet metal is usually hemmed over a rather substantial brace. In the case of some specific old cars, such as the Model A, specialty parts houses stock new replacement panels. Otherwise, it's a matter of repair.

Here is one place it pays to use the plastic rather than fight the inner reinforcement. There is seldom room to get a dolly, or even a pick of some kind, inside this bracing. The alternative is to weld up any cracks (they usually start at the upper and lower edges where this panel is riveted via a flange to the quarter panels), grind and lead if necessary, and straighten the flanged lip along the deck lid opening. To get a perfectly smooth contour often requires the use of plastic, usually more as a thick putty than anything else. When working such a large area, which has a very low crown in both directions, it is an advantage to rely primarily on large sanding files.

One area of preparation that is often overlooked about the deck lid is the flange lip itself. This should be cleaned very thoroughly with a rotary wire brush, both inside and beneath. Clean out all the old paint, rubber and cement, etc., then weld up the minute cracks that are sure to be present. Do not prime the lip heavily; instead rely on a thin coat of primer/surfacer and a thin coat of color to reduce its tendency to chip.

Quarter panels are the dead giveaway as to quality of bodywork on older cars. While rust is possible at the bottom edge, vertical waves are

4. Even when you don't suspect any rust in your lower panels, grind all the paint away just to be sure. The cancer may be hiding under 30 years of paint. This quarter panel looked good until grinding showed up some rust pinholes that would spread under the new paint unless taken care of.

5. The vintage car buff hates to cut his original flooring, but rust is usually worst here, and sometimes must be cut out. When you have a new steel piece made to replace flooring sections, make it of the same gauge and try to duplicate the contours and ribbing of the original.

6. In order to maintain an accurate restoration of an early car, you must constantly refer to photographs, books and antique car publications to be sure your work is a faithful duplicate of original body lines, etc.

7. Then there are the basketcases that have been butchered so badly in the past that you wonder if they're worth bringing back. This body had been completely gutted, and a whole new flooring substructure had to be fabricated. Original flooring was not available, but this strong repair job saves an otherwise wasted car.

4

5

6

7

Vintage Bodywork

common in the area around the fender opening. These imperfections may have been caused by a rear-end collision at some time, but many undamaged bodies also have them.

If the problem was caused by a collision (look on the inside of the trunk to find marks left by hammer or dolly), chances are the panel is stretched ever so slightly and will need a bit of shrinking. A typical example of this was covered under "Shrinking" in Chapter 1. When no previous damage has been involved, the low/high spots can be worked out with hammer, dolly and spoon. The beginner will find it difficult to get an absolutely perfect panel in this instance, since feel is the only way to locate the definite ripples. For this reason a thin coat of plastic filler may again be used as almost a putty. It is most effective.

FENDER BUGABOOS

Irregular fender lines are the worst enemy of the traditional hot rodder, since they are so prevalent and so difficult to repair. The problem is accentuated by a case of poor repairs. Older fenders display a marked tendency toward splitting, due to vibrations and lack of support.

About the only way to diagnose fender edge waves is by a critical eye looking down the fender line. This will disclose high and low areas along the edge, and will usually show if one end is out of alignment with the other. But it is not always a good proof, especially when the paint is dull. A sure-fire check is with either a plumb level or plumb bob. Position either of these vertical plumb devices at stations down the fender edge and make a chalk mark on the pavement below. Connect these marks with a line to determine how straight the fender edge really is. This plumb check will show up major ripples or waves, but it will not show small dings. Only the block sander will give them away.

Fender edge repair on older cars is best done with a hammer and dolly, at least until all the workable metal is straight. Because some fenders used wire in the rolled bead, it will be practically impossible to get each tiny dent out, so follow with a filler.

Often overlooked on the older cars modified as hot rods is the frame itself. Larger frame rails are susceptible to waves and ripples just like sheetmetal, and they can be straightened the same way. As can be seen in the accompanying photograph, anytime the holes in a frame are welded, distortion is likely to occur and must be removed. In this particular instance the 1932 Ford frame is being used beneath a 1929 roadster body, and it will be seen. Making it flawlessly smooth is a prerequisite to outstanding bodywork elsewhere.

HINGES AND DOORS

When it comes to the doors, older cars have a corner on the "bad news" market. Big, heavy cars may experience some trouble in keeping door alignment (usually sag results after several years), but most older

1. *Even if your car is rusted, the parts you have to buy at a swap meet to complete it may also be. One of the common answers is sandblasting. Though often done incorrectly, with bad results, fine sand and low pressure can yield a pristine, undistorted part like this splash apron.*

2. *Another derusting method rapidly gaining favor with the restoration crowd is chemical stripping. Entire cars can be dipped in stripping tanks that take off rust, paint and bondo without harming the good metal. This is one of the tanks at Redi-Strip of Los Angeles, where this Model T is to be relieved of its old finish.*

3. *So you think your panels are straight enough for black lacquer? This door looked fine until a guide coat of light primer was lightly scuffed with sandpaper to show many, many highs and lows that needed work.*

4. If there's no other way to do a good job straightening a door skin, cut out the inner structure so the outer panel can be worked with the hammer and dolly. When the work is done, weld the inner panel back in.

5. Rather than cutting up the inner panel, this door was fixed by drilling holes for a prybar to fit through in working on the outside skin. Never use newspaper stuffed into a door as sound deadener, though. Not only is it a fire hazard but the paper will hold moisture in the door, promoting later rust-out problems. Better to use boat-type pour-and-set foam.

6. One of the major problems with early open cars is door alignment. Corrections can often be made with varying shims placed under the cowl and body mounting bolts at the frame.

7. Especially when you don't have the original fenders that came on the car, check the heights and contours with chalk-lines on the ground.

8. Door alingment can be frustrating and time-consuming, but the answers aren't complex. Sometimes a simple bend against an object in the jamb can realign a hinge. See the chapter on MAKING IT FIT in this book.

cars were built with thin, lightweight doors. This means there will be trouble with alignment to some extent, but the mechanical door parts are likely to wear rapidly. A beautiful street roadster can have its image ruined by ill-working doors.

Alignment of a coupe or sedan door is not nearly as difficult as on its roadster counterpart, since the closed cars generally have three hinges to the roadster's two. Dual hinges became almost standard after 1936, but they were made stronger at the same time. Whether two or three hinges are involved, alignment will be handled in the same manner and is covered in a separate chapter.

Many times a sloppy-fitting door is due entirely to worn hinge pins. This may not be apparent when the door is opened and moved up and down as a check, since the wear is very little and limited to a small area of both hinge and pin. As a guide, if the pins haven't been changed (few have) on a car made before 1948, new pins will be needed.

Drive the old pin out and inspect for wear. Also check the hinge pin holes, as they may have elongated ever so slightly. If the holes are larger, it may be necessary to drill the hinge to a slight oversize. Pins are available from a number of sources, including Antique Auto Parts, 9113 E. Garvey, Rosemead, Calif., the local hardware store, and the local Volkswagen dealer. It is best to lubricate the pin with a dry graphite before installing it.

If the doors still sag after the hinge adjustments, there may be some other trouble. This is true of roadsters that have another body adjustment at the front body-to-frame bolts. By shimming between body and frame at the bolt nearest the door, it is possible to raise or lower the door in relation to the rear post.

Wooden framework doors have problems all their own when it comes to vertical alignment. After the hinges are checked and repaired, loosen the framework screws slightly. Swing the door closed, but do not latch it, and place a small jack under the door rear. By raising the jack in small adjustments, the door can be aligned perfectly with the opening. The screws must be retightened. If they do not hold, additional screws should be added. It also helps to pour a quality wood glue in the joints.

On larger wood-framed doors there will often be a diagonal support brace running from the top of the hinged side to the opposite bottom edge. Make sure this brace is rigid, and replace it if necessary. A piece of thin steel strap 1 in. wide may be added for more bracing if desired.

In many cases, the bottom of the door will stick out (see chapter on alignment). This presents a very special problem with wood-framed doors. Using normal screen-door tighteners available from any hardware, attach one end to the door top near a hinge

4

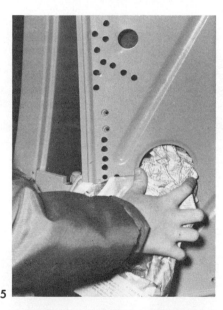

5

6

7

8

Vintage Bodywork

and the other at the opposite bottom, just like the brace. With the framework screws loosened, tighten this adjustable rod to the desired shape, then retighten the screws and add some glue.

Quite often the door may fit perfectly, but a worn latch assembly keeps the final fit sloppy. In the majority of old cars, the latching system is a simple sliding-bolt arrangement wherein a bar with a beveled end slides back and forth in the metal housing. This housing is comprised of two sides, in a sort of sandwich, held together by screws or bent metal tabs. When these tabs are carefully bent straight, the housing will separate. Every part of the latch should be washed and wire brushed, since rust is the usual cause of poorly operating doors.

The sliding bar tip may be worn and must be welded, then ground or filed to stock configuration. If a good arc welder is available, this tip may

be hardfaced to reduce repeat wear. Thoroughly lubricate the sliding bar sides and corresponding moving parts in the housing, then reassemble the complete unit.

The door post striker may also be worn and can be built up with weld as was the sliding bar. Since new parts are seldom available for older cars, this rebuilding procedure is often the only way to make doors fit and operate well.

Bringing a post-1948 car into outstanding shape is not as hard as with older cars, at least not from a sheetmetal standpoint. The larger body panels are easier to work with and alignment conditions are easier to control. Still, the newer cars present some special problems of their own.

After about 5 years, the rubber around doors and deck lids begins to deteriorate. The small rubber bumpers used to keep the hood in tension will crumble. Finding original replacements will be very difficult, since most manufacturers do not stock such parts for a long time. It is often

possible to locate these items in well established new car agencies, and occasionally usable rubber can be found on wrecked cars. When nothing else works, adapt rubber parts from newer automobiles. Most agencies stock a formed door rubber, and while this may not be exactly like the original, it will work. When attaching this type rubber, use the yellow 3M cement. It works far better than the black.

DEALING WITH WOOD

Many vintage cars, especially General Motors cars before 1935, take at least part, if not all of their structural strength from wood pieces that line the body panels on the inside. Indeed, in the case of cars of the 1920's, they were actually built out of wood, with sheetmetal panels tacked onto the outside of this wooden structure. Tack-on moldings hid the seams where the sheetmetal panels had been nailed into the wooden framework. The non-GM cars for the most part utilized steel bodies which

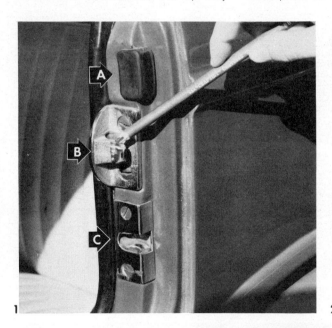

1

2

3

1. Three sources of early car door alignment are right here; A, the rubber door bumper, B, the striker, and C, the dovetail assembly. Worn striker tips can be built up with arc welding, rubbers replaced, and both striker and dovetail can be shimmed or moved slightly to affect a change in door fit and alignment.

2. Door fit and body rigidity were both improved on this roadster with addition of a crossbrace behind seat. Not seen here is turnbuckle (arrow) which provides for adjustment of the tension. Tension brought one door in and the other out. Both now fit.

3. Older hinge pins tend to wear and must be replaced as a rule. New stock pins can sometimes be located at new car dealerships that can be trimmed to fit early cars. Also you can check the antique parts houses.

1. Frame rails on non-fendered hot rod may have holes filled with brass or arc electrode, can then be ground smooth with disc sander.

2. If brass is used, it can cause a high point on inside of hole, which should be ground down in keeping with "supersanitary" code.

3. After rails have been welded, they should be straightened with a hammer. Low and high spots can be removed as with sheetmetal.

4. Even though it is much heavier, frame material can be treated just like body sheetmetal. Here brass was used to fill holes, then smoothed with file.

5. After final straightening, prime the rail and allow to thoroughly dry before proceeding with smoothing. Some mounting holes must remain.

6. Use glazing compound (putty) in thin coats to take care of minor low spots that remain. Keep amount of filler to bare minimum.

7. After the filler has dried, block sand the frame surface. Most stock rails will have edges higher than middle even when they are brand new.

8. Although this isn't the specific frame that received the treatment described, it is a good example of one that has been worked to sheetmetal smoothness. Because it's being restored rather than rodded, all frame mounting holes remain, although a quantity of non-stock openings were filled.

Vintage Bodywork

were strong in their own right, and *lined* these bodies with wooden supports, especially around the door openings and where the upholstery was to be attached.

Restoring either of the two types of construction means dealing with the problems of wood restoration, as well as the sheetmetal techniques described throughout this book. In the case of the steel-bodied cars, like Fords, the interior wood can be removed without destroying the body, and unless your wood pieces are in exceptional shape, you'll have to do this. Using the old pieces as patterns, you can purchase some sturdy hardwood like oak (unfortunately, increasingly hard to find today) and cut your own new pieces out, sanding them to fit the body precisely. You could also take your old pieces down to the local cabinet shop and have new pieces made to duplicate yours, if you don't have the tools at home for woodworking. There's an even easier way out, for those with the more popular years and models of Fords. A number of the antique Ford parts houses sell reproduction wood pieces for the Ford bodies with all the proper holes drilled, etc.

If you're restoring one of the Fisher bodies however, your problem is more serious. You might be better off to farm the whole task out to someone who specializes in antique car woodwork, although this work is naturally quite expensive. If your car has been fairly well kept over the years, you may not have too many wood problems. Commonly, you'll find places where water has collected and rotted out the wood in the lower sections of an early car, or where wood has cracked due to torsional stress on the car or simply to the gradual sagging of the body. When cracks are not too bad, meaning that no

wood is missing and the cracks are not in critical-stress areas, they can be reglued. There are a number of "super" wood glues on the market now that will do the job, and in fact should be used on even the joints that look OK. There's a tool used for furniture repairs that has a hypodermic needle-like point for squirting glue into wood seams and joints. Where a better repair must be made, the pieces can be held in alignment with clamps and drilled, so that glued dowels of wood can be driven in to stiffen the joint. Pieces that are rotted out must be replaced with new wood, of course, but only if a part of a long stringer is bad, can a new piece often be dovetailed and glued into the old stringer where you've cut out the bad section. Replacing *all* of the wood in such a body takes patience, and may best be left to a professional to handle.

"Woodie" station wagons are a problem unto themselves. The early ones were built entirely of wood and represent a major undertaking to restore, which is one reason why restored examples are so expensive on the antique car market. The later station wagons, up until the early '50's, were standard steel-bodied cars, to which wood was added outside for aesthetics. If yours has lived a well-cared-for life, you may have to do nothing more than remove the wood, sand it down, varnish it for beauty and protection, and put it back on the car when after the steel body has been restored and painted. Since this external wood is not structural, cracks can be repaired with glues satisfactorily, but replacing just a section of a wood piece will leave a non-stock seam that make detract from the overall restoration. Better to replace the whole piece. When replacing pieces of woodies, though, you must be more careful in your selection of woods than other restorers,

whose wood is never seen after the car is restored. Not only should the wood be of the exact same type as used originally, but you should do your best to find pieces with grain patterns that match your existing, good wood pieces. A seemingly heavy task, but a necessary one for a faithful restoration.

SEALING

One final area the body man will need to investigate is how well the body is sealed. Dust can enter a car

1. It's helpful in lining up the cowl and windshield frame on open cars, if you have a top; or at least the frame of one, to check with.

2. After your bodywork is done, you need to protect it from cancer from the inside; with undercoating, either from spray cans or a brush job.

3. Rotted wood is one of the banes of the early Fisher Body restorer. Although covered by upholstery in a finished car, the wood is part of the structural strength of the car and any rotted areas must be fixed.

4. Wood that is unfixable must be replaced with new wood of the same strength. Woodworker Bradley Brown is here making a new oak header piece for a '30 Cadillac, using the old, rotted piece as a rough pattern.

5. There are some good wood glues available now, and should be used on all joints. Cracks can often be fixed with superglue and clamps.

6. Where glue alone isn't enough to make a strong repair, holes must be drilled and wooden dowels driven in to strengthen a glued joint.

7. The roof area is where you'll find a lot of rotted wood. Here some of the original wood was saved by adding new pieces with a scarf joint that has been "glued and screwed."

8. While major woodwork, especially in structural areas, must be farmed out to professionals, most handy restorers can at least do some of the interior wood; like seat risers.

1

2

3

4

5

6

7

through the tiniest of openings, as can water. Seal around all leaking windows with special sealing compound, dousing the area with a hose as a preliminary check. Be advised that nothing will show up a water leak like a good rain storm, so the vehicle should be checked during a rain and the leaking area marked for repair when dry.

Dust can enter the passenger and luggage compartments from any opening, but the culprit is almost always improperly sealed doors and deck lid. To check for seal, close a sheet of typing paper in the door or deck lid. Do this completely around the sealing surface, and if the paper will pull out when the door is closed, that point is not sealing. This may be a problem of alignment, or the sealer may have failed.

The super sanitary car is the one which has received attention to detail. Not just the addition of new gimmicks, but the restoration of all stock items to like-new operation. It means, simply, that the car has been inspected from head to toe before being given that final nod of approval.

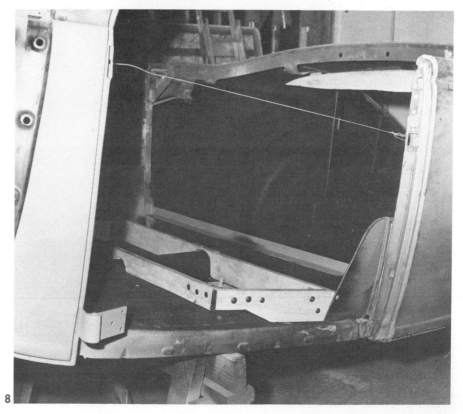

8

Vintage Bodywork

SOMETHING FROM NOTHING, RESTORATION TRICKERY

Problems in restoring a salvaged body may seem insurmountable to a body man whose experience has been limited to new or at least very recent cars. A late-model door, for example, damaged beyond salvation can be replaced by the simple expedient of ordering one from an agency, or it may be "skinned" with a replacement outer panel. But replacing a door on a car 20, 30 or more years old is a different can of worms. Diligent searching may eventually turn up another component, but more often than not it's in nearly as bad shape as the one it is to replace.

Sometimes it's possible to unite several assorted pieces into a single usable part. Using a door as an example again, one may have a structurally sound inner framework but with the outer panel badly rusted or shot full of holes. Another door scrounged from a wrecking yard or off a hulk rotting behind a barn may have a bent or badly deteriorated inner structure but a salvagable outer skin. The solution is to unite the best parts of each, and in restoration work this is often done.

Here are a couple of examples of what we're talking about. The first problem was with the left front fender of '36 Ford, almost as sound as the proverbial dollar except that the trailing edge had been trimmed away by some forgotten hot rodder who wanted to sport about town minus his running boards after the fashion of the day. The rear edge of the fender had been what they called "bobbed." When this fender was bolted on the car undergoing restoration, there was a roughly pie-shaped gap up to 8 inches wide between it and the running board. Still, the majority of the fender was in very good shape, and it was the best of several junkyard choices.

A second left front fender was obtained whose entire front portion had been the sad looser in a battle with something very solid. Someone had evidently tried to salvage this one by bashing the damaged surface into something not too close to original shape, grinding the metal to tissue paper thickness, then laying on heavy slabs of plastic filler. To a restorer, the front half of this fender was literally useless, but the trailing edge was rust-free and straight. This particular project, then, shows joining the better parts of the two identical fenders. The trick, and there really is one, lies in accurately joining the pieces so the alignment of bolt holes and final con-

1

2

tours is identical to the original, yet with as little metalworking as humanly possible.

FENDER SURGERY

To follow this sequence of events we dropped by the shop of Carl Green of Topeka, Kan. Carl is a young but experienced bodyworking technician who was about to perform the surgery illustrated. As the photos reveal, only ordinary body tools and equipment were used. One accompanying photo shows the bobbed fender which was to be repaired. Notice how the cut rear edge is rounded where the original "butcher" wanted some semblance of grace on his shade tree

reshaping project. It would have been time-consuming and wasted effort to transfer the outline of this irregular cut to the other fender, for there were no straight lines for accurate measurement and reference. So, the job was begun by cutting away even more of the fender.

Before work was attempted, however, the bobbed fender was solidly bolted to the car. This was not only to keep from having to chase the fender all over the shop floor when attacking it with hammer and dolly, but to hold rigidly in position during welding so that the tendency of the metal to shift around or warp when heated would be reduced.

Masking tape was placed on the in-

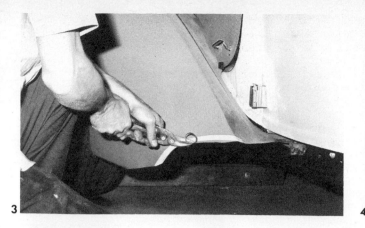

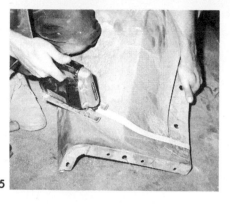

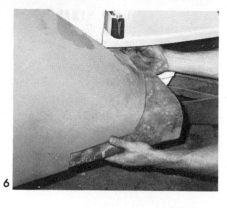

1. *It's obvious that a bit of work will be needed to undo some butchery perpetrated by a long-ago rodder. The trailing edge of '36 Ford front fender has been "bobbed," and our job is to restore it to its original condition.*

2. *Luckily, we found another fender. Its front portion was beyond salvage, but trailing edge was good and will be pieced onto bobbed fender.*

3. *Transfer of shape of fender piece needed would be difficult with curved edges, so it was further cut in a series of straight lines for easier measurement. Snips follow tape line.*

4. *Shape of needed piece was transferred to junked fender, but overlap of about 1 inch was allowed.*

5. *Saber saw makes quick work of cutting job; leaves a clean edge and no distortion of the metal.*

6. *Trial fit of severed end is with excess metal of piece slipped under edge of fender. When alignment was checked, an awl was used to scribe line which was carefully followed with aviation snips and grinder.*

7. *Tack welds are made at widely spaced intervals to prevent a great concentration of heat which would warp the metal and mean more repair.*

stalled fender to define straight-line cuts to be made. Snips, aviation snips if you prefer, were used to follow the tape's outline as shown. This eliminated the original curved edges of the earlier trimming job.

By careful measurement from various reference points on the original fender (the bolt holes along the flanged inner edge) more tape was placed on the spare fender. About an inch of excess metal was allowed for precisely matched trimming of the edges to be butted.

The slightly too-long fender segment was cut off with an electric saber saw, a useful body shop tool that does not bend or chew up the edges of cuts in body steel. The severed piece included one of the mounting holes on its inner flange, so it was bolted on the car right where it belonged. Precise measurements were next taken to assure perfect alignment, then the piece was clamped solidly with vise grips.

A sharp-pointed awl was used to scribe a fine line on the fender segment, using the cut edge of the other fender as a template. Next the piece was removed from the car and the line followed with the snips, then dressed off with the body grinder. Now the pieces could be accurately butted together without overlap. The segment was rebolted to the car, the mating running board edge was checked for alignment then, finally, welding began.

HAMMER WELDING

The fact that body sheet metal expands at approximately 6-millionths of an inch per degree of heat, doesn't sound like much. But when you realize a welding flame is about 1800° to 2000°F., some distortion is going to occur. Even the most carefully aligned edges of butted panels will spread from each other at one end when welding begins at the other. To prevent this, or to at least greatly reduce this tendency, a series of short tack welds are made at widely spaced intervals.

Carl began his welding procedure with one tack weld at each end of the cut separating the fender pieces. A third tack in the middle pretty firmly joined them and would prevent movement and misalignment through heat distortion. Then, by adding additional tack welds at alternate ends of the seam, the pieces became joined, yet without a concentration of heat at any one point.

As he completed each tack, Carl quickly put the torch down, but left it lit, and while the metal still glowed cherry red, he hammered it on top while holding a dolly underneath. This served to align the edges of the seam vertically and relieve the heat distortion stresses which would have accumulated during tack weldings.

When there were enough individual tack welds so the spaces between them were about 1 inch long, Carl welded up all the gaps, hammer-and-dollying each one as he went.

Although the technique and advantages of hammer welding are discussed in detail elsewhere in this book, it should be briefly mentioned here again. It might seem simpler to have welded up the seam, then bash it below the level of the surrounding metal, fill the valley with plastic filler, and carve it to final shape.

Vintage Bodywork

Welding butted panels, or joining adjacent edges where a rip might have been caused by an accident, means that a great concentration of heat must be applied. If this occurs in the center of a door or quarter panel, where there is a large and only slightly curved surface area, the radiating heat will distort the panel, probably beyond salvation. But by tack welding at widely spaced intervals first, as discussed, then filling in the gaps later after the metal has had a chance to cool, the heat will not spread and do irreparable damage over a vast area.

But welding with rod, as necessary in cases like the one illustrated, produces a built-up bead. To grind the bead flat with a body grinder would be to weaken the bond. But by hammering on the bead while it glows red and the metal is as pliable as butter, the metal of the bead is "moved" down into the seam. Also, hammer welding tends to shrink the metal im-

mediately adjacent to the welded seam which has "grown" through the application of heat. In effect, the technique returns to normal everything that welding upsets. True, hammer welding is time-consuming and, in the case of a professional body shop, more expensive, but the customizer or restorer generally has time at his disposal and wants the superior result that the technique will bring. Besides, this car will have the undersides of the fenders finished as smooth and distortion-free as the exposed areas. Hammer welding is the only way to wind up with both top and bottom sides as good as new.

Once the accessible areas of the fender seam had been entirely welded, and the two pieces had become one single fender, the fender was once more removed from the car. The difficult and inaccessible seam areas, such as the inner flange and the outer stiffening bead, could now be finished off with torch and rod.

Light surface grinding with a small, air-driven body grinder cleaned up

1. Gaps between tack welds are filled in, then hammer welded following the technique described in the text.

2. Weld seam is lightly ground to clean off weld scale and burned paint, and to show up high and low spots that are heated and hammered to shape.

3. Welding is complete and alignment of fender contours and bolt holes in frame and running board is assured.

4. No lead or filler was needed to bring fender to pre-paint condition, thanks to the careful hammer welding. Several heavy coats of primer/surfacer were applied, will be allowed to sit for considerable time until maximum shrinkage has occurred.

5. Rear fender has been bobbed like front one, though they came from two different cars. Worse, rear-end swap brought longer wheelbase so wheel cutout in fender must be moved back.

6. Electrical conduit, known as EMT stock, of ½-inch diameter, was curved around a tire until desired radius was reached. It will form new lip of fender cutout and is used as template for trimming the fender. Measurements to axle center served to properly locate conduit.

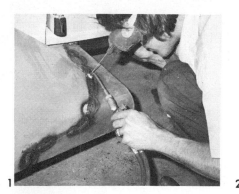

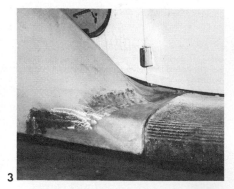

7

8

9

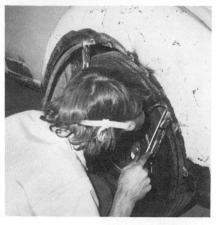

10

11

12

the welded seam of scale and burned paint, and also showed up small low and high spots that needed a little more dinging. These were places where heat distortion had moved the metal either above or below the desired level. Shrinking the spots by heating them cherry red then quickly hammer-and-dollying them, as when hammer welding, shrank the metal and brought it to proper contour.

Beyond this it would be a matter of dressing the area and preparing for paint, so we'll let the matter go for now and move to the second problem on the '36 Ford.

BACK TO THE BACK

One rear fender now on the subject car had been severely bobbed, evidently by another long-ago hot rodder that preferred cruising minus running boards. Again, the area that adjoined the running board had been completely eliminated, but this particular fender is a scarce item and neither a substitute nor a second fender, damaged in another area but from which the proper chunks could be salvaged, could be found. This would be purely a case of make-do.

As before, the first step was to temporarily but securely bolt the butchered fender to the car, then align and secure the running board. The huge gap between the two showed the area that would have to be entirely hand-formed.

But now came another vexing problem, one that many rodders restoring an older body for use on modern running gear might have to face. The rear axle was slightly farther aft than on the original car; the wheelbase had grown about 1½ inches when the late-model Chevy running gear and suspension had been united with the Ford chassis. What gave the new, longer stance away was the location of the wheels within the fender opening; they were too far back. Since the axle couldn't be repositioned forward, the fender had to go rearward. Not the entire fender, mind you, but only the wheel *opening*. Moving a *hole* might seem insurmountable to the bodyworking novice, but it isn't all that formidable, and here's how it was done.

THE CONDUIT TRICK

The outer edges of most older fenders have a rounded-under lip that strengthens the fender and prevents the start of vibration cracks. The radius of these rolled beads is approximately ½-inch in diameter. To change the beaded edge normally means hammering the rolled edge flat, making the repair or modification, then re-rolling the edge back under again with hammer and dolly. This is difficult, time consuming, and usually ends up with warped fender surfaces.

But there's a better way. Carl obtained a length of ½-inch diameter

7. Paint was ground from edge of fender, marking pen used to scribe trim line. Conduit was removed and line followed with aviation snips.

8. Conduit couldn't be curved sharp enough to follow rear part of cutout, so the piece was trimmed from fender and moved back. Note that radius of original bead or lip is same as tube.

9. Conduit is clamped inside of fender since cutout will not be flaired. For flaired look, however, the conduit would go outside fender. Metal is brazed to conduit to reduce amount of heat applied which could collapse or distort the conduit. All other seams were welded, however.

10. Initial tack brazes were made at widely spaced intervals. Object is to avoid a high concentration of heat which would warp metal, then impossible to hammer back to shape since conduit would prevent it.

11. Conduit extends into thin air, caused both by rearward shift of wheel cutout and portion of fender that was bobbed off for "racy" look.

12. Piece of 3/16-inch plate was cut from template and shaped to rear mounting flange of running board.

electrical conduit; a thin-wall, low-grade steel tube with a zinc coating to prevent corrosion. It can be welded or brazed without trouble since the coating quickly burns away. The EMT, as it's called, is pliable enough in ½-inch diameter, to be formed to almost any desired contour, and it

Vintage Bodywork

can be curved to a 1 foot or even smaller radius if you're careful and go slowly. Carl curved the conduit by the simple expedient of bending it around a tire, then worked it more between his hands until it assumed a smooth arch matching the curve of the original fender opening.

Next, the curved conduit was held against the rear fender and aligned by measurement from several points on the conduit to the center of the rear axle. It was clamped in place *outside* the fender and used as a template. A marking pen was run around the radius leaving a line on the fender to denote the arch of the new wheel opening.

Naturally, because the opening is being moved rearward, there was excess metal on the back portion of the fender, decreasing to nothing at the top of the arch, and a minus in front. Since you can't reshape a minus area, this was forgotten for the moment. The aviation snips cut away offending parts of the fender along the line just drawn. Next, the conduit was clamped in proper alignment *inside*

the fender where it was tack brazed at 6-inch intervals. At this point the front part of the conduit curved out into thin air, as the photos show. The conduit, if you haven't been paying attention, will form the new bead edge of the fender; it prevents the need to roll the metal under with hammer and dolly, and it provides greater strength in the bargain.

Brazing is best in a situation like this where a raw edge of metal must attach to the conduit. Welding, with its hotter flame, would distort the fender panel since its stiffening edge had been cut away, and the arched conduit itself might tend to wrinkle or collapse if too much heat were applied in one spot. By tack brazing at widely spaced intervals, though, the heat was controlled, and shortly the conduit had been solidly brazed where it joined the fender, or about half-way around the radius of the wheel opening.

Carl now had a rough outline of the area that would have to be bridged with new sheetmetal; one that coincided with the bobbed-off front edge where the running board must meet it.

1. Running board mounting flange is separate from fender sheetmetal for double-thickness strength. Plate is tack brazed to fender metal and forms basis of lower fender edge outline.

2. Fender "grows" as various-shaped pieces of sheetmetal are used to bridge gap between fender metal and conduit. Lower end of conduit was pushed inward to achieve final fender shape, then excess was cut off.

3. Nearing the end of the welding procedure, fender has good resemblance to original contours, but with wheel cutout moved back 1½ inches.

4. The areas of rework and complete fabrication are evident. Additional metal finishing is needed, but this will follow stripping fender of paint, scale, and grime to "sanitize" it.

5. Final brazing around running board mounting flange is done with fender removed from car for access.

6. Fender (along with other parts) was sent to Redi-Strip (12217 Woodruff, Downey, Calif.) for chemical stripping right down to bare metal. Secret process in no way affects the metal, as does sand blasting or acid processes. Process is quick and inexpensive, and the firm does work for Harrah's and other restoration museums. Items can be shipped to them. Our fender was primed on the underside, then we replaced it on car for final finishing steps. Plastic filler is used in a small quantity, here being mixed with its catalytic hardener.

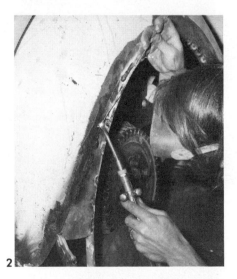

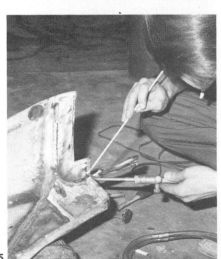

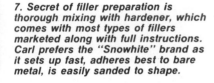

7. Secret of filler preparation is thorough mixing with hardener, which comes with most types of fillers marketed along with full instructions. Carl prefers the "Snowhite" brand as it sets up fast, adheres best to bare metal, is easily sanded to shape.

8. Areas of metal reworking are covered with a thin spread of filler; use a flexible plastic spatula. No more than 1/8-inch was wiped on, then most is filed and sanded off, leaving filler only in low spots.

9. Hardening time depends upon room temperature and amount of hardener added. Average time would be about 15 minutes. It can then be filed lightly with carrot grater-like file.

10. Carl runs his air file over the filler, but its stroke rate of 3500 per minute means going with caution. Machine uses rough-grit, dry production paper, is backed with a platen having one soft edge for tight radii as here.

11. No. 180 grit, dry-type paper on hard rubber sanding block brings the surface to final pre-paint finish. Fillers should never be applied then allowed to stand for considerable time, as overnight or a day or two. It continues to harden with time and eventually becomes too hard to work. Here it's actually still "green" but further hardening causes no shrinkage.

12. Several coats of primer/surfacer are applied, will be allowed to stand for considerable time. Final block sanding will show up very small high and low spots which will disappear with further priming and blocking.

The lower front edge of the original fender had been manufactured as a double-thickness, to provide strength where the running board bolted. Remember, all this had already been trimmed off.

A hockey-stick-shaped piece of 3/16-inch steel plate was cut using a cardboard template made from the rear running board flange. This produced a true lower edge contour of the missing fender portion, and it was tack brazed to the inner fender flange.

Various small shapes and sizes of 20 gauge sheetmetal were cut like a steel jigsaw puzzle to fill in the missing areas of the fenders. Carl preferred working with the relatively small pieces rather than a few large ones. Each was tack welded after being trimmed to fit between the cut edge of the fender and the conduit. He eye-balled the general contours as he went, using ingenuity, common sense, and several photos of '36 Fords that clearly showed how the rear fenders originally looked. When the pieces were all tacked in place, each seam was hammer welded as discussed previously. However, where

new metal was mated to the lip-forming conduit, it was brazed instead to keep welding's higher heat from buckling the thin-wall tubing.

The whole operation was brought to the roughly metal-finished stage in approximately 3 hours, as compared to the front fender on the same car that had required about 1 hour. Again, the body grinder cleaned the rear fender of weld and braze scale and burned paint, and disclosed some high and low spots that were then shrunk to proper contour with the torch, hammer, and dolly. Finally, the virtually hand-crafted rear fender was removed from the car so that the inaccessible inner flange could be properly welded. All that remained now was to permanently reinstall the fender, and prepare it for painting. It had been a tough job, one that certainly could have been eased had a complete fender been available. But it was a good lesson in making-do and proves that no matter how formidable a bodyworking job might be, fore-thought, patience and experience can make a complex operation really quite simple.

Louvering

How to make an apple-pie example of Americana— Louvers for a "Nostalgia Rod."

One of the more colorful trends in the street rodding world to surface in the last few years has been the "nostalgia rod." Dozens of old customs and early rods are being rebuilt and brought back to their former glory by rodders who remember fondly the era of "American Graffiti" and before. Not only that, but new rods and customs are being built from scratch to look just like they were built in the '50's. People are actually once again combing the swap meets for flathead Ford V-8 speed equipment, fender skirts, Carson top frames, Appleton spotlights and "flipper" hubcaps. The Good Old Days are being relived today by some automotive enthusiasts. One fad of the early rods that has never really died out but is now enjoying a revival of sorts is louvering. Back in the early days, a *car* was simply not a *machine* unless it had racy louvers punched into every panel that could be removed from the car and would fit into the local customizer's louver press. The most common application was of course on hood panels, where louvers served some practical purpose in letting hot air out of the engine compartment where a ⅜ by ⅜ flathead was always running just short of overheating. But many other panels were also punched out, such as deck lids, fenders and even skirts felt the

bite of the louver press.

The early drag racing cars made extensive use of louvers. Ostensibly the louvers were to make a car faster by letting the trapped wind escape, but they also held a psychological advantage in that the car with the most louvers and lightening holes just *looked* faster. Hot rodders always tend to emulate race cars with their street machines; and louvers became even more popular on the street than at the drags. There , the racers eventually found out that louvering the turret top of a '40 Ford coupe was expensive, but not necessarily effective in producing better performance. Since most of the hot rodding trends, especially in the early days, were started in Southern California, it's no surprise that louvering was started there, too. It's said by old-time rodders that the first guy they ever saw who had louvers on his hot rod had actually cut a panel out of a gymnasium locker and had welded this louvered panel into his hood! Luckily for the schools back then, customizers saw the popularity of louvers and built or bought the presses to turn out thousands of air slots for hot rodders and custom car owners. If your car had a hood, then it became *de rigueur* to "louver everything but the handle."

Now that the nostalgia-rod builders

are bringing back louvers to their former prominence, we thought you might like to see how this is done. Louvers are still a valid customizing technique for sheet metal, and still serve the practical purpose of letting out hot, underhood air. In that respect, they may even do something to improve your gas mileage, what with the high underhood temperatures cars are currently running; laboring as they do under a maze of plumbing and smog contraptions.

We took the top hood panels from our own '32 highboy roadster project car to Kent Fuller Manufacturing (19019 Parthenia, Northridge, Calif.) for the venting process, so we could show you what's involved. Kent explained to us that the actual punching of louvers is very simple, and that most of the work is in the layout and measurement of where you want the louvers to go. On our '32 hood, the panels are narrower at the front than at the rear, so the problem was how to install straight rows of louvers that seemed to match both the straight line of the hood centerstrip, and the *angle* of the panel's outer edge.

Kent Fuller has been around hot rodding since the very early days, and besides his wealth of knowledge in chassis building and aluminum-forming, he also has two louver presses together with the expertise in

1

using them. After a few minutes, studying and measuring our hood panels, Kent decided to stagger the rows of louvers (there would be two rows of louvers on each top panel) such that they were neither parallel to the hood centerline or to the outside edge. By splitting the difference between the two angles, the louvers "cheat the eye" and appear to be "right" with both edges of the hood.

Once you've settled on the width of the louvers and have decided where on the hood the rows will go, next comes the time-consuming setup of the press. The press has an adjustable guide along which the sheetmetal slides as it is fed through the press, and this must be adjusted to maintain the louvers at the desired angle and position on your panel. When the angle gets tricky, and you have to have more of an angle at one end of the panel than at the other, you may have to clamp a piece of metal to one edge of the hood as a spacer from the guide. This is what Kent did with our hood panels.

After checking the alignment of the male/female louver dies by louvering a scrap piece of aluminum, Kent and an assistant punched out our louvers—72 of them—in about five minutes. The dies have an edge that makes the spacing between the louvers an automatic proposition: You punch a louver and then butt the edge of this louver up against the die's outside edge before punching the next one. This keeps all the louvers spaced exactly the same distance.

If you live near a big city, you may be able to find someone in your area who is punching louvers, such as a locker company. By contacting the local street rod club, you may learn some additional clues beyond the yellow pages; or you could even mail your part to Kent Fuller. Expect to pay about 50¢ a louver at most places, and you may also have to pay $5 or more for a setup charge. We're not suggesting that you louver the hood of your 1975 car, but we do feel they are a legitimate customizing trick for which you may find many applications on specialty vehicles.

The one caution that we might give you is to have your panel completely stripped of paint and all bodywork done before you have it louvered. Naturally the hood must be flat and without waves or the louvers won't all be straight. Also, there should be no paint in the areas where the louvers will go, because after they are punched, the job of sanding the hood prior to finish-paint is made much more difficult. ♛

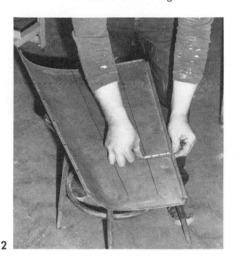

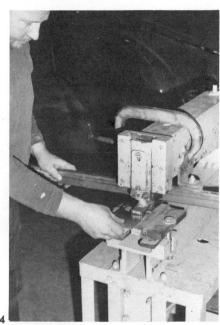

1. Louvering has been an effective custom trick for many, many years, and is now seeing a resurgence of popularity among street rodders, like Kent Fuller. Kent's nifty, original Volksrod features a louvered hood and even louvers in the fiberglass bed! This is accomplished by glassing a louvered metal panel into the bed.

2. Kent Fuller carefully scribes the guide lines on our '32 hood panel. By "splitting the difference" of the side and center angles, the rows of louvers cheat the eye and appear as parallel to the hood edges.

3. The most important part of the louvering process is setting the guide bar properly, so that the rows of louvers are straight, and are at the desired angle to the hood's edges.

4. After adjusting the guide bar, Kent checks the alignment of the male and female dies with a piece of scrap aluminum, before doing hood.

5. Usually some assistance is needed to keep the workpiece snug against the guide bar as the panel is fed through, one louver at a time.

6. To get the spacing and angles you desire, you may have to clamp some strap metal to the panel edge to space it from the guide bar.

The Traveling Fender Mender

How one man and a van make the kind of living that you've always wanted.

Okay, so you've got a decent job and you're getting by on your salary, but are you happy? Maybe you're one of those who'd like to step off the treadmill and open your own auto body and paint shop—sure would be great to be your own boss, wouldn't it? But, you say, look how much it costs to get started these days; so you head back to the old job every morning with a sigh, wondering how other guys manage to break loose and do it. Well, if you're willing to look at things from every angle, you're bound to find a way around the roadblocks, just as did Jim Byram of Orange, Calif.. When Jim got tired of working for someone else, he came up with a unique approach—a new twist to an old service—and got into business for himself on a minimum budget.

A native of Casselton, N.D., Jim picked up the fundamentals of his trade back there before moving to Orange in 1962 to work as a body man. It didn't take him too long to

figure out that there had to be a better way of making a living than working in a body shop. Not that he disliked his trade; it's just that there's something about the fresh air and being one's own boss that's especially appealing to the sense of freedom a newly arrived Californian feels. At that time, many used car lots found it more practical to peddle their wares with dings and scrapes intact than to hassle with a nearby body shop to get them fixed; they just knocked down the asking price enough to make the sale if the customer insisted. So Jim started moonlighting at used car lots, carrying his tools and equipment from lot to lot as he did the minor bodywork and spot painting right on the premises.

At this point, he realized that many new car dealerships had a problem that they were unable to solve. Almost every new car sale involves a trade-in, many of which have a number of dings and dents that need repairing before the cars are offered for

sale. But the new car dealership body and paint shop is a high-volume operation that's not really set up to cater to the used car department; so the trade-ins requiring minor exterior refurbishing to bring top dollar are worked on rather reluctantly by dealership body and paint men—and only when everything else is caught up, which can mean as much as a week or more. Yet, while the trade-in vehicles sit around waiting for attention, they're costing the used car department money, simply because they're not available for resale.

MOBILE BODY SHOP

The more Byram considered the problem, the more promising it looked to him. Jim soon came up with the idea of a mobile body and paint service that could come onto the dealer's lot, make the necessary repairs quickly and get trade-ins back on the lot within a few hours to a couple of days after the dealer received them. Essentially, it meant upgrading the

service he had been performing on used car lots. So, tossing his body and paint equipment into a beat-up 1947 Chevy van, he began making the rounds of Orange County dealerships to explain his idea; before he knew it, he'd acquired more customers than he knew what to do with. At this point, he built the van to serve as an efficient work station—and he's been his own boss ever since.

In fact, he soon outgrew the Chevy van and began looking around for something newer and more efficient;

2

1. *The Traveling Fender (bender) Mender at work—gifted with ingenuity. Jim Byram has made the great outdoors his body and paint shop.*

2. *An entire shop on wheels, his golden metallic-brown '73 Econoline was created from two wrecked vans and a Pinto. Hood scoop was taken from a Ford Torino, while the spoiler came from the rear of a Datsun 240-Z and is mounted upside down.*

3. *Early '72 Pinto seats mate perfectly with the Econoline seat base; late '72 Pintos used a slightly altered seat design that requires some modification. Pinto steering column and wheel were used.*

4. *Installing a camper shell window in the roof, Jim provided it with a snap on/off cover for those days when the sun's just too hot—van has air conditioning too.*

5. *Rear seat and quarter panels from Pinto were built into van against partition that separates workshop in rear. Portholes were installed forward of usual position—and partition window—in another camper shell window. Power tools store beneath seat.*

6. *The compartment behind the quarter panel on the passenger side hides his portable welding equipment; carpeted front flap folds down and you'd never know that it was there.*

3   4

5

6

Fender Mender

he hit upon a '65 Dodge van. A couple of years ago, Jim came across a '73 Econoline 100 that had been totaled. Because the engine and drivetrain had been salvaged from the wreck, Jim got the shell for a mere $15; he then picked up another total with a good engine, trans and rear end. Working in his spare time, Jim put the two together to come up with what appears to be a brand spanking new customized '73 Econoline—at a total cost to him of $1500 and 9 months of his spare time.

While he was building his latest mobile body shop, Jim decided to go all the way and make this one a van that could be used for pleasure as well as for business. He installed the seats from an early '72 Pinto (as well as the Pinto steering column), discovering that they fit neatly onto the van seat bases without modification. Building a partition across the van about 3 ft. from the rear doors, he installed the back seat from a Pinto to carry his family in comfort. Behind the carpeting along the side wall rests a 4-ft. cabinet that opens to expose part of the paint supply that he carries with him. A tool rack and a folding portable desk were mounted on the inboard side of the side doors, and between the side door and the partition he built in a small carpeted cabinet to hold his portable gas welding unit. Power tools are stored beneath the Pinto back seat, with the majority of hand tools carried in a tool chest behind the passenger's front seat. Visibility to the rear was provided by installing the plexiglas side window from a camper in the partition above the Pinto rear seat, and another such window was installed in the roof of the van over the driving compartment to serve as a sunroof. And to make certain that he didn't get too much sun, he also provided the sunroof with a snap-fit cover. Add all of this to the power steering and air conditioning and you've got a neat work/play vehicle that's lots of fun to drive.

But that's not all; he transferred his paint mixing equipment from the Dodge van to the back side of the Econoline's partition, providing music to mix by via a stereo radio with twin speakers mounted on the headliner. At the left side of his work space went the small air compressor unit he uses to run his power tools and spray

gun. One air tank was placed beneath the built-in bench, with two other air tanks mounted amidships under the van, one on each side. The spare tire found its home underneath, also. On the inboard side of the left rear door, Jim hung his masking paper dispenser; on the other door, racks were installed to hold his color formula and mixing books. An electrical outlet was installed under his workbench, along with several drawers to hold sandpaper, buffing cloths, tack rags, etc. The end result is a complete and self-contained body and paint shop that's capable of carrying out almost any minor repair you could imagine.

When Jim first went into the mobile body shop business, he had a lacquer mixing system in his van, but has since switched over to acrylic enamel only; as a result, he prefers to service Ford dealerships (Ford uses that type of paint exclusively). But restricting himself in this manner has not really hurt business; he has all that he can handle right now, with several other dealerships waiting in line to take advantage of his services whenever possible.

HAVE PAINT, WILL TRAVEL

To see just how Jim operates his unusual business, I accompanied him for a few days to watch his system at work. Most days go something like this: Jim arrives at the dealership in the morning and, as they're expecting him on that particular day, there's usually room provided somewhere on the used car lot where he can park his van. Checking with the used car manager, he finds out which cars need repairs and what should be done to them. Moving the cars to be worked on, he arranges them around the van in a circular fashion. He then hooks up his electrical outlet to the shop's power and also connects into their air line. The use of his portable

1. No usable space is wasted. Hand tool rack hangs on one door, while a fold-down desk and invoice rack on the other allow Jim to settle accounts right on the spot.

2. A cabinet behind the carpeted doors occupies the opposite wall and is used to hold paint and supplies in addition to those carried in the rear work space.

3. Jim sets up his mobile shop for work. The handle holding the left door open is attached to a broom—Jim leaves the lot as clean as he found it. Compressor hose and electrical cord are being removed from storage space under the workbench. Fold-down plastic keeps the bumper clean.

4. At the left side of his work compartment, we find the portable air compressor. The electrical box allows use of power tools; cord plugs into shop's power line. Drawers under the workbench hold miscellaneous small items such as sanding discs, buffing pads, etc.

5. With one air tank stored against the interior partition under the workbench, Jim has mounted two extra tanks beneath the van, one on each side for balance. Note the spare tire's location—every inch of space is utilized.

6. As Jim's compressor is slightly underpowered despite the extra air tanks, its use is reserved for those rare occasions when he's not able to hook up to the shop air line; here he connects the 100-ft. air hose to start the day.

7. With a well-equipped tool box, Byram can put his hands on almost any metal working tool needed.

5

6

7

Fender Mender

compressor is reserved for those rare days when the shop's air system is so loaded down that it can't accept another draw. Now he's ready to get down to business.

Working in a circular fashion, he begins the repair cycle on one car; when he reaches the point where he must wait for filler, body putty or primer to dry, he moves on to the next car. In this way, he's able to keep busy from one car to the next until everything is done—no wasted motion here, as time is money. Because he depends upon speed and quality to keep the used car manager happy, there are no shortcuts taken; while he could simply slap some putty over a ding and then paint it, he doesn't operate that way. It's drill a hole or two, pull out the ding with a knocker and then grind it smooth before using any putty.

Paint mixing is done with a variable-speed drill, adapted to fit over the mixing covers on the quart paint cans. As he carries a complete line of paints in the van, it's no problem for Jim to come up with any required color. For those who might wonder about the advisability of painting outdoors, remember that Jim restricts himself to minor repairs, which means mainly spot painting, and he's encountered no problems as far as dirt or dust is concerned. By using an acrylic enamel thinner and a bit of retarder, he's found that the enamel will dry before any dirt settles on it. And there is one distinct advantage to working outdoors with the spray gun: he gets better color matches—especially with metallics—than are possible when you're painting inside. While this may sound strange, it's true. Consider the fact that if you're working inside, you're trying to match fresh paint to what is most likely a fairly weatherbeaten finish on the rest of the car. So you get what appears to be a perfect match in the subdued shop light—but what happens when you get the finished car out into the bright sunlight, where the owner sees his car most often? Right, the match becomes a mismatch, particularly where the metallic colors are concerned. Going on the premise that most people are apt to look more closely at a car in sunlight, Jim works for a match under that illumination. No one has yet complained about the result in the years he's been at it.

By now, you may be wondering about exactly the same thing I did: why not outfit other vans in the same way and put a whole fleet of them on the road? After all, Jim's income is limited by the fact that he works

alone. There is a limit to what one man can accomplish in a week's work, especially if he happens to hit a rainy day now and then when he can't ply his trade on the lot. Well, Jim thought of this too, and toyed with the idea, but as he's really selling service, his employees would have to have the same kind of dedication to their work that he has; in this day and age, that type of dedication is a difficult commodity to come by. Nothing could ruin his reputation faster than a helper who failed to show up on the job, or one who did sloppy work. So he gave up the idea, feeling that the problems and possible risks were greater than the rewards.

Although not really novel to the California way of life—mobile shops servicing Orange County dealerships include transmission, upholstery and trim specialists—Jim has packaged his concept in a modern and up-to-date way that draws admiration wherever he goes. While you might expect a plumber on wheels to *look* like a plumber on wheels, this is one body and paint shop that looks as if it just came out of a custom car show—from its wide, flared rear fenders to the Torino hood scoop and Datsun 240-Z spoiler at the front. Maybe he can't make a million a year, but Jim Byram has reversed the usual pattern. Most of us would like to turn our hobby into a paying trade; Jim has turned his trade into a comfortably paying hobby. Do you know of any other body and paint men who get to travel in style, work in a different setting every day, enjoy the sunny Southern California weather at its best—and are paid for it?

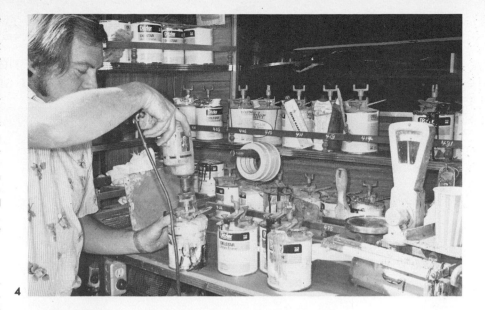

4

5

1. Even though Jim works outdoors, he still uses a mask when grinding or sanding, as breathing all that dust is just too much, indoors or out.

2. After pulling out the Mark IV's dented fender and smoothing the surface in preparation for a coat of body putty, Jim mixes up a small quantity at his workbench.

3. Smoothing the putty on the fender, Jim will move to another job while this one dries. Assembly-line technique lets him keep busy as he works his way around several different cars at various stages of completion.

4. Jim carries a complete line of Ditzler paints, allowing him to match any acrylic enamel on the spot. Paint is mixed using a variable-speed hand drill and a home-made attachment that fits over the mixing connectors on the can.

5. No guessing here—Byram uses scales and clean cups to mix his formulas right to manufacturer's specs.

6. After masking the area to be spotted, Jim shoots a coat of paint, and then it's on to the next job.

6

Painting Trivia

Some things you really don't need to know about painting—but you should.

The novice or beginner at automobile painting can be taken through the necessary steps in learning the proper application of the various kinds of paints, primers, thinners and reducers, by an old hand at the game. And the novice can be shown the fine arts of featheredge sanding, metal cleaning, paint mixing, and so forth. However, all of this may not necessarily teach him the *whys* of painting, with the result that at some future time, he may have to solve a peculiar painting problem without the guidance of an experienced professional. Thus, a few words seem to be in order to bring up points that a "green" hand at painting may miss as he learns the routines of sanding and spraying.

CAR PAINTING—WHY?

First, *why* are cars painted; to give them attractive coloring? In part, yes. But a car's color is only something added to a coating (which could just as easily be perfectly clear) that has been designed to prevent rust and corrosion caused by the sun, heat, rain, and cold, as well as salts and other harmful chemicals that a car normally encounters every day. Without paint, a car would be the drab grey shade of bare metal, scratched with imperfections caused by the die forming of the body panels, and ugly lines where welding or other methods were used to join the panels together. Within a very few days, the grey would start to turn a dull brown as rust caused by oxidation through exposure to the atmosphere started its dirty work, and eventually the metal would be eaten away completely, and what had formerly been a car would be nothing more than a collapsed heap of useless scale.

The paint—let's introduce the word finish since paint as referred to here, is actually several layers of different kinds of "paint"—is what protects the vulnerable bare metal from the elements. Technological advances in the field over the years have brought us modern finishes that measure as little as .004-in. (four thousandths of an inch!) thick, but which will stave off rust and other forms of deterioration for many years even under harsh conditions and with little care.

A car's finish may be built up with as few as two altogether different kinds of paint, or it may contain three or even more dissimilar layers. If we magnified a cross section of a body panel, we would find the metal, called the substrate, at the bottom, then a minimum of two layers above it. The top layer is, obviously, the topcoat or "paint" that your eyes see. But because topcoat finishes do not adhere to bare metal, an undercoating is necessary; a type of coating that will stick to metal, and to which the topcoat will adhere. This in-between undercoat, then, gives the topcoat something to stick to while it, in turn, is sticking to the metal surface.

UNDERCOAT

The adhesive quality or "stickiness" of an undercoat or a finish is a combination of the material itself and the surface to which it is applied. If you've ever tried to paint a piece of glass then had it peel right off, you realize that the surface, regardless of the material of which it is composed, must have a certain amount of roughness to it so the finish can get its "teeth" into the surface pores like the roots of a plant. The chemicals comprising the finish must actually flow down into the surface pores,

1. The mechanics of paint preparation and painting itself are fairly straightforward, but the budding spray painter is wise who learns the basic ins and outs, and whys, of automotive finishing.

2. The finish on a car covers lots of imperfections caused by manufacturing methods. The presses used in forming the body panels, and the methods in joining them together, cause scratches, dings, gouges and unsightly seams that only paint can cover. If, after all the parts are united into an automobile (as is being done here with a spot welder), but it is left unpainted, it would deteriorate to rust scale if some protective coating was not applied.

then harden to take permanent hold. This is why topcoat, no matter how good its condition, must be "roughed" with fine sandpaper before you spray a new color over it.

If we magnified our panel cross section even more, we'd see that the metal does not have a perfectly smooth surface. Rather, it's a series of hills and valleys in sawtooth pattern. Some of the valleys may be as much as a third or even half the depth of the metal. If we applied a thin undercoating film over the jagged surface, it might well flow down into the deeper valleys so that when it hardened, it would have very much the same jagged surface as the metal underneath. Now, if we put the topcoat on, it would also dry with a similarly rough surface with the result that reflected light rays would scatter in all directions, giving it a very dull appearance to the naked eye.

If we substituted some other substance for just plain undercoat, maybe we could brighten up the topcoat without a lot of tedious handwork. In the old days, back before

1924, automobile bodies and fenders were actually hand finished; brushing on a thick layer of color-impregnated (usually black) varnish. When it hardened, the surface was rubbed with an abrasive comprised of pumice and water, then another coat was added, then another and another. This lengthy process sometimes took as much as a month, but even so, the final finish would soon become dull and begin to crack, often within a year.

Unless new finishing techniques and materials were forthcoming—and quickly—the automobile industry

3. Paint—more properly "finish"—includes pigment (for coloring) mixed with a binder, which by itself is clear. Even when thinned down to spraying consistency, too heavy an application will cause runs or sags.

4. Enamel is especially hard to spray properly since it stays soft for an extended period, unlike lacquer paints. Too heavy a topcoat may sag like this even after the painter has hung up his gun and left.

5. Many things can happen to the new finish coat if its chemicals are not compatible with the old finish, or the wrong undercoat, or if the finish is incorrectly mixed and/or applied. Right side of panel has a "cracked" finish, caused by excessive film thickness (too much paint), materials not uniformly mixed, the piling on of succesive coats without proper drying time in between, or the wrong thinner or reducer additive. On left of same panel is an example of sandscratch swelling. It's caused by improper surface preparation; if too coarse a sandpaper is used to "scuff" the surface, solvents in new finish will exaggerate swelling of the old.

would flounder under stacks of unfinished body parts. The most important development to come from all of this was the development of the modern spray gun and new materials that could be thinned down to air-spraying consistency. Another advancement was the special compounding of an undercoating that had not only the desirable adhesive qualities, but also a filling ability to allow it to get down into the metal surface irregularities, and it dried with enough film thickness that its surface could be sanded smooth. Now the topcoat could be added and it would harden or dry with as smooth a surface as the sanded surface of the undercoating over which it was sprayed. This new kind of undercoat was termed primer/surfacer, and it's what you'll usually find as the bottom layer or substance in our painted panel cross section.

SEALER

There are many types of undercoats, topcoats, etc., and each utilizes many different chemicals. When mixed together, or at least applied over one another, these chemicals are not necessarily compatible with each other. A new topcoat sprayed over an older factory finish may crack, blister, peel, flake, or result in other undesirable effects. Though the old finish had dried long ago, one or more of the chemicals in the new topcoat may "excite," activate or melt into the old one and cause all kinds of problems. To prevent this, a coating of what is called sealer was developed. Sealer is well named,

since it actually seals the old finish, and chemicals in the new topcoat cannot get through it to attack the finish underneath. Thus, a car that has been repainted might have a cross section that consists of, first, the metal or substrate, the original primer/surfacer, the original finish, a layer of sealer, more primer/surfacer and, lastly, the new topcoat. It's very much like a multi-tiered sandwich that grows as each layer is applied.

An automobile's topcoat—the only visible part of the finish—consists of a powdered substance called *pigment* that is mixed with a liquid known as a *binder*. Essentially, the pigment in most paints is evenly distributed throughout the binder which, by itself, can be perfectly clear. Some paints, however, use pigment whose individual particles are heavy enough to settle down through the binder. This is why paint should be thoroughly stirred before use: to evenly distribute the pigment particles through the binder. Now, this mixture of materials could probably be spread with a spatula or at least a good stiff brush, but it's too glue-like to be sprayed with air pressure through a conventional gun. So another additive must be introduced to "thin" down the pigment-holding binder to spraying consistency. Thinner is the general term used in automotive circles, but actually thinner is used for lacquer-based finishes while reducer is used with enamels.

PIGMENT

A good example of pigment is lampblack. If you've ever rubbed your

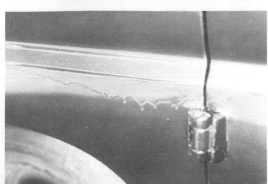

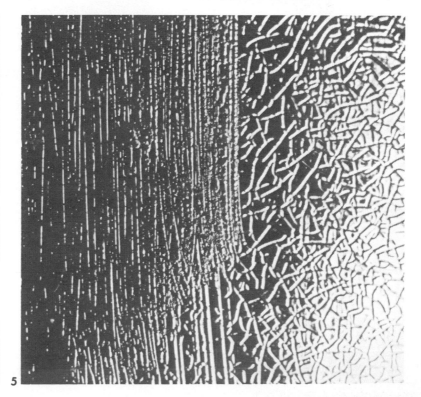

fingers inside a kerosene lamp, you know how fine the particles are because they're so hard to wash off. We've all heard that Henry Ford announced that anyone could have any color car he wanted, as long as it was black. But Henry was wrong on one point; black isn't a color. Not a single color, that is. It's a combination of all colors. It reflects very little or no light so the eye registers on it as black. On the other hand, white is the absence of color. Anything that appears white to the eye is reflecting all the light rays. When you see the color red, for example, it's because all the light rays striking the surface are being absorbed except those that reflect back to the eye in the hue we know as red.

It isn't our intention to get into the very deep subjects of light waves, the color spectrum, the human eye, and related discourses, but the point is, what you see when you look at a car's finish (or anything else, for that matter) are merely light waves of various intensity that reflect on the eye's retina, the sensory membrane that receives the image. It is the immediate instrument of vision, and is connected to the brain by the optic nerve.

TRICK FINISHES

The "trick" finishes, such as the metallics, Metalflake, and others, have an additional element introduced to the binder that produces sparkle, glitter or irridescence. It may be finely powdered aluminum, steel, or other ground-up materials. When these particles are mixed in with the binder and pigment, they reflect light brightly from their faceted surfaces. They may

1. Any smooth surface must be roughed up so topcoat finish can get its "teeth" into it and hang on. Here's an example of a new topcoat applied over an old one that wasn't sanded thoroughly, or not sanded at all.

2. The Metalflake products come in a series of coarseness or flake sizes. This is a coarse job with light reflecting from particle surfaces.

3. Lacquer-based paints are the spray painter's dream, since they dry rapidly and are less conducive to runs or sags than enamel paints. However, gun air pressure causes mottling of the surface which dries too rapidly to settle down smoothly. Thus the lacquered surface must be polished to give it sheen. Fine-grit rubbing compound, best applied by hand, is used first, but carefully, since it is highly abrasive and might cut through paint film. Buffing with ordinary corn starch will bring it to a reflective sheen and, finally, a very lightly abrasive polishing compound will finish the job.

be evenly distributed throughout the paint film where extreme dazzle or a silvery appearance is wanted, or they may settle, through their weight, to the bottom of the binder film after it has been applied to a surface, in which case the sparkle is reduced. In some cases, the particles are relatively large—a hundred times the size of a particle of pigment—and the paint must be frequently agitated in the spray gun to keep the metal bits from sinking to the bottom of the gun cup. In the case of a very coarse Metal-flake, it may even be necessary to add a handful of marbles or ball bearings to the gun cup so that shaking will provide the agitation needed.

AGED FINISHES

An automobile finish that has aged through long contact with the atmosphere, that has been minutely scratched by dusting, and washed over the years with water containing harmful chemicals, will appear dull since the surface is no longer as microscopically smooth as it once was. To restore the surface, an abrasive must be applied to cut down the sawtooth-like surface. This operation naturally removes some of the paint film thickness, since the "highs" are cut down to the level of the "lows."

But remember, the topcoat film may be only .004-in. thick, so be careful you don't reduce the film thickness to the point where air-borne chemicals can penetrate it and damage the metal beneath. Special abrasive compounds have been developed for automotive finishes, but be selective in your choice since the cutting ability of the compound relates directly to its abrasiveness or grit. The finer the grit, the less paint film will be removed with a given amount of elbow grease.

Whole books have been written about automotive finishes; theory, techniques, materials, equipment, and so forth. Much of this information is disseminated by the makers of the products involved, a lot of it free, so the seriously interested but would-be painter is well advised to gather up the folders and booklets handed out by dealers and distributors, study them, then put the words into practice. Don't forget your library or book store, either. There's a mine of painting information available.

Remember, automobile painting can be a rewarding and self-gratifying profession, because no matter how complex the engineering, or how beautiful the design of a car, it is the *color* that people see. ✦

4. Magnified cross section of painted panel shows base or substrate which is the metal itself. Topcoat is the finish that you see and which gives the car its painted color. Between is the undercoat, a necessary intermediate which topcoat adheres to, and which in turn adheres to substrate.

5. In actual practice, the substrate is not smooth. Topcoat would have the same rough surface if an undercoat were not applied which could be sanded smooth. It's called primer/surfacer.

6. Some topcoat finishes are not compatible with primer/surfacer, so a coat of sealer must separate them.

7. An older car may have been repainted once, twice or more. This is a cross section of a re-paint job where original topcoat gouges or dings have been filled with primer/surfacer then sanded smooth before new sealer and topcoat were added.

8. A new or highly polished topcoat will reflect light waves uniformly, and the eye sees it as being bright.

9. An older, weathered surface will reflect light waves indiscriminately. Since not all reflected waves reach the eye, surface appears dull.

10. Metallic paints contain powdered metals whose faceted sides reflect light brightly but at various angles. This produces highlights or "hot spots" which give these types of finishes their spotty brilliance.

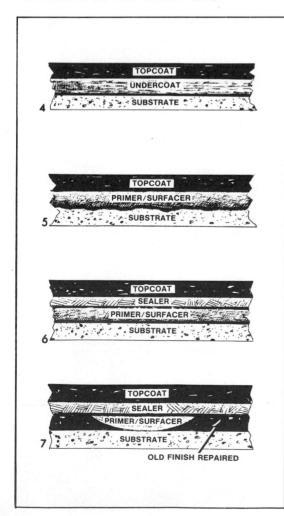

4 TOPCOAT / UNDERCOAT / SUBSTRATE

5 TOPCOAT / PRIMER/SURFACER / SUBSTRATE

6 TOPCOAT / SEALER / PRIMER/SURFACER / SUBSTRATE

7 TOPCOAT / SEALER / PRIMER/SURFACER / SUBSTRATE / OLD FINISH REPAIRED

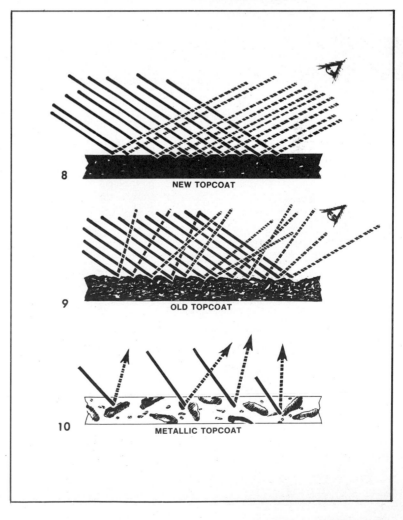

8 NEW TOPCOAT

9 OLD TOPCOAT

10 METALLIC TOPCOAT

Selecting Spray Equipment

If you're not a full-time painter, you don't need high-dollar new equipment for high-quality results.

If you're like the average rodder, you like to do as much work on your car as you can, and that may range anywhere from dropping in a different engine to refinishing the body and maybe even shooting your own paint.

Sure, top quality spray outfits are available new at premium prices, but the point is, no one has to buy the ultimate in spray equipment, and in new condition, when he has no immediate plans about going into the painting business full-time. To do a respectable job, all one needs is good equipment, which also means equipment that is tailored for the type of work you have in mind.

This is akin to saying if you plan to race at Indy, don't try to make the starting line up with a Pinto, just because it happens to be an automobile. You have to take into consideration the type of paint you'll be applying, be it candy, 'flake, lacquer, enamel, epoxy or acrylic. Then you can go about the task of selecting the proper spray paint equipment.

The reason for this is because the type of paint you will be using has a direct bearing on the equipment necessary to apply it. All spray guns are not alike, nor are hoses, compressors, regulators and so forth. Sure, we know, your good buddy Charlie borrowed a portable spray outfit from his uncle last month and applied a super lacquer job to his 'Vette. And old Tom rented a similar outfit just the other day and did a respectable job on his roadster.

Now, we're not knocking these guys nor their home-applied paint jobs. In fact we are encouraging the idea, and this is the prime reason for this story: to explain how to select *compatible* spray paint equipment so you can do a respectable job at home.

What you may not be aware of is the fact that the spray equipment these two guys used was most likely balanced, or as we just stated, it was compatible, matched for the type of paint that was going to applied, and therefore was capable of producing the results they were after. Of course this does not relieve them of the responsibility of learning how to use spray equipment proficiently. Because *applying* paint is material for another section, we'll pass on this matter and concern ourselves solely with selecting compatible spray equipment.

First we must have a spray gun, one large enough to properly paint our machine, so let's see what is available. The guns most of us are familiar with feature the paint cup attached to the gun, but there are also remote cup guns, where the paint cup or pot can be held in one hand while the gun is in the other. Most painters prefer to set the remote pot on the floor, as this is one reason why this type of gun/pot combination was developed: to reduce the weight the painter has to support in his one hand and to give him more freedom of movement. Another advantage is that the remote cup can be of greater capacity than hand-held types, saving time with fewer refills.

There are also bleeder-type guns, where air passes through the gun at all times, preventing pressure buildup in the air lines. This apparatus is used with small air compressing outfits of limited capacity and pressure. The trigger controls only the flow of paint in this type of gun. A nonbleeder-type spray gun is equipped with an air valve which shuts off the air when the trigger is released. It is used wherever a pressure-controlling arrangement (regulator) is present in the compressed air supply system.

A spray gun that mixes and ato-

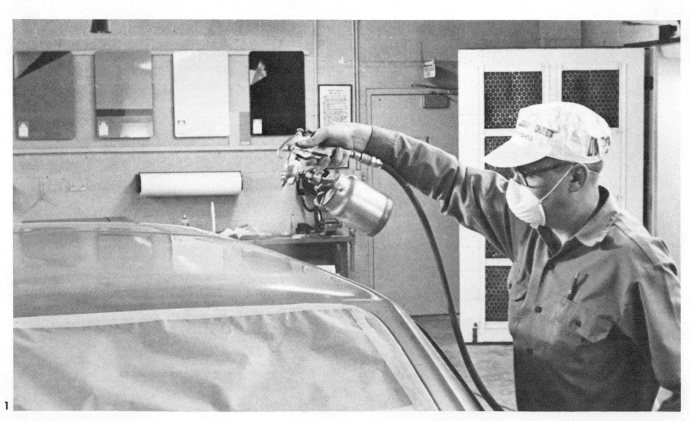

1

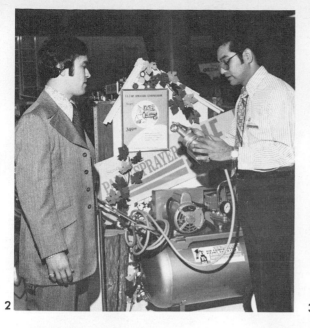

1. Bodywork and painting can be a rewarding profession or a fun hobby, but whether pro or amateur, you must select the compressor and equipment best suited to the work you do.

2. Shop around for your spray paint equipment, comparing price vs. the cfm and pressure requirements for the jobs you'll be doing. Don't forget to watch for sales in the big stores of Sears and Montgomery Wards also.

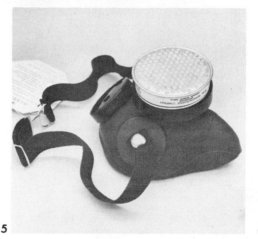

3. This inexpensive Sears homeowner spray gun is for small jobs. It needs 2 to 5 cfm at 25 to 50 psi pressure; it's non-bleeder type of gun, and works with pressure or siphon feed. Cost is about $15.95; it's designed for use with a ½- to ¾-hp compressor, and it has a screw-on cup.

4. A better Sears gun is this unit, their semi-production model, wich goes for about $28.95. It converts from pressure to siphon, needs 4 to 9 cfm at 35 to 50 psi, is for use with 1- to 2-hp compressor, and comes with internal and external mix nozzles. Higher priced competitive guns offer more nozzles, are frequently more precise, and can spray types of paint these can't. The Sears guns are well worth their prices, though.

5. When spray painting, be sure you select an air respirator designed for this kind of work. All respirators are not alike; this happens to be a Binks replaceable-cartridge type.

6. This Binks #69 gun is fitted with a 1-qt. siphon cup. It is a standard production gun, and is ideal for lacquers, enamels, acrylics, etc.

7. Air compressors come in a multitude of sizes; some electric, others are gasoline powered. This Binks Lo-Boy is indicative of portable models available. Horsepower rating of the compressor is only one aspect that you must be concerned with. The other is the cfm displacement it is capable of. Note that this model has a belt guard, which is highly recommended.

Spray Equipment

mizes air and paint outside the air cap is referred to as an external mix gun. This is the most common gun used in painting cars, as it is the only type suitable for fast-drying paints such as lacquers and can be used for applying almost all paints. An internal mix gun is used where low air pressures are employed and where slow-drying paints are to be sprayed.

Finally, we have suction feed, pressure feed and gravity feed guns. A suction feed gun is one in which a stream of compressed air creates a partial vacuum, allowing atmospheric pressure to force paint from the attached cup into the spray head of the gun. A pressure feed gun is one with an air cap not designed to create a vacuum. The paint is forced to the gun by air pressure from a tank, cup or pump. Gravity feed guns feature the paint cup on top of the gun, and are used for specialty work. They feature siphon- or suction-type air nozzles in their design.

Retracing our steps a bit, it would appear that a suction feed gun, fitted with an external mix air cap and fluid tip, would probably be the wisest choice for most guys interested in painting their own cars. If you can afford, or have access to, a large enough air compressor, then a non-bleeder gun would also be the right choice. How much you spend for a gun is relatively unimportant, though you shouldn't expect to get top quality work from some gun that may have cost only $20 new, if such an animal exists.

You will have noticed that brief mention has already been made of air caps and fluid tips. It must be emphasized that no matter how expensive your spray gun, or how large the compressor, if the air cap and fluid tip selection you're attemping to use is incorrect for the type of paint to be sprayed (and the rate of flow required for that particular job), you're in a heap of trouble.

A spray gun is a tool using compressed air to atomize sprayable material and apply it to a surface. Air and paint enter the gun through separate passages and are mixed and ejected at the air cap in a controlled pattern. There are various styles of caps producing different sizes and purpose of the cap is to atomize the paint as it leaves the gun. Rather than delve too deeply into which size or type of cap would be best for the paint you're going to use, we'll suggest you check with your local spray equipment dealer or friendly professional spray painter.

Once you've settled on a gun, fluid tip and air cap package for the paint

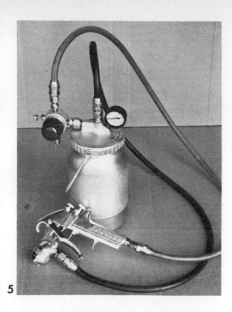

5

6

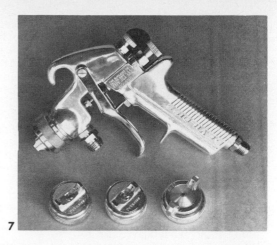

7

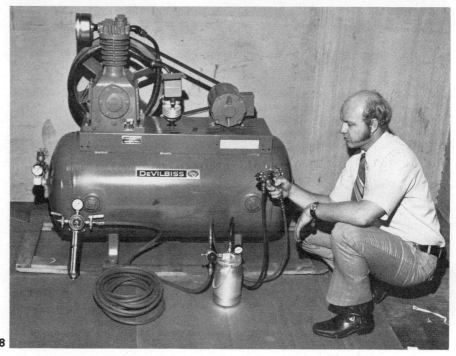

8

9

1. This is the Binks model No. 7. It's a first-class spray gun featuring a drop-forged aluminum body. This heavy-duty gun will spray any type of automotive finish. The price is about $103.95, including a 1-qt. siphon cup.

2. This is a custom assembly, made up of a DeVilbiss MBC gun and a Sharpe's cup. This cup features a bleed hole inside the cup lip; won't cause drips on surface when spraying.

3. With the Sharpe's cup removed from the DeVilbiss gun, the internal bleed tube is visible. Its purpose is to prevent paint from spilling through the bleed hole when you're shooting at a downward angle.

4. Siphon or suction cup guns must have a bleed hole in the paint cup cap. This is to allow atmospheric pressure to push down on the fluid in the container forcing material to spray gun, working with the air nozzle which creates a partial vacuum at the face of the fluid nozzle in the cap.

5. This is a pressure feed cup with a DeVilbiss JGA-502 spray gun. This type is ideal if the gun is in frequent use, or if the spray painter might tire from a heavier gun.

6. This gun is equipped with external mix air cap, indicated (arrow) by the fluid tip extending beyond face of the air cap. This particular gun is the suction feed type.

7. Included in the top line of DeVilbiss spray guns is the JGA-502, shown here with a few air caps. It features a forged aluminum body for strength, is available in both suction and pressure feed models, and is known as a high capacity gun.

8. Clifford Watne, L.A. Branch manager of DeVilbiss, demonstrates one of their stationary 2-hp compressors. When you're doing a lot of painting, units of this size are necessary, otherwise a smaller one is adequate.

9. This selection of Binks air caps illustrates the variety of those available. Factors such as volume of air, type of paint to be sprayed and volume, type of feed system, etc., have a bearing on the air cap best suited for your specific needs.

you're going to shoot, the next objective is to select an air compressor and hose that will supply the air consumption requirements for same. Compressors are rated according to their output of air, which is measured in cfm (cubic feet per minute); this expressing the amount of work that can be accomplished in a given period of time. The pressure (or the force) necessary to move the air is measured in psi (pounds per square inch). The air delivery (cfm) is one consideration which determines the type of air cap and the amount of atomized paint which can be sprayed per minute. Thicker or heavy-bodied paints require high air pressure for atomization. Most paints, such as lacquers, enamels and primers, require lower pressures.

The two most popular types of compressors are the diaphragm-type and piston-type. The diaphragm-type compressor usually develops pressure in the 35 to 40 psi range, and is suitable for small home jobs. The piston compressor, on the other hand, will

Spray Equipment

provide working pressures up to 200 psi. A piston compressor will produce approximately 4 cfm for each unit of horsepower.

For the sake of clarification, let's select a couple of different makes of spray guns suitable for our work, and then determine the size of compressor required. Binks offers a standard-production spray gun, Model 69, that is priced at under $100, which includes a 1 qt. siphon cup. It is used with 5/16-in-I.D. air hose. The nozzle setup recommended by Binks for this gun, where lacquers, enamels, synthetics, acrylics and all commonly used materials will be used, is No. 66 x 66SF. This combination requires 11.4 cfm of air at 50 psi pressure to perform properly.

A comparable gun is the DeVilbiss MGA-150, set up with their 51E nozzle combination. This gun is excellent for all refinish jobs, metallic color matching, lacquer, enamel, etc. It utilizes the same size lines as the Binks gun, though it requires 7.7 cfm of air at 50 psi pressure to work properly. It costs about the same as the Binks model, slightly under $100, and comes with a 1 qt. cup.

At this point we know that these guns will consume 11.4 and 7.7 cfm respectively at 50 psi pressure. But this does not mean that the compressor must be capable of maintaining only 50 psi to be suitable for these guns. It must be putting out more pressure, the additional amount being dependent upon the air hose I.D. and overall length. This is because of a pressure drop in the hose, due to friction between the flowing air and walls of the hose; as well as the pipe line and passages it travels through. An accompanying table of air pressure drop figures shows the importance of this factor. Other charts illustrate the size of air compressor necessary with various air-operated devices.

According to one chart, if the only device you will be operating is either of these spray guns, then you would need a compressor rated at at least 1 hp, maintaining 80 to 100 lbs. pressure. It must be pointed out that this is true where the spray gun will be operated intermittently—that is a few minutes at a time—or at least with pauses now and then, to allow the compressor to maintain its pressure and volume. Should the gun be in operation continuously, then you would need a 3 hp compressor.

If an air gauge at the compressor tank outlet registers 50 psi, with a 5/16-in. I.D. air hose connected up, you would find that a pressure drop of 3½ lbs. is incurred 10 ft. away from the tank. At 25 ft. out, the drop would be 5 lbs. and at 50 ft., 10 lbs. Therefore, if we were to use 50 ft. of 5/16-in. I.D. air hose with either of these spray guns, the compressor would have to maintain 70 psi in the tank at all times. Taking into consideration the 13 lb. air pressure drop at the gun with this length and size of hose, we would end up with 57 psi, enough to operate the guns as they were designed (with the air caps discussed). Use of ¼-in. air hose, rather than 5/16-in., would cause a severe pressure drop and air starvation at the gun.

Should you be thinking of running a shorter air hose, thereby reducing air pressure drop at the gun and the requirement of having to run high tank pressures, let us put this idea to rest. Compressors are rated at a standard air temperature of 68°F.

1

2

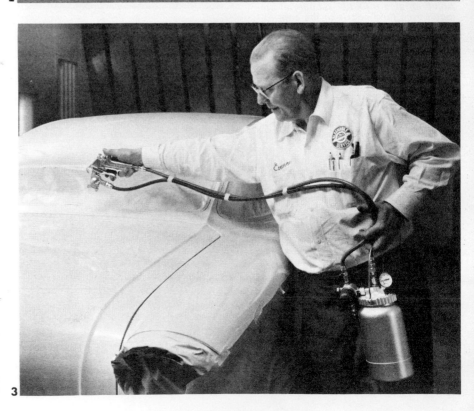

3

When air is compressed, it heats up rapidly, and the higher the working pressure, the higher the heat generated. The temperature of discharged air can range from 150°-500°F. One way to reduce this heat is to run at least 25 ft. of air line from the tank. But because this cooling will likely produce condensation, water will be present in the line. Naturally you would want to remove this water from the hose, along with any dirt and/or oil that may be present. This can be accomplished by installing an air transformer, condenser or extractor: a device for filtering these contaminants from the air in the line. So now we have at least 25 ft. of line (preferably pipe of the specified inside diameter, installed so it runs slightly downhill from the compressor tank, permitting any contaminants to flow freely into the extractor) connecting the air tank to the water, dust and oil extractor. From this device you would run the flexible air hose needed to operate your spray gun.

Regulation of air is very important. Less air is consumed when used at low pressure than at high pressure

4

5

1. The Marson Corp. produces this production-size spray gun (MCK model) suitable for all automotive uses.

2. Regulation of air is extremely important. If pressure changes as little as five pounds on a metallic job, the shade of the paint will be changed and the job ruined. These DeVilbiss regulators are independent and have a capacity of 30 cfm.

3. For production work, a gun with the paint cup separate makes the job easier on the painter's arm. Also, there is no chance of dropping paint out of the siphon hole onto the car and the cup can hold more paint. The cup is sometimes attached to a belt.

4. Gravity-feed guns like this Sata generally have a larger orifice, and thus are best suited for spraying a heavy or thick paint like the epoxy primer/surfacers used to fill over pitted or sandblasted body panels.

5. If you plan to run other tools from your compressor, such as this air-powered sander, you'll need a much larger compressor than required for painting. Those air tools eat up a lot of air pressure, and fast.

6. When your requirements lead you to a compressor of over 2-hp, you'll probably wind up with a gas-powered unit like this Sears 3-hp if you want to stick with a portable spray outfit.

7. Especially ideal for engine painting, spot repair, and touch-up work, is this tiny DeVilbiss EGA gun. It requires only 2.3 cfm of air at 30 psi on suction.

8. Marson produces this tiny spray gun and cup, their Finer 70 Model, which is ideal for custom spraying, touch-up work and other small jobs.

6

7

8

Spray Equipment

Therefore, if a tool (such as our spray guns) can be operated at 50 psi and your air compressor maintains the pressure between 80 and 100 psi, a regulator should be installed to control the air being supplied and at its lowest operating pressure. Consequently, by using a minimum volume of air this will allow lower operating costs.

Oil and water extractors and pressure regulators are available as independent units, or can be purchased as a single unit. In any event, they should be installed at the end of the 25-ft. line, where the flex hose to the gun begins. We have previously mentioned that it is best to have that initial 25 ft. of line for air cooling actually in pipe. If you're wondering what the story is with portable air compressor units . . . well, there is no way you can run 25 ft. of pipe and still be portable. You can run 25 ft. of air hose from the air tank into a transformer, or extractor, though, and another 25 or more on to the gun. In fact, this is the way to go if you're going the portable route and want the best possible paint job. The initial 25 ft. of hose should be laid out flat on the deck and not draped up and over objects on the way. If you haven't a water extractor, as the condensation can build up in the lower parts of the hose; then air will suddenly blow water into the gun, ruining a good paint job. Even an extractor won't stop a surge of water.

The final piece of equipment you should avail yourself of is also one of the least expensive. It's an air respirator with replaceable filter. Nothing can ruin your health faster than spray-painting without a respirator. If the fumes (atomized paint) don't get your sinuses first, they'll eventually get to your lungs. After all the coins are laid out for the professional equipment, maybe the salesman will toss in a respirator free. Anyway, ask him. Don't be the first guy in town with metalflaked lungs. 🐱

1

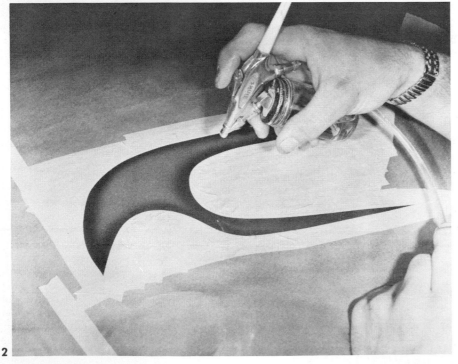

3

4

2

1. The smaller guns can be used for touch-up work, but their forte is really in custom painting, where they are used for shading, detailing and when you're using a number of colors and don't want to mix a whole batch of each color for a regular-size gun.

2. When the trick painter has need of some truly fine work, he usually uses an airbrush gun. Don't let the size fool you, these little babies are almost as expensive as other guns.

3. The Metalflake company markets an economy airbrush called the MiniGun, which can be used with a compressor or with its own can of propellant.

4. More versatile than the MiniGun is the Metalflake SuperGun, which is an all-metal, professional-quality airbrush. Both guns are single-action types in which the paint and airflow are both activated with one button.

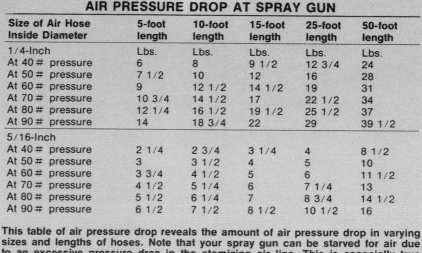

AIR PRESSURE DROP AT SPRAY GUN

Size of Air Hose Inside Diameter	5-foot length	10-foot length	15-foot length	25-foot length	50-foot length
1/4-Inch	Lbs.	Lbs.	Lbs.	Lbs.	Lbs.
At 40 # pressure	6	8	9 1/2	12 3/4	24
At 50 # pressure	7 1/2	10	12	16	28
At 60 # pressure	9	12 1/2	14 1/2	19	31
At 70 # pressure	10 3/4	14 1/2	17	22 1/2	34
At 80 # pressure	12 1/4	16 1/2	19 1/2	25 1/2	37
At 90 # pressure	14	18 3/4	22	29	39 1/2
5/16-Inch					
At 40 # pressure	2 1/4	2 3/4	3 1/4	4	8 1/2
At 50 # pressure	3	3 1/2	4	5	10
At 60 # pressure	3 3/4	4 1/2	5	6	11 1/2
At 70 # pressure	4 1/2	5 1/4	6	7 1/4	13
At 80 # pressure	5 1/2	6 1/4	7	8 3/4	14 1/2
At 90 # pressure	6 1/2	7 1/2	8 1/2	10 1/2	16

This table of air pressure drop reveals the amount of air pressure drop in varying sizes and lengths of hoses. Note that your spray gun can be starved for air due to an excessive pressure drop in the atomizing air line. This is especially true where a ¼-inch hose is used, when the gun is designed for a 5/16-inch hose. Don't assume that pressure recorded at tank is the same at gun. It is not.

CFM & PRESSURE REQUIREMENTS

Type Device	Maximum Pressure Required	Average Free Air Consumption c.f.m.
Body Polisher	100	2.0
Body Sander	100	5.0
Dusting Gun (blow gun)	100	2.5
Spray Gun (suction feed)*	100	11.0
Tire Inflation Line	150	1.5
Vacuum Cleaner	150	6.5

* Check air consumption of your particular gun with manufacturer

Spray guns aren't the only devices that require a specific amount of air to operate properly. This chart lists some common air operated tools that might be found in a small shop or club garage. If two or more of these devices may be used at once, then you must total up the free air consumption figures before selecting a compressor.

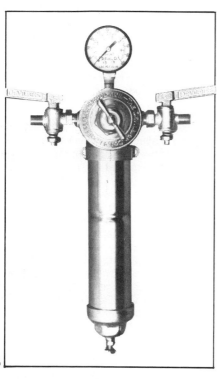

HOW TO FIND THE RIGHT COMPRESSOR

Compressor Pressures to Per Square Inch		Free Air Consumption in Cubic Feet per Minute of Total Equipment (Intermittent Operation)	Free Air Consumption in Cubic Feet per Minute of Total Equipment (Continuous Operation)	H.P.
Cut In	Cut Out			
		Up to 3.5	Up to 1.2	1/3
		3.6 to 6.6	1.3 to 2.1	1/2
		6.7 to 10.5	2.2 to 2.8	3/4
80	100	10.6 to 13.6	2.9 to 4.1	1
		13.7 to 20.3	4.2 to 6.0	1 1/2
		20.4 to 26.6	6.1 to 7.4	2
		26.7 to 39.5	7.5 to 14.0	3
		39.6 to 58	14.1 to 21.5	5
		Up to 9.0	Up to 3.2	3/4
		9.1 to 12.0	3.3 to 4.0	1
		12.1 to 15.6	4.1 to 5.2	1 1/2
140	175	15.7 to 21.0	5.3 to 7.0	2
		21.1 to 33.0	7.1 to 11.0	3
		33.1 to 46.4	11.1 to 18.3	5

Having noted the highest pressure required to operate any tool (up to 100 psi, or 175 psi), next seek out the total free air consumption figure under either the intermittent or continuous column. To the right of this figure is the minimum size air compressor you'll need to operate.

5. This Binks model 86-940 oil and water extractor (air dryer) is compact yet has a 30 cfm capacity, sufficient for spray painting a car. For single-gun operation, it features dual filtration and comes equipped with an air regulator.

6. When you're spray painting a car, it's essential that all water, oil and dust be removed from the air before it gets into the paint. Use of an air transformer (or extractor) such as this DeVilbiss P-HB is a must. This unit incorporates an air regulator and features two outlet valves. It has a 15 cfm capacity and, like others, a replaceable filter.

Paints, Primers, and Preparation

Shining the luster of creative gems, quality paints demand careful preparation and sacred application.

As the slogan goes, "Paint's come a long way, baby." But then again, it had to. There once was a time, and not so long ago, when automotive finishes consisted of primitive mixtures of varnish and pigment (such as lampblack) and were applied to the boxlike bodies by brushwork. Ah, yes, those were the good old days of hand-rubbing each coat, with pumice and water, after it dried. Obviously, this was time-consuming and produced nothing but bottlenecks and unhappy bean counters. One of the first to find an answer was ol' Henry, hisself. Ford discovered that the fastest dryer of 'em all was black. So black it was, take it or leave it, until the middle '20's, when Chevy (and others) forced Ford to offer a more varied palette.

Over the ensuing years, a zillion paint manufacturers have been hard at it, developing new paints, and compounds and faster, easier methods of applying, mixing and caring for their products. Today most car manufacturers use acrylics, either enamel or lacquer, and bake the material on the bodies to ensure a diamond-hard surface that will generally outlast everything, including the inroads of inner body rust.

It shouldn't come as a great surprise that automotive painting isn't all that hard if you follow or look into some of the ideas we're going to be exploring in this particular yarn. Suffice it to say, most painting is merely preparation. The better you prepare the surface for the final top coat, the better the chance of achieving that "custom paint job" look. Consequently, we'll begin our discussion of paint types and characteristics with an inside-out look at the materials used in creating that firm foundation on which all good paint jobs rest.

KNOW YOUR BASE

We naturally assume that the reader is interested in repainting his or her car or parts thereof. If you are going the stocker route, there are several things to consider: Do you know what type of paint is currently on your car, and/or will it be compatible with what you are planning to put over it? There are two down-'n'-dirty ways of determining what you've got there in the way of original paint. First is the factory-provided I.D. method. Every car shipped from Detroit or imported has a paint and color identification number(s) or letter(s) "tabbed" to the body, firewall, hood, front fender splash panels, door posts, instrument panel braces, crossrails or—get this—stuck behind the spare tire. Once you've located the I.D. plate, copy down the paint number, even if you're *not* going the

stocker route. The important thing is to determine what you have on hand; no, make that body. The reason behind this seeming madness is simple. Neither straight nor acrylic lacquer will go over enamel in color-coat form. The only time you can place the "hotter" lacquers and acrylics over enamel is when the enamel is factory-baked original and is fully dried, "clear through." The other quick-'n'-dirty method is simply this: Put a large drop of lacquer thinner on the doorjamb and watch it closely. If the paint should soften when it comes in contact with the drop of thinner, you've got lacquer there, podner. By the way, take the penciled-in numbers or letters to the local automotive paint store. They are supplied with an up-to-date accounting of all the stock automotive finishes from the various manufacturers.

BEGIN BY CLEANING

Once you've determined what type of paint is on your car's bod, then it's just a matter of formality to choose a compatible type of paint, thinner, primer and sealer to begin the second phase of our paint type and characteristic piece. Stripping the old paint is one thing we won't be covering here, but we would like to remind you that the surface must be smooth, free of defects, and have enough tooth to allow the primer to stick on tight. Most automotive refinishing brochures or catalogs—obtained through writing the various paint manufacturers or snaffled from your friendly local automotive finishes stores—suggest you start by washing your car,

1. There are a number of good paints on the market, all capable of doing the job for you, so choose one type and stick with it, for intermixing brands usually has poor results.

2. Most of the major paint companys produce brochures and books on the lines of products they sell which are excellent sources of painting information as well. Write for 'em.

3. In picking a paint to do your car, the first step should be to determine exactly what type of paint, lacquer or enamel, was on your car originally. Your body ID tag will give you the number you need to determine the type, and color if you are planning to repaint with the original color.

2

3

thoroughly. Once the surface has been dried with compressed air, lintless rags, the sun or whatever comes to mind, wash the surface with a "prep-coat"-type material. This solvent does a couple of good deeds. First, it helps remove any residual wax, grease or dirt which might have been missed in the washing. Second, it treats or neutralizes any acids or foreign matter which would ultimately bubble up through the fresh top coat. These prep coatings also form a film which conditions the metal and allows it to accept primer more easily. However, never use these solutions in conjunction with plastic fillers. The porous nature of the fillers causes the material to soak in, then bleed through, with primers applied.

Rarely do we have a perfect surface to work with, especially considering the age and conditions of the cars generally in our possession. Time, and untender, unloving care have resulted in the nicks, scratches, gouges, pit holes and burrs which must be removed—or the final results will look like the Grand Canyon in miniature. We'll start with the stuff you'll need if the surface is marred by deep nicks or gouges. These are called putties. They generally feature the same composition as the "primer-surfacers" but are loaded with a greater amount of solids. Putties are applied with a—you guessed it—putty knife or squeegee. Then there is a whole family of primer-surfacers.

PRIMERS AND SEALERS

What these do is provide a good adhesion base between the virgin metal and the primer coat. All good primer-surfacers must provide good stick, drying speed (they should be ready to sand in no less than 30 mins.), good sealing qualities (to keep the original top coat from bleeding through), settling resistance (that means the solids or pigments won't settle to the bottom of the spray gun

tank); and build and/or fill minor surface flaws. Naturally, there are two types of primer-surfacers: lacquer and enamel. One features a fast-drying lacquer base, the other a synthetic resin base, taking longer to dry.

There is one last type of undercoating, employed before the primer goes on, and that is your sealer. Sealers are simple. They are made from material specially formulated from resins which, when dry, resist the action of the solvents in the paint. In other words, they form a surface shield between the original paint and the new material. This shield keeps the old paint from "bleeding" through and contaminating the fresh primer or top coat. There are special bleeder sealers used to cover colors that contain a bleeding dye pigment, such as maroons and deep reds. A hint here is that you can make "spot checks" by using a spot of white to see if there is a "bleeding" color present.

There are primers and then there are primers. You don't, let's say, use the same primer for aluminum as you do for steel. And you don't use an enamel primer with a lacquer top coat. Primers are used for only one good reason: to help bond the color or top coats to the surface of the metal. Primers are generally available in all forms, from enamel, lacquer, acrylics, special plastic urethanes and epoxies, zinc chromate, to even vinyl primer washes. These vinyl primer washes are employed on the spangled galvanized bodies of buses before an enamel primer or primer-surfacer goes on. Zinc chromates are used in conjunction with aluminum. For instance, should you have a gennie steel body with a fancy fabricated aluminum pickup bed, the zinc chromate primer keeps the electrolytic action of the two rubbing together from occurring. Again, when using primers of any type or style, always consult the manufacturer's recommendations as to percentages of thinning and

discussions of which spray gun line pressures work best.

THINNERS AND REDUCERS

In the interest of definition, thinners are used for "diluting" lacquers and reducers are used for "diluting" enamels, and are not interchangeable. There are some exceptions, however. You can purchase a number of all-purpose thinners/reducers which can be mixed with both types of paint. But, generally, one cannot use a thinner in an enamel paint, nor a reducer in a lacquer paint. The secret to using thinners and reducers wisely is to use a product that is completely compatible with the paint being thinned or reduced. The best results are always achieved when a specific paint is diluted with a thinner/reducer especially formulated for that specific paint. This allows the ingredients in the top coat to flow out to their maximum effectiveness. What you should look for when selecting one of these thinners/reducers is to be sure that the material will pass through the spray gun smoothly; atomize easily with the compressed air and travel well between the run and the painted surface. The thinner/reducer combination should also provide an excellent resistance to settling; that is, it should keep the paint in suspension and allow it to flow out and level to a smooth, dead-on surface. And, naturally, it should resist sagging. Consequently, the diluters must quickly evaporate into the atmosphere and leave behind them a smooth, tough and durable surface.

Weather plays an important part in the selection of that "right" reducer; that "thinking ahead" thinner. Unless you have access to a spray booth equipped with a full-tilt boggie climate-control system, you must consider the effects on your painting from two weather-bred situations: temperature and humidity. We'll give you a couple of "fer instances" here.

Paints, Primers

Should you find yourself confronted by a hot, dry day, you're going to be painting under a fast-dry condition. The other extreme is the cold and humid day. Then you'll be confronted by a slow-drying situation. Just down the scale from fast-drying to slow-drying are the hot, humid days or the warm, dry ones. These are quick-drying conditions, but not as quick as a hot, dry day. Same for a cold, dry or a cool, humid day. These are slow-drying periods, but not as slow-drying as a cold, damp day. Therefore, on a hot, dry day, use an extra-slow-drying diluter. On a cool, damp spring morn, try a fast-drying thinner/reducer combo. Thankfully, you don't have to use "PP's" generalities as a guide. All the leading paint manufacturers have "compensation" charts specially tailored for the changes in the weather.

REDUCTION PROBLEMS

Mother Nature can delay or speed up the drying process, but using the wrong thinner and/or reducers can and will do a lot more than that. A genuine, by-the-numbers foul-up in the mixture will ruin tens of hours worth of careful preparation. If you use too hot a mixture, it will evaporate too fast and you can expect to see a sorry case of orange peel, blushing and even overspray. Orange peel is a name for a surface condition which exhibits a rough, orange peel-like appearance. This is caused by the thinner/reducer evaporating so fast that the paint droplets dry before they hit the surface and have a chance to flow. With lacquer or acrylic lacquer you can wait a minute, resand the surface, then start again with a cooler mixture. With the slower drying enamels, you're going to have to wait a while before you can repair the foul-up. Blush is a lacquer phenomenon. It usually happens under

hot, humid weather conditions. What generally occurs is that some of the thinner evaporates before it hits the surface. This process causes heat to be absorbed out of the moist air, giving off a cooling condition which allows moisture to be formed within the spray stream itself. As a result, the droplets of water are trapped in the paint, causing the surface film to have a dull, hazy appearance. As for overspray, this unwanted condition is similar to orange peel. The paint is going on so dry that the edges of the spray pattern will not melt together, and you get a delineation between the adjacent spray patterns.

Then there is the condition of the "too slow" evaporation. A too-slow situation is typified by spot repair rings, scratch swelling, sags or runs. Spot repair rings are peculiar to metallic finishes. The slow drying, due to the use of a wrong thiner/reducer in the mixture, causes the flakes of metal to move out and form a clearly visible ring. A slow-drying mixture also induces sand scratching swelling. What happens here is that the wrong thinners/reducers tend to penetrate into the old, original finish, making all the surface imperfections quite apparent. And then there's the traditional bugaboo of sags and runs. Runs or sags are caused by too moist a mixture. When this rich mixture reaches the painted surface, it flows or runs like crazy. The mixture also weighs too much, causing it to slide or sag down the surface.

Most manufacturers swear by the basic rule of "choose the slowest drying thinner/reducer you can handle without incurring the wrath of sags and runs." By following this golden rule, you can be assured of a smooth surface without having to worry about the above foul-ups. But again, check with the manufacturer's recommendations: they have those nice little tip sheets filled with exact

types and dilution percentages to use when dealing with their products.

LACQUERS

Be they lacquer or enamel, all paints are made of three basic ingredients: pigment or color, binder and solvents. The pigment is the coloring portion; it serves to produce the hiding value of the paint as well as to protect the binders. The binder is what the manufacturers call a non-volatile film-forming material which carries the pigment and gives the color its toughness, gloss and durability. Then there are the solvents. These dissolve the binder so the pigment will flow over the surface. When the solvents (or thinners/reducers) evaporate, they help dry the residual pigment and binder.

Lacquer and acrylic lacquer—the acrylic is a plastic-based material; straight lacquer is made from a combination of cellulose, resins and a sticky substance deposited by tree-dwelling insects in Asia, called Lac—has generally been the hot rodder's friend. It is easy to use. But it's also quite brittle, which necessitates the use of a plasticizer to give it more elasticity. But its fast-drying characteristics make it an ideal covering for those not blessed with a spray booth or a tightly sealed garage. The acrylic portion of the lacquer family is much like the straights. It dries quickly, but its plastic base causes the material to undergo a chemical change when the paint dries and unites with the surrounding atmosphere. Consequently, acrylic lacquer must be sprayed on in light coats for maximum gloss, unlike the fewer, heavier coats commonly employed with the straights.

Lacquers dry from the inside out. The evaporation of the solvents as they move into the air cures and dries the binders and pigments Therefore, many a professional painter will lay on the lacquer, then color-

1. If you will be applying primer over a bodyworked area that is bare metal, you'll have to treat the bare areas with a metal conditioner first. It etches the metal so paint adheres.

2. Another treatment, this one for bare and painted surfaces, is a wax and grease remover like Prep-Sol. Use it and a tack rag before any painting.

3. When you're bodywork is done, you can use a glazing putty to fill the pinholes and scratches in the bondo. The glazing putty is actually just very thick primer and should never be applied thick, or without first laying down a coat of primer on the metalwork so the putty will stick.

4. Sandscratch swelling is a paint problem that occurs when too rapid a thinner is used in the paint and the soft paint sinks into the cuts.

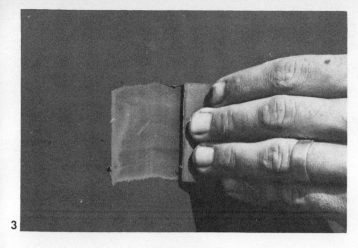

sand it within a week's time. This sanding opens up the pores and speeds up the drying process.

ENAMELS AND EPOXIES

Enamels (both straight and acrylic) differ from lacquer because their basic ingredients are varnishes (varnish produces that instant sheen) mixed with alcohol, turpentine and/or amyl acetates. Now you can see why you must use enamel reducer with enamel and lacquer thinner with lacquer. Where enamels generally outperform lacquer is in the durability department. They live, especially when baked in an oven, like gangbusters. Enamel is hard to apply. Line pressures, proper mix, weather, etc., can have a good/bad effect on the medium. But once the application part has been mastered, you can spray on the enamel and forget it. No color-sanding, rubbing out or fast oxidation will haunt you when the enamel is used.

As we've mentioned before, the best enamel jobs are the super-baked ones and are generally far superior to the more common air-dry jobs. This is because the surface can be kept free of flying foreign matter and the infrared lights speed up the oxidation of the enamel's binders.

Lately we've seen large numbers of eye-catching variations within both lacquer and enamel paints. Admixtures like metallics and metalflakes are part of the program—as are the candies—and are sprayed on in translucent layers. But nothing has become more interesting to the rodder than today's generation of epoxies and polyurethanes. Like the acrylic enamels, which use a catalytic compound to speed up the drying process, the diamond-hard breed of epoxies combines pigment with a hot-reacting catalyst. The catalyst works in the same manner as it does with fiberglass or plastic fillers. When the catalyst goes off, it literally ''kicks'' the pigment into an extremely hard, extremely tough and durable finish.

We understand epoxies have be-

come almost standard in heavy-duty or commercial (trucks, trailers, stationary engines, tanks, you-name-it, they've painted it) use. But many of the pro trendsetters have stayed away from these paints because of the limited amount of available colors.

What's so neat about the epoxies is that their special primers feature super flowout characteristics which make them attractive to the guy whose car body is still filled with scratches. The long flow of the material fills the sanding scratches, and, because it's plastic, it won't shrink with drying or age. Epoxies can be sprayed over lacquer or enamel if a special epoxy sealer is used, and it can be mixed with metallics, metalflake and pearls.

The racers love these types of finishes because they resist the inroads of nitro and alky. Consequently, if the stuff can do this, it can also ward off nicks and scratches, making it dynamite for undercarriage or chassis applications. Rocks, flying debris and

road grime find it tough going when they come up against the bulletproof nature of epoxy. But the plastic paint has its drawbacks, especially if the base coats are lacquer and you're spraying a clear epoxy over the surface. Unless the lacquer is thoroughly dried, the pressure generated by the seeping vapors will literally lift the paint off the metal.

As in any general discussion of paints, primers and preparation, we must treat the subject generally. Time, space limitations, the almost infinite variety of paints and their supporting casts make it nearly impossible to explore them in depth. But there are any number of catalogs, brochures, pamphlets and pocketbooks offered by the paint manufacturing industry to the general public. Consequently, we're providing a cross section of the painting publications. information is available in the preparation They should serve as a guide to what of primers and paints. 𝕎

Repainting: A to Z

A new paint job is more than some sandpaper and a squirt gun. Here's the right way to apply a new finish.

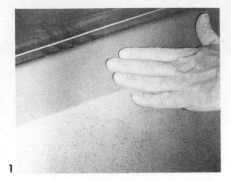

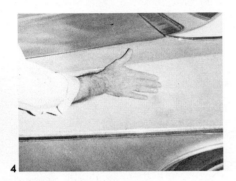

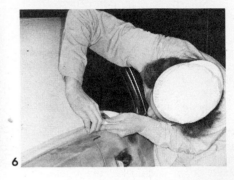

1

2

3

4

5

6

Properly taken care of, factory paint jobs can retain that new-car look for up to 4 years, but few of us are that faithful in keeping our car cleaned and polished. More likely, we rely upon the local car wash to do it for us, and there's nothing more destructive to the paint surface than continued use of commercial detergents on the finish, and if you don't believe it, ask any confirmed show car addict and watch him shudder.

Repainting most late-model cars will give them an entirely new-lease-on-life appearance and it's something you can do quite easily yourself, providing you're willing to spend the time and effort to do the job right. Or, if you don't feel competent to shoot the paint yourself, you can cut costs considerably by doing the surface preparation and masking before turning the car over to a paint shop for the actual top coat.

To show you exactly how a top paint shop would approach the problem of a repaint job, we went to Larry Davidson, a well-known painter in Los Angeles. We followed a 1972 Dodge through the process from start to finish, as you'll see in the accompanying photos. At the same time, we asked Larry to draw on his 18 years' experience as a painter to give us some practical hints that will help you to do the same thing at home. So

follow along as we start surface prep.

There's no great mystery to pre-paint preparation; the major aspect involved here is an expenditure of time and careful effort, but the better the prep job, the better the finished paint job will be. If there are any minor dents or other areas to be repaired, now's the time to take care of them. In the past, it was standard procedure to recommend that all chrome trim and ornaments be taken off prior to sanding. With all trim removed, the entire body gets paint protection and as wax and grease build up around the trim, removal of the chrome can make your preparation job easier. But lately, Detroit has been throwing painters a curve ball by cementing both trim and emblems to the body of many models, and trying to remove all the chrome in such a case can get you into more trouble than it's worth. About the only shops that remove trim completely today are the custom painters, but if you take a bit of care in sanding and masking, there's no reason why you can't get just as good a final result with the trim left on as with it all removed.

SANDING

Provided the surface is in good condition and does not require paint removal, begin surface preparation by

sanding. The idea here is to rough up the old surface sufficiently to provide a good tooth for the new top coat. If you're a real glutton for punishment, you'll hand sand the old surface with a block, #400 wet-or-dry paper, and water. But the amount of time and effort involved in this step can be considerably reduced by using a pneumatic jitterbug sander and #220 paper. Sand each panel horizontally from left to right; avoid using a circular motion since it's likely to leave an unwanted pattern of sand scratches that will show through the finished coat.

Once you've gone over the entire surface, blow off the sanding dust with compressed air and wash the body down with a solvent-type cleaner like Pre-Kleano or Prep-Sol. This will not only remove any contamination you may have missed while sanding, but it accentuates the tooth of the old paint surface and gives the new paint something to "bite" into for good adhesion qualities. While you may be tempted to remove the dust by washing the surface, don't. No matter how well you think you've managed to dry it off, there's always the possibility that water will remain between the panels, in door jambs, etc., and when you begin spraying, the water will mix with the paint—then you've really got problems.

1. Our demonstration car was a light poly gray 1972 Dodge Coronet Custom which had the appearance of a speckled Easter egg; vandals had sprayed acid all over the body.

2. Starting from the front and working backward with a jitterbug sander and #220 grit paper scuffs up the finish quickly and is just as efficient as hand sanding, but it sure is a lot faster.

3. Wearing a respirator mask is a good precaution to take; with all the foul air we breathe these days, the lungs can do without sanding dust. Use extra caution when sanding up to the chrome edges. If you're not handy with an electric/air sander, you may want to hand sand those areas.

4. Check the sanding job by touch; if you've cut too deeply or sanded unevenly, this will tell you faster than trying to spot it visually.

5. Use compressed air and a soft cloth to remove all sanding dust. Pay special attention to all joints and crevices, then wash body down with a solvent cleaner.

6. Start masking the chrome strip that separates the body and vinyl roof with ¾-inch tape. Be sure to press tape down securely to prevent paint from seeping underneath.

7. Mask the chrome trim next. Run the tape in one piece from front to rear. You'll need three strips to do the trim properly.

8. Use 2-inch tape to cover the chrome trim on the wheelwells. Run it across the trim and press up underneath. Do one side of the car before moving to the other side.

MASKING

Once the sanding and surface cleaning has been completed, the car is ready to be masked. This step is of equal importance to proper surface preparation, because careful masking is the mark of a craftsman; if you're sloppy, the finished paint job will show it regardless of how particular you've been up to this point. Begin by masking all trim, door handles, and other ornamentation. Use just masking tape for this, and pick a width that will cover the parts as completely as possible. Run the masking tape the entire length of the body trim, then use a razor blade to break the tape at each panel joint where the chrome breaks. Open each door and fold the tape over the edge of the chrome; use another small piece of tape, if necessary, to complete the job.

If the car has chrome on the wheelwells, mask those too. Use covers for the wheels if you have them (old seat covers work well); otherwise, use paper and tape. Now turn your attention to the side windows. With a hardtop, fasten a sheet of masking paper (never, never use newspaper) on the outside with a strip of tape at the bottom of the window, then fold it up and over the door chrome, and tape it securely from the inside. With sedans that require paint on the door frame, you'll have to mask just the glass—do this by applying paper to the lower half of the glass and then to the upper half;

run a length of tape on the overlapping edge to seal it completely. Finish the window by taping the paper at each side.

Open the hood and run a strip of tape along the top of the grille, then drape a sheet of masking paper across the front. If a color change is involved, you'll also need to mask off the engine compartment so that the hood lid can be painted. Do the same to the trunk area to mask off the rear bumper and taillights. Again, if you're changing colors, be sure to mask the inside of the trunk with paper so that the trunk lid area can be painted.

If the car has a vinyl roof, you can mask the windshield and rear window without any special attention, since you'll also cover the roof with paper. Start from the lower portion of both and overlap each succeeding piece, then tape all open edges securely to prevent overspray from working its way in. To mask a vinyl roof, run a sheet of masking paper lengthwise on each side, and then tape the seam down the middle.

The whole procedure can be done almost as quickly as it can be described, but it's best that you take your time, especially when masking off those areas directly adjacent to the paint—nothing marks the work of an amateur quite as quickly as a door lock or handle that wasn't properly masked. Be sure to go over each area carefully and press the tape down securely to make sure that it adheres properly to prevent paint from leaking under the tape.

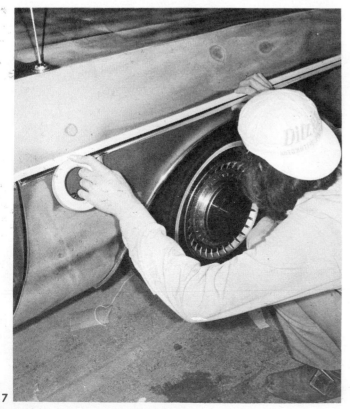

7

8

Repainting: A to Z

PRIMING

Once masking is completed, you're ready to shoot the primer. Use a good grade of primer-surfacer to grip the metal surface tightly, and to provide a firm base for the top coat. Mix the primer-surfacer according to directions on the can, run a tack rag over the entire surface, and then spray a medium thin wet coat. While beginners have a tendency to spray a heavy coat they shouldn't do it, because it won't dry uniformly. Although the surface will appear hard, the primer-surfacer close to the metal will not dry, and it can cause pin holes, poor top coat adhesion, and other defects. After flash-off, a light sanding with dry #400 grit paper is in order. Do this by hand, and follow by blowing out all crevices and mouldings with compressed air, then give the surface another wash down with Pre-Kleano or Prep-Sol.

At this point, some painters would prefer to wait about 30 days before applying the top coat. This delay gives the primer a chance to completely dry and shrink, but on a repaint job where you didn't have to go down to bare metal during surface

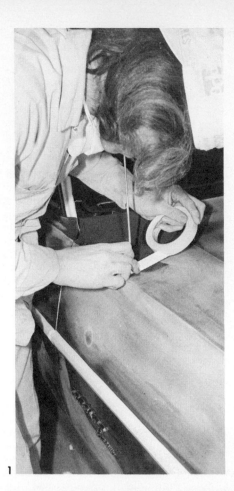

1

1. Mask the radio antenna base, then run tape up one side of antenna and down the other, pressing together.

2. Masking the windows on this hardtop is easy as the window frame is chrome, not paint. Fold paper over top of door and tape to window.

3. Break the tape at panel joints and fold it over. If necessary, use another small piece of tape to cover the end of the chrome strip.

4. Mask side lamps by running tape around outside edge, then fold tape inward and cover remainder of lamp with additional strips of tape.

5. Use extra care when taping door handles and locks. Careless masking shows up here first, since almost everyone looks at these as they unlock or open the door.

6. Run paper across grille, fold down over bumper and tape in place.

7. Cover the windshield by lifting the hood and draping masking paper inside. Note that all seams are taped to prevent overspray from penetrating.

8. As parking lamp is set in the splash pan beneath bumper, it must be masked separately. Run tape along outside edge, fold inward and cover with another strip.

9. Trunk is masked the same as grille. Taillamp placement in rear bumper makes rear of car easier to work on.

2

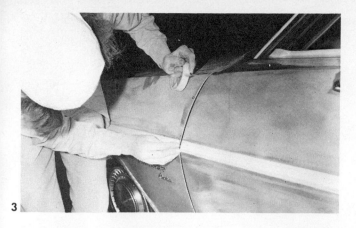

3

4

5

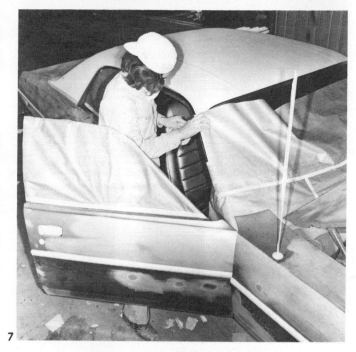

6

7

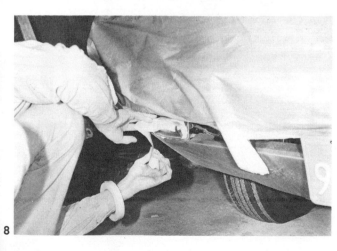

8

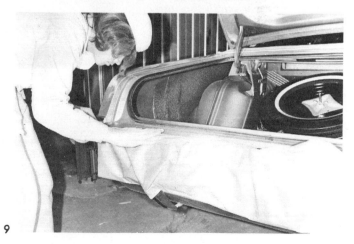

9

preparation, it really isn't necessary. And in today's fast-moving world, it isn't economical either.

PAINTING

Now you're ready to apply the top coat. In most cases, a gallon of paint will be sufficient to do the job once it's properly thinned. Be sure to apply the same type of paint as originally used on the car. While it is possible to spray acrylic enamel over acrylic lacquer without creating problems, you'll really be in trouble trying to put lacquer over enamel, as the hotter solvent in the lacquer will cause the enamel underneath to lift. Generally speaking, Ford and Chrysler use enamels while GM continues to prefer lacquers. Your best bet is to determine the color code and model year from the certification label and take this information to the paint dealer. This label is usually located at the rear edge of the driver's door or under the hood on the firewall or fenderwell. If you want to change colors, the dealer can help you select one that will do the trick without complicating your life any further.

Since acrylic lacquers dry by solvent evaporation or "flash-off", their drying time is rapid, and the fresh

Repainting: A to Z

topcoat will attract a minimum of dust and dirt. But acrylic enamels dry more slowly and in two stages—solvent evaporation and oxidation of the binder, and complete drying can take up to 8 months or more. After the first 24 hours, a new enamel finish reaches a state where it's "sensitive." Any damage that's done to the new paint surface during the week or so of "sensitivity" can't be repaired without lifting the fresh enamel recently applied.

If you're going to apply acrylic enamel, here's something to think about. A new hardener additive has come on the market in the past 18 months worth considering. Ditzler calls its version Delthane DXR-80, but other paint manufacturers have their own similar formulas. DXR-80 contains xylene, cellosolve acetate and polyurethane and provides a catalyst action to the enamel. This additive markedly increases the gloss of an enamel coat while reducing the curing time considerably. It also prevents wrinkling and will lengthen life expectancy by about 50%.

After an enamel finish containing

1. *Mask rear window as shown, fold as necessary, tape each seam to prevent overspray from seeping in.*

2. *Run 2-inch tape along chrome trim on roof above doors and fold in and under to form paint-tight seal. Only top remains to be covered.*

3. *Bring paper folds together at side of bumper and tape securely in place. Don't forget bumper guards which extend to rear splash pan—use tape only to cover them.*

4. *One strip of paper extending from windshield to rear window is taped in place as shown.*

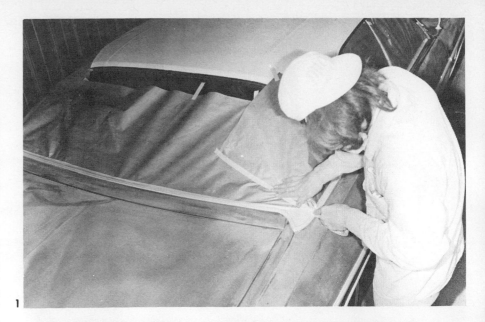

1

2

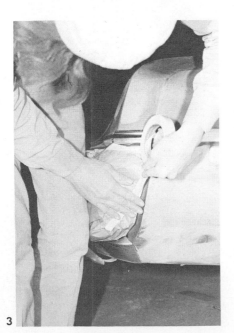

3

4

DXR-80 has been on the car for as little as 24 hours, you can send it through the nearest commercial car wash without fear of ruining the finish; something no one in their right mind would do with a straight acrylic enamel finish that fresh. You can even spill battery acid on the new topcoat without damaging it. As DXR-80 counteracts the period of sensitivity, any scratches, scrapes or other damage that might occur during the first 7 to 10 days after application can be easily corrected by respraying, because the fresh enamel underneath won't lift.

While this hardener additive does have a lot going for it, there are a few disadvantages. If you can't spray in a dust-free area like a regular paint booth, using DXR-80 can cause problems. While regular acrylic enamel will dry to a state where dust won't affect it in about an hour, the additive increases that initial drying period to about 4 hours. As its fumes are very strong, you must use a cartridge-type

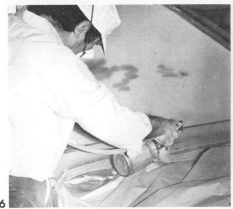

5. The second sheet is overlapped and taped in place. Masking tape seals seam on roof and overlaps on front and rear glass areas is also taped. Masking job is now complete.

6. If a color change is involved, engine compartment and insides of doors must be masked to allow painting of hood lid and door jambs without overspray problems.

7. With major masking completed and ready for the paint booth, the '72 Coronet is well on its way to recovery from the acid bath.

8. Checking final details, Larry discovers one spot unmasked. Removal of lettering is impractical as it's glued in place, but care in applying tape will give as good a final result as if you'd removed the lettering.

9. Before priming, the entire surface is gone over with a tack rag. Compare used one (right) to new one to see what you don't want to leave on the car.

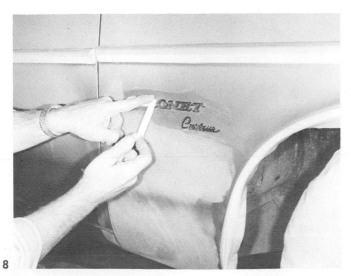

Repainting: A to Z

respirator when spraying or the chances are excellent that you'll be quite sick before you finish shooting the car. The final disadvantage is one of cost; DXR-80 sells for $40 per gallon, but a pint ($7.50) should suffice for the average car.

Once you've selected the correct color and type of paint, it must be mixed and reduced or thinned to a spraying consistency. When you buy the paint, have the dealer put it on a power-driven shaker to completely mix the pigment with the binder and solvent. Then by the time you get around to using it, a good stirring with a clean, flat-bottom paddle should be sufficient. Follow the directions on the can as to type and quantity of solvent or reducer to use; the wrong type will give problems, just as

an incorrect quantity will also ruin the finish coat. Add the solvent slowly and stir well, mixing paint and solvent together. Then, when you fill the spray gun cup, use a strainer to trap and remove any foreign matter or contamination that might be present.

Just before spraying the top coat, run a clean tack rag over the surface again; chances are good that you'll really be surprised when you see how much dirt and dust has accumulated. If you're doing the job piece-meal and shot the primer some days before, you should also wash the surface down again with Pre-Kleano or Prep-Sol before tacking. When you're ready to start spraying, bring the air pressure up to 65 pounds for acrylic enamel (45 for acrylic lacquer) and spray a test pattern to check and adjust the gun correctly. This can be done right on the masking paper used on the car. Initial adjustment for

normal work is made by backing off the fluid screw about 2½ turns from its fully closed position; final corrections are then made with the fan ad-

1. A medium-thin wet coat of primer/surfacer is applied to the entire surface, one panel at a time. Note use of wheel covers to protect wheels from overspray.

2. After the primer/surfacer has flashed off (about 20 minutes), Larry hand sands the entire body with #400 grit paper. Too much pressure here will cut right through to the old paint, or worse, to bare metal.

3. The final prep step before applying the topcoat is a last washdown with a solvent cleaner. Rub on with one cloth, wipe off immediately with another clean one.

4. It may seem like a lot of tacking but any good painter will tell you that this little cloth is his best friend. You can't be too cautious at this point.

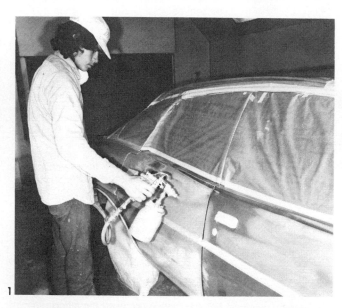

1

2

3

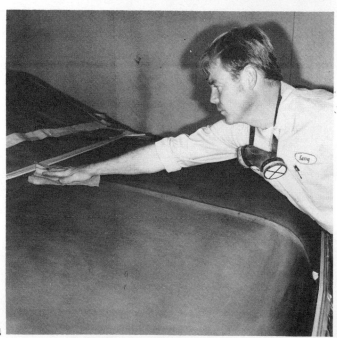

4

5. *Be sure to strain the paint when filling the gun cup. Any contamination or foreign matter in the paint at this point could clog the gun or, worse, force its way through the gun onto the surface.*

6. *Air pressure is adjusted for spraying acrylic enamel; final adjustment is made at the gun.*

7. *Larry opens up the fluid adjust screw about 2½ turns from its fully closed position to shoot his first test pattern.*

8. *If you get a pattern like this, you need to adjust the fan; your pattern is too round and too heavy.*

9. *The fan adjustment is located above the fluid screw and should be opened about one turn at a time.*

10. *Here's the pattern Larry will use to shoot the car. It allows him to work about 8-10 inches from the surface and gives uniform coverage without distortion.*

justment screw. A correct pattern should be uniform, have good atomization, and no distortion.

While you can spray a car in a variety of ways, Larry suggests starting with the hood area, then moving to the left to do the fender, across to the right fender and up that entire side of the car, stopping at the rear and moving across to the opposite side to pick up the door panel next to the left front fender, down that entire side of the car to finish up on the trunk. In this way, no single panel sits with paint on it long enough to make blending a problem. If you start at one point and work your way 360° around the car back to that point, there's a good possibility that when you reach the point where you first started, drying will be sufficiently advanced to make blending difficult. This is especially true of non-profes-

sionals, who tend to work slower than the fellow who earns his daily bread with a spray gun. Three coats should be sufficient with acrylic enamel; acrylic lacquer usually takes four or five coats for a good finish.

Working with correct temperatures is very important if you expect the final result to be perfect the first time around. If you're fortunate enough to have access to a regular spray booth (often you can rent one on a weekend), your problem is solved because you can control the heat, but working at home in the garage or backyard means that you'll have to pick your day carefully. For best results, the temperature should be close to 75, but even if the air temperature is right on the button, remember that direct sunlight on that metal body is going to raise its surface temperature quite a bit above the ideal. If you have to

5

6

7

8

9

10

Repainting: A to Z

work outdoors and can't place the car in open shade, better look for a retarder to slow the drying process.

Beginners have a strong temptation to remove the masking paper and tape as quickly as possible in order to get a look at their handiwork, but the pro will leave it on until he's sure that it's dry. Besides the possibility of leaving ragged edges where a straight line should be, there's always the chance that sanding dust in a fold of the masking paper will sprinkle out and onto the not-yet-dry paint. So be patient and let lacquer set for at least an hour after applying the final coat; enamel should have 2 to 3 hours to set before you attempt to unmask it.

DETAILING

The final step is that of detailing. Color sand lacquer finishes by hand, then machine polish and wax. Enamel is an entirely different matter because of its very slow drying qualities. Wait at least 48 hours before detailing an enamel finish, and never color sand it or you'll lose the gloss. Keep the car away from commercial car washes; if it has to be cleaned, do the job with cool water and very soft rags; dry it carefully with a chamois, because water left on an enamel surface will spot the paint. (This can happen with lacquer too.) Avoid waxing enamel for from 5 to 6 months to give the paint a good start toward drying. Of course, if you used DXR-80 with your paint, you can wash or wax the car 24 hours after spraying—another dandy reason for using the hardener additive.

So, now you know what goes into a professional repaint job and what you can expect to receive for the $150 or so you'll be charged. If you decide you'd like to do it yourself, we've laid the route out for you to follow. One last caution—if you have any inclination at all toward the cheaper paint jobs that are offered these days, take a second look at what they include in the way of preparation and application; auto painting is still one area in which you get what you pay for—from A to Z. 🐞

PAINT SHOP DO'S AND DON'T'S*

Dirt has an affinity for wet paint. Here are some often-overlooked dirt sources in a presumably clean spray booth.

DIRTY CAR. Even though a car has been thoroughly cleaned, dust can and will blow out from under the fenders and other places where it is trapped. Steam or pressure cleaning of a car's underbody is a good investment toward a dirt-free new finish.

POOR HOUSEKEEPING. Dust will accumulate on the walls, ceiling and floor of a spray booth. Test such areas for dirt by wiping with a facial tissue. A spray booth is no place for discarded sandpaper, masking paper, etc. These are good dirt harborers. Wet the floor with a hose before spraying a car to keep the inevitable under-foot dirt down where it belongs.

SANDING IN A BOOTH. It happens more often than you'd think possible. Even wet sanding in a paint spray booth will leave dirt-filled mud, which will become dust looking for a new home when it dries.

EXHAUST FAN RUNNING WITH BOOTH DOOR OPEN. Spray booth exhaust fans expel air up and out a duct, but this air must be replaced. It can only enter through the filters—but if the booth door is open, the air will come through the opening of least resistance and bring outside dirt with it.

DUSTY EQUIPMENT. Overspray dust from previous paint jobs will settle on air hoses, pressure regulators, portable heat lamps, and so forth. Keep such equipment clean at all times.

PAINTER'S CLOTHING. If the painter wears street clothes, or lint-catching clothing, dust will find its way onto the newly painted surface. Starched coveralls or clothing of synthetic cloth are preferred.

DIRTY PAINT. New or thoroughly cleaned containers should be used for mixing paint. Old cans, thinner which has been allowed to stand uncovered, are good dirt sources.

CHEESE CLOTH. Paint strainers are specially made of materials that won't collect dust. Never substitute cheese cloth which often contains lint.

PAINT VISCOSITY. Follow manufacturer's instructions for thinning paint to proper spraying consistency. Paint with too much thinner or reducer results in excessive overspray, which settles back on the car.

SPRAY BOOTH FILTERS. Dirt and dust will gradually collect, and eventually clog, spray booth filters. Filters should be changed frequently.

UNSEALED BOOTH LEAKS. It's possible air and accompanying dirt can enter a spray booth through wall or ceiling joints not properly sealed. Check all seams if dirt is persistent, yet all other good housekeeping measures are followed.

WRONG END FIRST. Some painters prefer starting at the front of a car, others at the rear. Whichever end you prefer, make sure that end is the farthest from the exhaust fan. Always spray working in the direction toward the fan.

DUCT DIRT BUILDUP. Some types of exhaust ducts may gradually become partially clogged with dirt and paint overspray. This lessens exhaust airflow and velocity and an inefficiency in carrying off overspray from the present paint job.

DIRTY AIR LINES. Old air hoses, regulating equipment, undrained condenser chambers—all may harbor dirt, water and/or oil. Inspect and clean regularly.

STATIC ELECTRICITY. In the winter, or when humidity is low, a car may carry a small charge of static electricity that attracts dust like a magnet. After a car is in the booth, run a wire lead from the ground terminal of the car's battery to a positive ground, like a water pipe.

SPRAY CAP FUZZ. Overspray may build up on the gun spray cap. If it isn't wiped off, it can blow off in gobs and cause a bad paint blemish.

DUSTY MASKING. Never use newspaper for masking; one of the first rules a novice painter hears. Still, the practice persists. Many a non-thinker will carry a stack of old newspapers into the booth, and drop the bundle where paper lint gets onto everything.

POOR TACKING. Always use as clean a tack rag as possible; they're inexpensive in relation to a repaint job. Also, after spraying the edges of doors and lids when shooting a new color, tack the car's exterior again to catch dirt that may have been blown from crevices.

EXCESSIVE EXHAUST. Follow the spray booth manufacturer's instructions for the *minimum* velocity of air exhaust by the fan. Excessive air agitation is conducive to dusty conditions.

DIRTY OLD YOU. Got dandruff? Wear a tight fitting cap. Skin flaking off from a summer tan or other condition? Wear pants without cuffs; those cuffs are great dirt collectors.

*BASED ON "DIRTY PAINT", COURTESY THE DEVILBISS COMPANY, TOLEDO, OHIO.

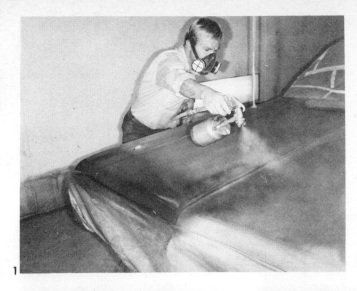

1. As Larry is using DXR-80 in the paint, he's wearing a double-cartridge respirator. Filters should be changed after the car is completed, because fumes render them useless.

2. Larry works from the left front fender (facing car) around to the right rear, then switches over to the left front door and back to the trunk area to avoid blending problems at the finish area.

3. Larry allows the new enamel finish to set for 2½ hours before he starts unmasking. Patience in getting to this step is one big key to a good job; hurrying the unveiling can cause many tricky problems.

4. Major areas like the doors are left until all trim is uncovered, as problems are most likely to show up in the smaller areas.

5. The roof paper comes off last and it's still a keen sight, even to an experienced painter like Larry.

6. Here's the finished car—you can't tell it from new. Now you know why good paint jobs cost money!

POSSIBLE CAUSES	WRINKLING OF ENAMEL	ORANGE PEEL	BLUSHING	LIFTING	CRAZING	FEATHEREDGE CRACKING OR SPLITTING	MOTTLING	ADHESION LOSS & CHIPPING	RUNS OR SAGS	SHRINKING OR SPLITTING OF PUTTY	PINHOLING
Materials not uniformly mixed		●				●	●	●			●
Wrong reduction or thinning (amount or grade)		●	■	●	●	●	●	●	●		●
Improper substrate cleaning or preparation				●		●		■		●	●
Wrong gun adjustments or technique		■	●			●	●		●		●
"Piling-On" in heavy or wet coats	■					■	■		■	■	■
Contamination (air or feed lines, shop tools, original finish, etc.)								●			●
Effect of old finish or previous repair				●	●	●					●
Poor shop temperature (too cold or too hot)	●	●	●		■	●	●		●		●
Improper dry (fanning air, wrong force dry or bake)	●	●	●	●		●					●
Flash time or recoat time between coats (too long or too short)		●		■			●	●	●		●

REMEDIES (R)											
ADHESION LOSS AND CHIPPING Remove the finish for an area considerably larger than the affected area and refinish.								R			
BLUSHING Add retarder to the reduced color and apply another double-coat.			R								
CRAZING Over-reduce with thinner blended with retarder and apply wet double coats until crazing pattern disappears.					R						
FEATHEREDGE CRACKING OR SPLITTING Remove finish from the affected area and refinish.						R					
LIFTING Remove finish from affected area and refinish.				R							
MOTTLING After color coat has set up, apply another double-coat using fast evaporating thinner or reducer at high pressure.							R				
ORANGE PEEL Rub with rubbing compound when thoroughly dry, or sand down to smooth surface and refinish, using a slower evaporating thinner or reducer at a lower air pressure.		R									
PINHOLING Sand down to a smooth finish and refinish.											R
RUNS OR SAGS When thoroughly dry, sand down to remove runs and refinish.									R		
SHRINKING OR SPLITTING OF PUTTY Remove putty in affected areas and reapply using thin coats.										R	
WRINKLING OF ENAMEL Remove wrinkled enamel and refinish.	R										

Causes & Remedies

POSSIBLE CAUSES	BLISTERING	CHECKING	CHALKING	CRACKING	DISCOLORATION OR STAINING	SAND-SCRATCH SWELLING	WET SPOTS (DUE TO WAX, GREASE, ETC.)	FISH EYES	WATER SPOTTING	"BLEEDING"	CRATERING
Materials not uniformly mixed		●	●	●							
Wrong reduction or thinning (amount or grade)	●		●			●			●		
Improper substrate cleaning or preparation	■				●	■	■	●			●
Incorrect use of additives (type or amount)	●	●	●	●							
Contamination (air or feed lines, shop tools, old finish, etc.)	●				●			■		●	■
Effect of old finish or previous repair	●	●		●	●	●	●	●		■	
Excessive film thickness	●	●		■					●		
Washing finish prematurely or with untried cleaners	●				●				■		
Exposed to harmful materials (chemicals, industrial fallout, etc.) or prolonged exposure to sun light		■	■	●	■						
REMEDIES (R)											
BLISTERING Sand affected areas to a smooth finish, or in extreme cases remove finish down to the metal and refinish.	R										
CHECKING If proper gloss and smoothness cannot be restored by slight rubbing or polishing, sand the affected area and refinish. In extreme cases, area may have to be removed to primer.		R									
CHALKING When this condition is encountered, rub and polish the surface to remove dead pigments and scale.			R								
CRACKING Sand affected areas to a smooth finish, or in extreme cases remove finish down to the metal and refinish.				R							
DISCOLORATION OR STAINING Rub with rubbing compound and polish, or in severe cases sand to primer and refinish.					R						
SAND-SCRATCH SWELLING Sand down to smooth surface and apply clear or gray automotive sealer before refinishing.						R					
WET SPOTS (due to wax, grease, etc.) Remove finish from affected area and refinish.							R				
FISH EYES After affected coat has setup, apply another double coat of color containing "FEE" fish eye eliminator. In severe cases, affected areas should be refinished.								R			
WATER SPOTTING Rub with rubbing compound and polish, or in severe cases, sand affected areas and refinish.									R		
BLEEDING Apply two medium coats of bleederseal in accordance with label directions and apply color coat.										R	
CRATERING Sand affected areas to a smooth finish and refinish.											R

■ — Most Common Cause

The Perfect Blend

Few professional painters can actually blend without difficulty; but here are some tricks.

Repainting a spot repair or even an entire panel with acrylic enamel can present a problem, especially if you're working with a metallic finish. The repainting itself is easy enough—the problem arises when the paint has dried—it doesn't quite look the same as the rest of the car. To the novice painter, the first thought that pops into his mind at this point is simply that he somehow got the wrong paint. If only the answer were that simple!

It seems logical enough if you buy a can of the same paint that's on your car, that it should look the same when applied, right? Ah, but there's a slight rub here—a factory-applied finish is very thin (about .004-in., *four thousandths*, at best on late models) and baked on at high temperatures; your repair is neither thin nor baked. Depending upon the age of the paint job involved, this difference in application techniques, along with aging, fading and a few other factors, combine to create a real disparity in appearance. Actually, the application difference is sufficient to cause a problem even on a brand new car, despite the fact that the repair paint used is exactly the same formula as that the factory applied to the car.

Any professional painter will tell you that unless you blend the new finish into the old, your chances of

avoiding this effect are about one in four. Sounds simple enough, but you'd be surprised to learn how few professional painters can actually blend without difficulty. In theory, blending is elementary enough. The human eye will notice a disparity only if there's a reasonably sharp, clear breaking line between the old and the new. Bridge that line by blending and even though the difference still exists (to a lesser degree), the eye will not usually notice it.

In essence, blending a paint finish is much like featheredging a repair spot before painting—do it well enough and you can't tell where the damage was; once the repair has been made. But if you don't featheredge, the repair spot catches the eye immediately, regardless of how many coats you've applied over it. To make the entire job of blending easier for the novice, we went to one of Los Angeles' top painters to get his slant on the problem. And sure enough, there are a couple of tricks that you can use to good advantage.

Let's suppose that the damaged area extends over two panels; we'll take the hood and front fender as an example. The problem of blending here can be completely avoided (depending upon the car involved) if you backtape. Pick a high crown line beyond the damaged area and face it

with masking tape applied so that one-half of the tape's width will form an extension of the crown line (this works best on late-model or boxy designs). If you taped that crown line in the usual manner and then painted, you'd wind up with a sharp edge, once the paint dried and the tape was removed. Blending would avoid the sharp paint line but backtaping is much easier than blending and leaves no sharp paint line.

You simply paint up to the taped crown line and, as the paint strikes the surface under pressure, it hits the masking tape extension and bounces back, so to speak. Without the masking tape extension, the paint would just lie there and build up. When you look at a metallic paint area with a high crown line running through it, there'll be a slight difference in appearance anyway, because of the difference in the angle of light striking it. Backtaping takes advantage of this optical difference and the eye can't tell that you've "cheated" on it a bit. Clever? You bet, but it's also amazing just how much a sharp painter can get away with by using a crown line to his advantage.

But suppose that you can't avoid the blend; here's another little trick to help you make it easier. Begin by shooting a single coat, follow with a double coat and you're ready to

1. This 1973 Mustang requires blending into fender panel on passenger side, and will be blended into door panel on driver's side.

2. Masking tape is lifted along the entire crown line to assure that paint can "bounce" when it's sprayed. Backtaping on high crown line of fender saves painter a blending job.

3. Factory paint is a green-gold metallic poly and is scuffed lightly, not sanded, where backtaping is used.

4. Larry sprays a single coat over the entire surface. This will be followed by a double coat and then the blend coat.

5. Fender is blended about one-third of the way into door panel using a color blend coat.

6. Blend line is extended further into door panel by a coat of clear.

7. Blend is completed using a weak coat of clear mixed with a fast-acting reducer and shot to end of door panel. This prevents color mottle and produces a perfect blend.

blend. This is also a single coat and you'll shoot color about a third of the way into the adjoining panel where the blend is to take place, gradually fading from the single coat application to nothing. Change from color to clear at this point and shoot a thin coat about two-thirds into that panel, again fading to nothing. Follow this with a coat of clear, mixed 1 part to 10 parts of a fast reducer, and shoot it all the way to the end of the blend panel.

If you try to blend using just a color coat, you'll find it difficult to trigger the gun smoothly enough to obtain the gradual fade necessary, and you might even wind up painting the entire panel as a result. Then you'll have to start all over again and blend on another adjoining panel. When blending metallics, the possibility of ending up with a color mottle is ever-present, but extending the blend line with clear solves both problems, giving a nice smooth blend even if you're not an expert.

As paint reduction with metallic colors is very critical, here's one other tip that has a great bearing on the amount of blending that you'll have to do: Follow the paint manufacturer's directions to the letter when reducing the acrylic enamel for spraying. Too little reducer will give you a darker-than-desired color; too much will over-lighten a metallic paint.

When shooting a regular color, reduction is not as critical, but the blending process is much the same. If the area to which you must blend is faded, your blending problem will be somewhat greater, but rather than tamper with the paint formulas, try buffing the old paint before you start shooting. Since buffing brings up the remaining gloss, it salvages whatever life remains in the old coat and reduces the degree of blending that's necessary to bring the two paint areas close enough so that the eye will not be disturbed by whatever slight difference remains once you're finished.

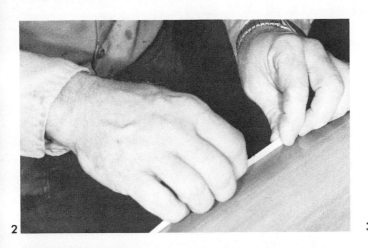

2

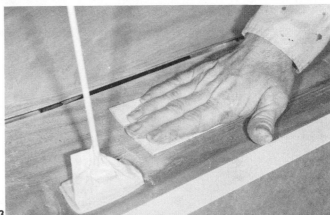

3

4

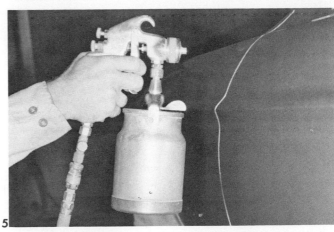

5

6

7

Custom Paint Ideas

The heart of the art of frozen action spotlights a 20-year fad that now marches to a different drummer.

Twenty years ago, customizing was the biggest rage on the automotive scene, and one of its hottest aspects was custom painting. Flames were "in," with scalloping, striping and other unusual effects decorating the reworked chariots. Rock and roll tunes of that era syncopated with the chorus of hammers as youngsters tore off front ends and grafted on new ones, reworked rear decks, fins and taillights, sucked factory interiors into the nearest garbage can with large vacuum cleaners that blew in new and exotic ones which made Detroit's own garish taste look *haute couture* by comparison. The whole transformation was wrapped in candy apple and driven slowly down the street for all to see. Names like George Barris, Dean Jeffries, and Big Daddy Roth wafted out of Southern California to influence an entire generation of backyard customizers.

Somewhere along the way, the bubble burst, the magic faded, the dream tarnished and by the '60's, we were on a performance binge from which there seemed no return. Big blocks got bigger, hemis became super hemis and the ponies grew into overpowered muscle cars. Customizing as an art slipped into its Dark Ages and custom painting faded from view, as will all exterior finishes when exposed to the effects of long neglect. But contrary to what you might have heard or read, custom painting never really died; in fact, it's alive and well and is now spreading across the country once more. Performance has had its day and, in the face of tougher emission regulations coming out of state legislatures and Washington, it's heading into oblivion, at least in the opinion of many observers.

With today's car enthusiasts seeking a new means of expressing their automotive personality, it looks like custom painting is on the verge of winning over another whole generation. The big revival came about with the sudden surge of interest in vans about 1970, and now it's spreading to the street machine crowd. Even staid dealerships in California have embraced it, hiring local painters to decorate their new cars before placing them on the lot for sale.

The new breed of custom painters look at their work as having descended directly from the traditions established 20 years ago by men who are mostly out of the business now, but

the techniques have changed somewhat, as well as the effects sought. Flames have returned with a vengeance, but scalloping? Once the most initiated and overused of effects, lacing now seems restricted to those production painters who cover boxy van surfaces for dealers eager to cash in on a new trend; no true custom painter who values his name does lacing today, unless the customer absolutely insists on it.

What seems to have emerged this time around is a combination favorites and new art forms. So come along as we delve first into the basics and then turn to the latest and hottest in custom painting with an eye toward the do-it-yourself painter.

SURFACE PREPARATION AND PRIMING

If there's any such thing as a key to a successful paint job, it's proper surface preparation, and this is especially true of custom work, according to Walt Prey, who operates Walt's Studio of Style on Woodman Ave. in Van Nuys, Calif. Also known as the "Wizard of Van Nuys" for his imaginative painting designs, he has a lot of advice for the would-be custom painter and all of it learned through years of experience and careful experimentation.

Basically, the job shop and custom painter both do the same thing; the primary differences between their work rests in the amount and kind of preparation and the top coat materials used. As the surface to which he will apply his paint has to be as flawless as possible, the custom man has

to be meticulous—no waves, dents, or scratches to mar the end result.

In preparing a car for a custom finish, the painter can't afford to disregard any part of the car, if he's going to turn out that distinctive appearance that justifies the considerably higher cost involved. Chrome trim, the door, hood, and deck lid rubber, ID plates on door sills, etc. should all be removed and the inner surfaces wet sanded completely with No. 320 grit paper. Rough places are then worked over with No. 00 steel wool before cleaning with a good grade of wax and grease remover.

Exterior panels must be prepared with an eye toward perfection, so the entire car should be wet sanded with a rubber block and No. 320 grit paper. If high and low spots are present, sand to the metal in the high spots, using the original paint as a low area filler. Using the original paint as a filler in this way helps to guard against a premature failure caused by loading paint on the panel. If a high spot can't be worked down with a light filing, it should be worked with a hammer and dolly, but such spots are unlikely unless there has been previous panel damage.

A sanding block about 10 inches in length seems to be ideal, especially if the car has several low-crown panels like those of the ever-popular Impalas. Curves and longer ripples that might otherwise be missed will show up nicely by using the larger block. If a dark color is to be the finish coat, removing all such blemishes is an absolute necessity, as darker colors have a tendency to accentuate rip-

1. Trick paint jobs can be done with standard colors or paints that are trick in their own right. A large selection of custom paints is available from Sem Products, Inc. of Belmont, CA. In addition to their Aero-Lac line of pearls, candies and flakes, they also have two-tone transmission pearl pigments to mix with any clear system and Design Colors for op-art.

2. Most trick painting and detailing is done with an airbrush, which allows you to only mix small amounts of paint when you are using many colors in a panel. These two by Metalflake are relatively inexpensive and can be used either with a compressor or with their own can of propellant.

3. A product of the van era, mural paint jobs are increasingly popular, and are even showing up on passenger cars and street rods, like this fine self-portrait on a '47 Plymouth rod.

4. Flames have been around for many years, but new variations are always appearing, like the design on this sedan delivery, on which the woman's hair flows back with flamelike tresses.

5. When the overall body color of the car is the same as the flames, then what you have are "reverse" flames, because what is actually painted on or added is the darker paint between the flames. Geometric shapes between the flames were done by fogging over cardboard stencils.

ples, and nothing looks worse than an otherwise top quality finish resting on a wavy panel. This is especially true when repainting production fiberglass bodies like the Corvette, which come factory-equipped with their share of ripples.

Once the car has been completely sanded and is ready for priming, wash it down with a good solvent cleaner. Primer by itself is designed simply to cover bare metal, not to act as a scratch filler, so it's a good idea to shoot primer-surfacer instead. This will fill minor scratches, without reacting chemically to any of the original paint left on the car. Primer-surfacer has other advantages; it allows the use of glazing compound if necessary (glaze otherwise lifts enamel) and gives a good strong undercoat that grips both bare metal and the original paint while providing a good tooth for the new coat. Incidentally, if glaze is used to bring up low spots, it should be applied in thin coats that are given ample time to dry between applications, because it cracks when built up too thickly.

Primer-surfacer also works as a non-sanding sealer when applied over a lacquer finish, cutting out the sanding requirement before shooting the finish color coats. Just remember that primer-surfacer is a synthetic enamel and so it does not flash-off like lacquer primer; plenty of time should be allowed for it to dry and shrink before sanding and painting is attempted. Just prior to sanding, a flash coat of a different color primer is shot. This dries quite rapidly and when the car is block sanded, the difference in color shows up any high or low spots that might have been missed during the original preparation. Very fine wet paper is used for this—No. 320 grit for enamel, and No. 400 or No. 600 is used for lacquer.

COLOR COAT APPLICATION

Shooting custom color coats is pretty much the same as shooting any other topcoat, but techniques do vary somewhat, depending upon the type of paint being used. In most cases, it's a matter of building the color desired by applying coat after coat. Where three to five coats will suffice for the average repaint job done at the corner spray booth, the custom painter will often shoot 35 to 40 coats or more. Candy colors provide a good example; as they are translucent, a highly reflective underbase is the secret. The four common

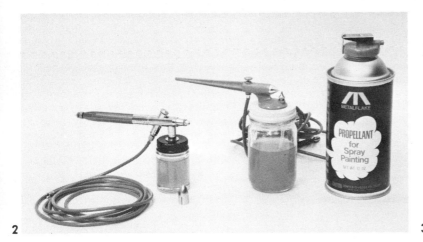

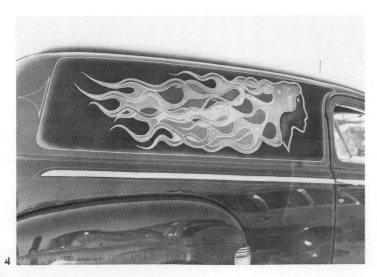

Custom Paint Ideas

underbases for lacquer are gold, copper, silver, and pearl or white metallics. Each works in combination with the candy toners for a specific effect. A copper underbase darkens the final color, giving a rich, warm tone. Gold provides a vivid brilliance underneath any color, yet leaves a definite warm sparkle. Silver gives the final result a deep chromed look while toning down the color.

Pearl auto finishes are also unusual and popular. These contain synthetic pearl pigments that have an iridescent-like play, unobtainable with ordinary dyes and pigments. The pearl pigments give a two-color play when used over white or light pastel backgrounds, and strong single color effects over black or some other dark bases.

The underbase is mixed·50/50 with a good slow drying lacquer thinner and then shot under low (40 lbs.) pressure. To keep the underbase from bleeding, a sealer is applied after the underbase has dried. All candy colors except Pagan Gold and Mother of Pearl can be used over any of the underbases; pearl has to be used over a gold or silver base and gold can only go over a gold underbase. While the exact tone depends upon the particular toner used and the number of coats applied, you can get a good idea of the final color while the paint is still wet. Custom painters simply shoot coat after coat until they get the desired effect and often can't remember the total number of coats applied.

The color or topcoat should be mixed 1:1 with thinner and applied at a pressure between 50-65 lbs. Fog the color on slightly dry, then cover with clear so that it will flow together. After 8 hours' drying time, an intermediate color sanding with No. 600 wet grit paper is followed by a couple of surface flow coats, mixed 2 or 3:1 with a slow-dry thinner. Final color sanding and rubbing out should be delayed for about 15 days to give the paint sufficient time to dry and shrink.

Enamel has long been considered the best of all general purpose paints, and it's even better suited to cars since the introduction of acrylics. But custom painters haven't had much luck with enamel in the past, and until Joe Andersen found a way to mix and apply enamels in all the candy colors, they shied away from it, preferring to stick with the lacquer. Because enamel flows much better than lacquer, it tends to cover minor scratches and nicks that a lacquer would miss. And once the color coat is on, pearl highlighting can be sprayed on selected spots to empha-

1

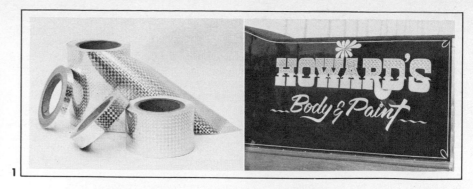

2

size the custom color. In addition, enamel requires no color sanding or rubbing. As the amount of labor is considerably less than that required for lacquer, enamel paint jobs are much easier and less expensive to apply; enamel can cut the cost for a good custom paint job to about two-thirds that of lacquer and three-fourths that of metalflake.

Metalflake is a highly reflective paint base available presently in 36 colors to which tiny particles of metal, glass, or mylar are added for a distinctive reflective quality. There's also a special prism flake, which reflects rainbow colors, that is becoming more and more popular. When Metalflake was first introduced, there were only two cuts of flakes available; this has since been expanded to four. The coarsest flake particles are approximately one-quarter the size of a small straight pin head while the smallest are really tiny, some taking approximately 385 million particles to make a single pound of flake.

To reduce color spotting; Metalflake should be applied over a primer-surfacer of the same general tint. The flake is mixed with thinned acrylic clear (the clear should be mixed about 1½:1 with thinner), to about 12 ounces of flake per gallon of reduced clear. Because the flake is heavy, it settles rapidly to the bottom of the mixing container and must be thoroughly agitated before being poured into the gun cup. The same settling

will occur in the spray cup, although there are two methods of keeping the flakes in suspension. One is to put marbles or bolts in the cup, and after making several strokes, agitate the gun well. The other method is to hold a rag over the nozzle, forcing air back into the cup to ''burble'' the mixture and thus keep it suspended. You won't have this suspension problem with mylar or prism flake, since it's much lighter. For those of you who plan to spray a lot of Metalflake paints or other metallics, you can make or purchase an attachment for your spraygun to agitate the metallic particles. It's like a stirring rod inside the paint cup which is kept stirring the paint by air power, which you bleed off from the air hose just before it enters the gun itself. These little ''windmills'' work great.

A couple of heavy coats of flake are sprayed on, at least enough to get 90% coverage over the underbase. Always spray flake and metallics very wet, because this lets the individual flakes lie down properly. Allow about 5 mins. setup time between each coat, and remember to keep the flakes in suspension by agitating the gun often. Spray away from the car until the flake mixture starts to flow from the nozzle, then arc the gun onto the panel and shoot the coat.

Flake is sprayed at a rather low pressure, usually between 25 and 30 lbs. A general utility spray gun nozzle

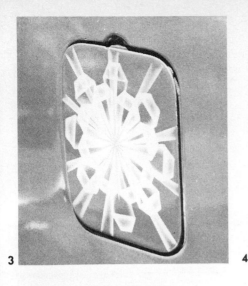

3   **4**

1. Especially neat for lettering and signs, but also usable with other paint ideas, Metalflake's SpecTrim tape reflects all the colors of the rainbow under changing light.

2. Pioneers in the custom paint field, Metalflake offers a complete system, with such special effects paints as Vreeble, Glowble, Mirra, Spindrift, Eerie-Dess, pearls and candies.

3. Can't afford a whole custom paint job? How about a little airbrush detailing in small areas. Touches like the stenciled burst design on this gas filler door can set your vehicle apart with out the expense of an overall trick paint job.

4. Maybe there's a striper in your town but no custom paint facilities. You could lay out a neat design like this and have the striper outline it with simple and effective striping.

and cap should be used, such as the DeVilbis No. 043, No. 30, or No. 306. Binks guns have equivalent nozzle/cap combinations. It's important to spray flake with an even pattern to avoid ''heavy'' streaking. Along with the wet application, this tends to flow the flakes smoothly and cuts down on the amount of clear required for a smooth final finish.

After at least 30 mins. drying time, blow off the loose flake. Rub the surface by hand while blowing to smooth off rough edges that might be standing up but don't sand. Apply about seven full coats of clear acrylic, letting each coat set up from 5 to 10 mins. After the last coat, the paint should air-dry overnight, then seven more coats of clear are applied. If a color toner is to be used, it should be sprayed during the initial coats of clear, because the toner must be well below the surface where it's immune to final sanding. Fourteen coats of clear seems to be a lot, but that's what the manufacturers recommend, although custom painters often do not spray that many. Clear has a tendency to break down after a year

or so, and the more that's used, the more susceptible it will be to checking. The answer is in keeping the clear well protected with a good quality wax.

It's best to shoot flake with acrylic clear, since the acrylic stays wet long enough for the flake to lie down and also has excellent lasting qualities. Lacquer clear can be used, but it tends to turn amber with age and breaks up much sooner than acrylic. Another advantage in using acrylic clear is that it can literally be melted back together, that is, any cracking can be flowed shut. Spraying more clear over the surface will not do the trick, but fogging on several coats of wet thinner will. This makes the surface cracks flow together again, and the clear looks as good as new.

It is possible to sand the final coats of clear after thorough air drying, but not for 3 to 4 weeks. This lets the paint harden really well. Block sand the finish with No. 220 grit wet, followed by a No. 340 grit wet, until the clear is perfectly smooth. If the flake has been prepared as directed, it won't require much clear to give a smooth finish. When sanding, don't cut through to either the toner or flake. Wash and wipe the finish dry, tack off and apply a light coat of thinner with 15% clear added. Once this final coat has dried, use rubbing compound and a machine buffer.

Now that we've got some of the basics down, let's take a look at the current scene and the ''trick'' paint techniques that gave custom painting its strongest revival in the past two decades. There's something for every taste and pocketbook described on the next few pages.

PANEL PAINTING

An oldie brought up to date, panel painting has never had it so good; its popularity ranks high on the list of today's favorites. Walt demonstrated panel painting for us with a car

known far and wide in Southern California as ''Gypsy Rose.'' It had been brought back to his shop for a complete redo, and the basic scheme called for twin panels on hood and deck lid set into an overall candy red finish, with roses of different sizes and styles laid across the panels on veiled vines.

Once the car has been prepared for spraying, the first step is to apply a white underbase. Abalone pearl mixed with gold murano pigment and clear is then shot over the underbase to provide the best reflective qualities for the candy red. After the pearl has dried, four coats of clear are sprayed over before proceeding. This trick serves a couple of purposes; if you goof further on down the line, the mistake can be sanded off by removing the clear and there's no damage to the undercoats. Clear also tends to smooth out acrylic lacquer and keeps it from puddling as you build the surface up coat by coat. Once the clear is dry, wet sand the entire surface with No. 400 grit paper and wipe dry with a clean chamois.

The panels are then masked off, and once you try this, you can appreciate the artistry in Walt's style. Regardless of who builds the car, the dimensions of one side are never exactly equal to those of the other side and trying to lay out dual panels on a deck lid can drive you crazy, if you attempt to do it by measurement (the scientific way) alone. Yet for those without experienced eyes that can lay out equal dimensions freehand, it's the only choice. Just plan on measuring, taping, remeasuring, and moving the tape several times until it looks right. At this point, the chances are good that the two sets of measurements won't match, but if it looks right, that's where the action is. One important hint: use the car's body lines, even chop them up a bit if you have to, but don't ignore them in deciding what size paneling to use and

Custom Paint Ideas

where to place it. Done properly, you can improve what the boys in Detroit did; ignore the lines and you'll just have an eyesore on your hands.

Once you've laid out all the panels and taped them as we've shown you, cover them with masking paper. Do a neat job and keep the paper as smooth and taut as possible to prevent overspray or a puddle of candy color from working its way down un-

der the tape and onto the panel. At the same time, press the tape down well all over. When masking is completed, it's a good idea to shoot the interpanel color as soon as possible, because if it's left too long, the tape will loosen by itself, and even if you remember to go over it again, pressing it down before you spray, its best adhesion qualities disappear with passing time.

The gun you use will depend pretty much on your own personal preference; Walt sprays with a Binks 69

equipped with the standard No. 69 nozzle, as he feels that a larger gun shoots too much paint, and leads to the possibility of streaking and other problems. For our project, candy red was mixed with clear and color thinner until the right depth of color was achieved, and then the mixture was sprayed over the unmasked surface. Twenty coats of the candy red and a final, even coat of clear brought the panel trim to perfection.

Unmasking can be a tricky project; if you lift the tape while the candy

HOW-TO: Panels and Decorations

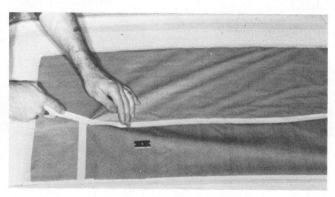

1. While surface preparation is being completed up front, Walt begins laying out the panel shapes for the deck lid using ¼-inch masking tape.

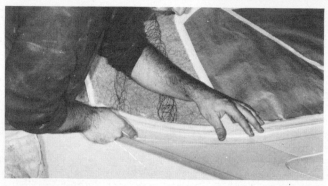

2. Good eyesight and judgement are greater assets here than a ruler. Precise measurement does not necessarily mean that the finished job will look right to the eye.

3. Walt uses small pieces of masking paper to cover the panels and then he tapes the seams carefully so that overspray or paint puddles won't seep underneath.

4. Candy red is sprayed on one coat after another to build the panel outline to the color intensity required. A final coat of clear covers everything.

5. After drying, masking paper is removed and finish wet sanded before the reverse masking is started. Walt sneaked some gold veiling when we weren't looking.

6. Special care is taken with the reverse masking operation since the candy red color must be totally covered before the application of panel fade can begin.

lacquer is still drying, the paint surface is rubbery and you may tear large sections off while unmasking. But wait too long and the edge becomes too brittle; lifting the tape then causes a very ragged edge. One hour seemed to be just right (temperature and humidity play a role here) and the few ragged edges that did occur (some always will) were easily sanded out smooth. Let the candy lacquer dry good and hard (about 4 hours minimum) before attempting the reverse masking. Otherwise you'll run the risk of lifting the candy surface with the tape when unmasking and that makes a horrible mess.

Reverse mask the candy surface in the same way you originally masked the panel and then spray the color fade on the panel by concentrating on the outer edge and gradually working your way in toward the center in layers, applying fewer and thinner coats as you move inward. Work slowly and when your color fade is just the right intensity, shoot a coat of clear and let everything dry. Un-

masking is as tricky here as it was once before, because this time you have two surfaces that can be damaged if you're not careful, and trying to touch up the resulting mess can be fatal for the novice painter.

If you're going to decorate the panel as we did, do so before removing the masking. Let the clear dry for about 15 mins. before starting work on the panel. Since ours was to contain roses, Walt used a pressure feed gun and a special veiling nozzle to apply a veiling that would simulate a

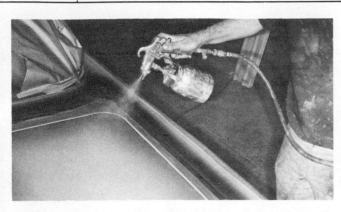

7. Candy pink panel fades are applied by working inward from the outer edge, with fewer and thinner coats used as the center of the panel is approached.

8. Veiling is tricky and requires practice before you commit gun to panel, as any change in air pressure or distance from gun to surface can alter the pattern.

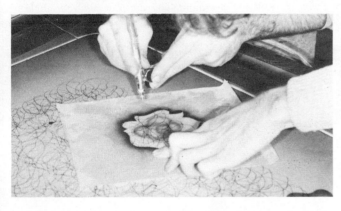

9. Rose application is done with template and airbrush. Masking tape will not hold the template tightly enough for sharp outline, so it is held by hand.

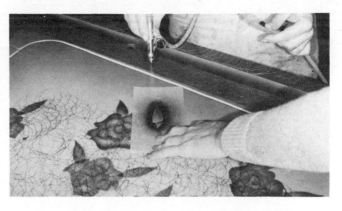

10. After scattering roses on the vine of veiling, do the same with different sizes of leaves. Use two or more shades for leaves to add variety and realism.

11. The rose pattern springs to life when it is outlined with black lacquer. Then Walt adds further realism with the black lacquer twining he's applying.

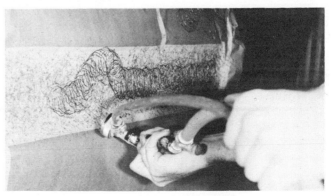

12. After the cobwebbing has dried, veiling is done with the same equipment. Lower air pressure makes the difference between the two effects with a veiling gun.

Custom Paint Ideas

rose vine. If no decorative effects are planned, remove the reverse masking carefully and you'll have a color fade away panel floating in a sea of solid candy color. At this point, everything is done, but come along with us as we consider panel decoration next; this is great for further emphasis.

DECORATIVE EFFECTS

As mentioned, our panel was veiled for effect before applying the roses. Veiling is done with a thick, syrupy lacquer made especially for the technique. It's mixed with color toner and sprayed under pressure from 18 to 30 lbs., depending upon the effect you want. The veiling nozzle spins the thick mixture out without atomizing it, and the resulting effect is that of a wiggly stream of paint. The size of veiling depends upon the distance the gun is held from the surface and how slowly you move it. The effect varies from that of a thin rope (fast movement) to a squiggly-like mud puddle (practically no movement).

Before applying veiling to the surface, shoot some on a scrap panel or masking paper to adjust pressure, determine the correct distance and pace of movement for the effect desired. Once you've shot the veiling, let everything dry and then carefully remove the reverse masking. For further effect, make an outline template of whatever you choose for decoration. Use thin cardboard that can be bent around a contour surface if nec-

HOW-TO: GOP Art

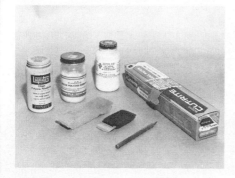

1. Tweety the Painter of Newhall, Calif. gave us some expert advice on using the Gop-Art technique. Here are all the materials you'll need to start.

2. Using Liquitex Gloss Polymer, our friend brushes six coats on the artwork that he has cut from a magazine. Wait at least 25 minutes between coats.

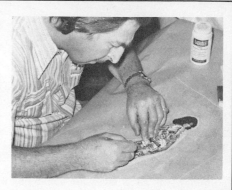

3. When the six coats (applied in alternating directions, of course) have dried overnight, you can cut out your picture with a razor or X-Acto.

4. Place the art in lukewarm water. Soak until the paper backing comes off with light rubbing. The thicker the paper, the longer you soak it.

5. After the decal has been dried flat—overnight—between two sheets of waxed paper, brush the backside with another coat of polymer medium.

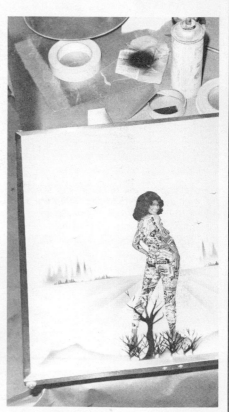

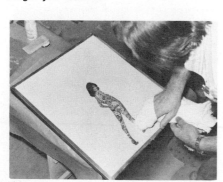

6. Carefully locate the decal on the panel you want, squeezing out the air bubbles as you go, and wipe off excess polymer with a damp rag.

7. Once your decal has dried in place, you can add any artwork or other paint ideas you like. Tweety is spraying through stencils here.

8. When finished, cover with clear spray. Apply light; then build up. Tweety uses polyester or epoxy for clear; warns to watch for air bubbles.

essary, and then cut the outline with a sharp razor blade or X-Acto knife for good clean lines.

The template is held in place (taping won't work here if you want sharp lines), and an airbrush is used to outline it. With our roses, Walt began by spraying a small center spot of color. After outlining the rose, the center spot was used to build color detail and shading. The roses were scattered on the vine and then templates of various size leaves were used to increase the realistic effect. Roses were sprayed in burgundy, pink, and red; leaves were sprayed in yellow and green.

Colors were mixed 50/50 of toner and color thinner, with just a dash of retarder to slow down drying a bit. This can be mixed in clean baby food jars for convenience in pouring into the small airbrush cup, but if you drop one, the broken glass makes a real mess. A better idea is to use a standard paper coffee cup, but pick the one you use with care. Styrofoam cups disintegrate completely and im-

mediately under the action of color thinner. If the cup has a waxed surface, everything goes well but the paint will never dry; the thinner dissolves and absorbs the wax, which will completely inhibit drying action.

Once the roses and leaves have been sprayed, outline them by hand with a brush and a mixture of black lacquer, retarder, and thinner. Outlining snaps the pattern to the surface and adds detail, as leaf veins and rose petals are brought out with the black lacquer. By the time you've fin-

HOW-TO: Acrylustrations

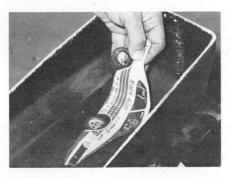

1. Use a picture from a magazine that has good quality coated glossy paper. We goofed; tape the page down to be sprayed before cutting out a picture.

2. Mix Metalflake clear acrylic with Metalflake lacquer thinner at 50/50 ratio. Steve Young of Crazy Painters in Bellflower, Calif. did job for us.

3. Spray surface of picture with 2 or 3 coats of clear. Now you see how we goofed; picture wants to blow away. Cut out picture after clear is dry.

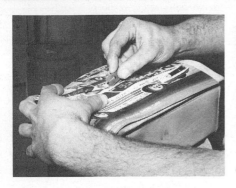

4. After coating is good and dry, the cut out picture is soaked in a warm water bath to remove the backing paper. Type of paper will vary time.

5. Rub backing with thumbs; the paper will eventually peel off. Note weak color saturation after white paper was removed; white ink was too thin.

6. With paper removed you now have a decal. Weak white areas will allow color of mounting surface to show through. Consider when choosing pix.

7. We solved problem by air brushing a thin coat of white paint on the back of our decal to give the colors an opaque white background as before.

8. Front half of decal has been backcoated with white paint; note how color has been improved. This will be a necessary step with light pictures.

9. Apply light coat of clear to back of decal and mounting surface. Place decal in position, squeege lightly, seal with several coats of clear.

Custom Paint Ideas

ished the lacquer outlines, everything is dry enough to shoot a couple coats of clear for protection, and you're finished.

While lace panels have gone out of style for all but the vanners, cobwebbing is very much alive and continues to take new and different forms as painters experiment with the technique. The cobweb effect is basically achieved by spraying acrylic paint that has not been thinned. Depending upon the manufacturer, there's a difference in the thickness of acrylics, but while it is possible to thicken a can just by leaving it uncapped for awhile, don't give in to the temation to cut the paint when straining it into the gun cup, even though the straining will take considerable time.

The type of gun used is not too vital, but you should use a large nozzle/air cap combination. Any paint equipment sales or rental store will know what you require when told that the paint must be sprayed very thick and at low pressures. The amount of air pressure used depends entirely upon the effect desired and the area to be covered, but 15 to 20 lbs. is a good starting point. If covering a very large area, the pressure can be increased to widen the fan coverage but not too much, because the higher pressure tends to break up the paint and ruin the cobweb effect.

Run a few experiments with the equipment before committing your ideas to the panel. Moving the gun in different patterns will give different types of webbing; overlapping strokes will give other types, as will varying the distance from nozzle to surface. To get just the effect you want, practice with different movements, distances, and manners of application; once you hit upon the one that pleases you, move onto panel and continue handling gun in same way.

Speed of application is vital in cobwebbing. With the base coat ready, apply a final coat of clear with a slow thinner or even a retarder added. This coat must remain wet while the webbing is applied, and so speed is of the essence. Spray the webbing onto the wet clear and let it dry thoroughly before adding the top coats of clear. If you don't, the wet webbing smears and runs when more clear is added. Build the finish with clear acrylic and do the final finishing as you would with Metalflake.

Just about anything can be done with the web effect and, recently, Walt has taken to applying cobwebbing with a veiling lacquer and veiling gun. This is done by simply increasing the air pressure to around 40 lbs. and tinkering with the fan adjustment

until just the right point is hit upon. Variations such as this have helped keep cobwebbing a current favorite with the "in" crowd.

MURAL/CARTOON APPLICATION

While cartoons and murals also made their appearance on the custom scene courtesy of the current van craze, they're now found on insert panels of Mustangs. Corvettes, and other street machines as well as custom show cars, and variations such as three-dimensional nudes have already made their appearance. Although the techniques used to create these two different effects on an automotive panel are quite similar in nature, only the mural painting seems to be original in nature, and so a word of caution is in order here.

Cartoon characters like Yosemite Sam and Snoopy, ever-popular favorites these days, are all copyrighted; transferring their likeness to your car is illegal without permission of the copyright owner. If the thought of the Roadrunner dashing across your hood appeals to you, consider the small, authorized decals before emblazoning a painted likeness for all to see; you can bet that Chrysler paid Warner Brothers a healthy sum for the use of that particular character.

Other than subject matter, the primary difference between these two effects rests in the method of application. Although the tools are the same, cartooning is done primarily with a lettering brush and bulletin colors, with the air brush reserved for creating detail and adding a dimensional effect to the flat character by shading. Murals are created mainly with an airbrush and bulletin colors. The use of the lettering brush here is to create small sharp details like birds flying over ships in the ocean, or trees bending in the breeze.

The application of either is pretty permanent, since they must be done directly on the panel surface. While you can shoot a coat of clear first, any red or purple colors you might use are likely to stain and ruin the

1. The traditionalists among flame enthusiasts prefer the short, fat flame licks such as here; and they seeem to look best on older vehicles.

2. This simple, but effective stripe on a Datsun pickup was done with one color and creative use of ¼-in. tape.

3. The shadowed strobe stripes, often seen in a band around the belt of a custom van, are easily created by spraying around cardboard cutouts and objects, such as this round paint strainer. A simple technique but it can work well with the right colors.

entire effect. And once you've applied the mural or cartoon to the panel surface and the paint has set (it can be completely removed with solvent during the first 24 hours), the only satisfactory way to remove it is by sanding off the entire decoration down to the bare metal. With care, it is possible to sand the design off without damaging the original finish, but when the panel is sprayed to restore its color balance with the rest of the car, a bas-relief of the design will reappear in the new finish, as the bulletin colors really grip into the paint base underneath.

PIN STRIPING

Probably one of the reasons that pin striping never seems to go out of style is that it invariably gives a touch of style to any automobile, as long as the basic rule of not violating body lines is observed. Another reason, of course, is that applying a pin stripe to a car is inexpensive when compared to other forms of exterior customizing. Like pattern painting, pin striping also came roaring back into prominence not too long ago with the van movement. California new car dealers immediately embraced it, especially those who sell import lines and mini-pickups. Bolt-on accessories for both were and still are limited in type and variety, and customers flipped over a simple pin stripe added to the rather plain looking imports.

The movement spread to the domestic minicars like Pinto and Vega, and pin striping is now so popular that new cars arriving from the fac-

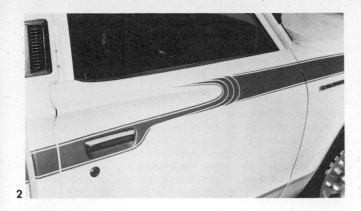

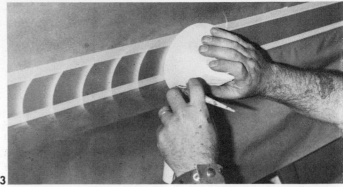

tory carry at least a single or double stripe applied in Detroit; dealers simply wipe these optional stripes off with lacquer thinner and then send the car back to their own striper, who redoes the striping with somewhat less conservatism. In their enthusiasm, some dealers even forget to scrub the extra charge for the factory striping from the sticker price when they tack on the additional charge for their own efforts, and the customer winds up paying two charges for one stripe.

While pin striping is one of the simplest customizing paint techniques, it's also one of the most difficult to do correctly. Actually, there are two different basic styles of pin striping; the simple panel outline and the more stylistic, flowing form that accentuates the car as a total entity. Most pin striping provided by dealers is of the panel outline variety and armed with an aerosol can of lacquer and a roll of die-cut striping tape, the weekend painter can duplicate the effect at home with ease. This is done by simply laying out the tape to achieve the desired pattern and then removing the center third of the tape to expose the area to be striped. A few shakes of the aerosol can, a squirt or two of lacquer held a few inches from the surface and you've run a neat, clean pin stripe along a panel. Let it flash off and then coat with clear lacquer for protection.

Any overspray can be wiped off with a cloth dampened in lacquer thinner, and providing you let everything set an hour or two before removing the other two pieces of tape, you've got a good job. But don't spray the paint on too thick or you'll have a messy problem or two develop. If it's too thick, the fresh paint may run under or over the tape and give problems. A thick coat that does not run is no better; once you start waxing the car, wax will build up along the edge, giving the stripe a chipped appearance. When you try to remove the excess wax, the paint stripe will actually chip. Spray just enough for an even color coat and stop at that point.

Those who make a living striping cars use a graphic art finish known as bulletin colors, which were mentioned in connection with murals and cartoons. These are designed primarily for application on outdoor signs to give sharp lettering on vertical surfaces. Bulletin colors have a brilliant color quality, solid hiding properties and a quick set-to-touch time that keeps runs to a minimum. But don't let anyone mislead you; while panel pin striping can be done in the backyard, the stylistic, flowing pin stripe is an art like any other form of custom painting.

Unless you have an artistic flair or twist in your nature, you'd better stick to the aerosol can and die-cut striping tape and panel outlining . . . but we thought you'd like to see how a pro pin stripes a car with nothing more than a camel hair sword brush and an occasional strip of masking tape used as a guideline. A striper who works in this manner has two things going for him that the average auto enthusiast lacks. He can visualize exactly what he wants to achieve and once he sets brush to surface, it's a non-stop process from beginning to end. In addition to the ability to preconceive the pattern, he has a talent or knack with that floppy little brush that allows him to work freehand, using just a finger as a pivot point. And if you don't think that's a talent, just give it a try.

CUSTOM COLOR STRIPING

OK, we've shown you the latest in painting techniques that can help you to express that dash of individuality that separates your car from all the others of the same make, model, and color on the road today. But perhaps you don't really care to go that far down the road in placing your own personality on the hood of your car for the whole world to see. Perhaps all you really want (or can afford) to do is a stripe down each side, like that available from the showroom floor. If so, this is the easiest of all to do, and we can help you here by passing along a few hints on how to design and apply that custom touch

while saving a bundle in the process.

After all, dealers pay an average of $45 to the painter for that type of work and as most at least double the cost to the new car purchaser, what we're about to discuss can run you $90 or more off the showroom floor, plus the finance charge. For that kind of money, you can afford to rent an airbrush and spray gun and do the job yourself on a Saturday afternoon. On that basis, the chances are good that your per-hour savings will turn out to be the best wage rate you've earned in several moons. So read on and count the bread you can save.

Probably the most difficult aspect for the non-professional painter is in developing a type of stripe that really helps the car's appearance. Remember our oft-mentioned caution about using instead of destroying the car's body lines, and try running a strip of masking tape along the front fender to the rear. Try to follow the panel contours without breaking any major styling lines. Now run another strip of tape along the bottom of that contour parallel with the top strip. This will give you a basic pattern of approach and let you see where a flourish or two can be added for effect. Generally speaking, the stripe should get larger as it progresses toward the rear of the car; this helps to accentuate the car's appearance of forward motion while at rest and lets the stripe flow with the rest of the body design.

Chances are good that bringing the stripe to a point near the front of the car will add to the effect you're seeking and you can add a flourish by running it up and over the roof to connect with the stripe on the other side. Your stripe may be a solid line or even a broken one; you can add a scallop or two, or insert any other individual touch that does not detract from the end result. Once you've settled on a basic design after suitable experimentation, the next task is to lay it out exactly on the car's surface. But before beginning this, wash down the general area to be painted with a good grade of wax and grease remover and a clean cloth. As with any

Custom Paint Ideas

paint work, this surface preparation is extremely important to the success of the end result.

Laying out a basic horizontal stripe is best done by measurement; you won't find enough variation in panels here to make eyeballing it necessary as you'll be working across several panels in a narrow band. Use a ruler and felt-tip pen to lay out guide marks for the tape and then double-check your measurements at each step along the way, as a ¼-in. deviation from one end of the stripe to the other can really foul things up for you. After laying out the pattern and

taping it, the next step is that of masking. Complete masking is not necessary in this case, since you're not going to shoot that much paint, but a good 18 ins. on either side of the stripe should be covered. If you should also decide on a hood and/or deck lid pattern to complement the side stripe, you'll wind up masking most of the car anyway. As in masking for any other type of paint work, all seams should be secured with tape and all tape should be pressed down well. A photographic print roller is handy for this, because you can roll the tape throughly to make sure you'll get a clean, sharp edge and the rubber roller will not harm the paint surface.

A plain stripe doesn't have quite enough snap to really accentuate the car, so you can add a simple pin stripe to your design. The pin stripe will be sprayed with an airbrush and a suitable contrasting color to that planned for the basic stripe. If you really want to economize in renting equipment, you can shoot the pin stripe with a spray bomb just as easily. Use acrylic enamel and mix the paint 70/30 with reducer for an ideal spraying consistency. Airbrush the pin stripe, going over each section several times until you've got enough coats on to bring up the color bright and full. Then clean your equipment while allowing the paint to dry for an hour or two. If you really want to be

HOW-TO: Mural Painting

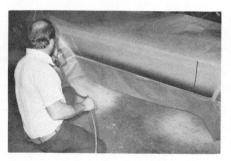

1. Our mural how-to was shot at the Jalin Custom Painting shop in Van Nuys, Calif. by Orv Dittman. Here Orv has cleaned and masked off a panel.

2. Tape seams over the door are cut and the door jamb masked off to prevent any overspray from finding its way inside. Mask inside of door also.

3. Masking paper is secured around the outside of the panel area to prevent any overspray from settling on the dark brown metallic finish of the Pinto.

4. Orv begins the mural application by shooting a light or mist coat of dark blue across the top two-thirds of the panel—this is the first of seven colors.

5. Once the dark blue has "flashed off," Orv then shoots another mist coat, but this time with powder blue, taking care to create a blochy effect.

6. Now a piece of tape and masking paper is run across the panel length in a random up-down fashion; this will create the horizon line, as you'll see.

7. Two shades of brown are sprayed, one mist coat at a time. When the masking tape and paper are removed from the panel, you have a horizon line.

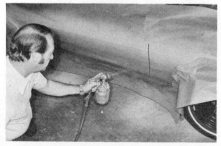

8. Mist coats of orange, yellow and white follow in quick succession, creating what looks like an unsightly mess to the uninitiated eye, but all to a purpose.

9. Because Orv does not tape his template in place he'll require the help of assistants to position and hold it while he works with gun and airbrush.

on the safe side, let it set overnight, because our next step will be to run ½-inch masking tape over the pin stripe area, leaving just the basic stripe exposed.

Once this is done, you're ready to shoot the basic stripe. Start spraying at one end and follow the stripe right along to its end. If yours is a continuous stripe, so much the better, as you can move right around the car in a 360-degree motion. Two to three coats of acrylic enamel should do the trick; commercial shops spraying the same kind of stripe for dealerships only shoot two. After the final coat has set, remove the masking tape that covers the pin stripe and then shoot a couple coats of clear over

both to protect the finished work.

Wait about an hour before removing the tape, but use the utmost caution if you have to see your work that soon. A better idea is to let everything set for several hours or even overnight before the unveiling. You won't have the same unmasking problem here as when shooting candy colors on panels, because your stripe won't be as thick. Acrylic enamel doesn't have the same rubbery drying quality as candy lacquer, but it's still a good idea to unmask carefully, regardless of how long you've let the finished paint set. Peel a corner of the masking tape free and pull it at an angle in the opposite direction of the freshly painted sur-

face. Check your finished work; should you find any flaws such as a chip on the door edge, a camel hair brush and a dab of paint can be used to touch up.

So now that you know where the action is, it's time to step outside and take a good look at that plain jane you're driving. We have given you enough hints so that it can be transformed into almost anything you want to make it. And if you want to, but don't dare—take it to the Wizard. He'll even let you watch as he weaves his magic spell. Whichever way you decide, there's one thing for certain—the days of drab looking cars have gone and almost everyone is shouting, ''Long live color!''

10. The basic outline of the desert scene is shot with the spray gun using a narrow pattern spray. If you use aerosol cans, be sure to check the nozzle size.

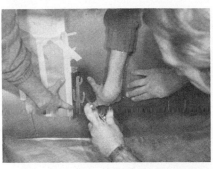

11. Aerosol cans are available with either wide or narrow nozzle patterns and can be used in place of the gun and airbrush, which Orv uses for detail.

12. A mountain and waterfall are added to the rear of the panel scene using a separate template. The gun creates the pattern line; airbrush the detail.

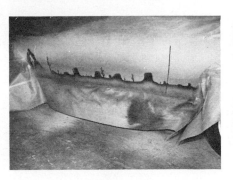

13. The mural is now allowed to dry, as Orv has finished all but the fine detail in less than five minutes; it takes longer to change paints than to spray them.

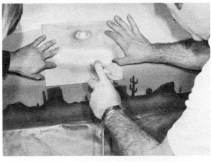

14. Clouds are placed at random using the airbrush and white paint. Shadowing their edges with blacks and oranges adds dimension to their presence.

15. Birds are added in the sky by using white and then black alternately; spray the bird pattern with white and then add a little black at each wing tip, etc.

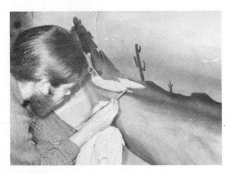

16. Now the detailing is added with a lettering brush and bulletin colors. Plants, rushing water and details of the rocks are done by hand.

17. After a few coats of clear for protection, the mural is finished and the tape can be removed to see the overall effect. Here, on dark brown metallic as a body color, the desert mural scene seems to work particularly well, and brings this Pinto its share of admiring looks.

Spray-Can Trickery

Professional results every time with proper color selection and application will stamp you as an aerosol acrobat.

I doubt that there is even *one* of our many readers who hasn't, at one time or another, used aerosol spray paint. For the nonprofessional painter, it is unquestionably the most common method of applying paint to any type of surface. But that doesn't mean that professional results can't be obtained with the spray-can paints. Through careful surface preparation and application, and the proper use of colors, almost anyone can obtain beautiful results. Take, for example, that stripe or panel you've been wanting to put on the side of your van, or the tank and fenders of your bike that you'd like to paint some wild exotic color. And speaking of wild colors, you can get just about any of them in spray cans these days—metalflakes, pearls, candies, etc.—take your pick.

Aerosol spray equipment has improved dramatically in recent years and is available in three basic types, with differing variations of these types produced by many manufacturers. One common type is the all-in-one can which contains both the propellant and paint in one compact unit. Another example is a kit with three different spray cans, a base coat, a second (candy or metalflake) coat, and a third can of clear to protect the results. The third type contains an aerosol pack and an auxiliary, integrated receptacle or jar for holding paint which may be obtained in bulk and diluted accordingly.

The bulk of sprayable paint mediums offered today which are applicable to custom panel painting are acrylics. Acrylics or acrylic lacquers are the ultimate in custom paint mediums: easy to apply, colorful and fast-drying. The types of spray can acrylic mediums available to date are the following:

Solid or Opaque Colors—These may come as standard colors or in the guise of touch-up auto paint in a full range of colors. Current manufacturers of these opaque mediums include *Tempo, Martin Senour* and *Lubritech,* to name a few.

Candies—Candy is a transparent color medium which offers an exciting finish with rich depth and color saturation, governed by the number of coats applied. A base coat must initially be applied under the candy, which serves to enhance the candy effect, adding to the richness of the translucence. Varied compatible or contrasting colors may be added under the candy coat to heighten visual effects. Candies are a bit more difficult to apply due to their transparent nature, and the margin for error in application is virtually nil. They are available in spray can form from a variety of manufacturers.

Metallics and Flakes—Many sophisticated and opulent metallics are available today which give the paint a glitter that is both dazzling and eye-catching. *Glitter Flake* by Lubritech is an excellent metallic and is obtainable in all-in-one spray cans. For paint buffs who dig the richer, more metallic Metalflake finishes, complete metalflaking kits are available and may be obtained from Metalflake, Inc., Box 950, Haverhill, Mass. 01830, and Cal Custom, 23011 South Wilmington Ave., Carson, Calif. 90745. The flake application utilizing these excellent kits is simple and foolproof, enabling one to realize a finished job akin to that produced with professional spray equipment.

Pearls—A few pearlescent paints are available today in spray cans, one of which is manufactured by Metalflake. Pearlescents are made up of special color-radiating iridescent particles suspended in clear acrylic. This paint transmits rich iridescence which is extremely lustrous. Pearl is usually applied over a ground or base coat and can be obtained in various colors. Combining pearls with candies broadens the color and effect spectrum.

Vreeble—*Vreeble* by Metalflake is a paneling medium unlike any other and is distinguished by its lightning-like crackle finish. *Vreeble* is sprayed straight from the spray can in the same manner as with standard spray can acrylics. As it dries, the "crack-

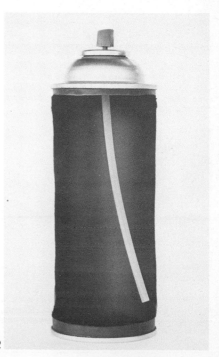

ing'' results, caused by the inclusion in the paint solution of a common acrylic ingredient which inhibits shrinkage. The degree of cracking can be controlled. The thinner the coat applied, the smaller the crackle pattern. Heavy coating results in larger cracking effects.

SPRAY CAN APPLICATION

First, decide what sort of effect you wish to achieve. If you cannot create a design in your mind, look at pictures of van paint jobs you like and try to duplicate one which strikes your fancy. Then mask off the panel area to be painted with tape and masking paper. Tacked-on newspaper or brown wrapping paper also serve well as large-area masking mediums. A common practice in van painting is the masking off of a central horizontal strip on the van, usually about 18 ins. in width. This area must then be sanded down, starting with 220-grit paper, dry; breaking through the top paint coating or layer and vigorously sanding into the factory paint job. It is imperative that all the factory top coating be removed, as it may contain silicone or wax protectives which will interfere with acrylic overpainting and ruin the paint job applied. It is advisable to use a primer-sealer after sanding and prior to custom painting. (NOTE: Enamel paint and primer can be applied over lacquer. But if lacquer paint or primer is sprayed over enamel, its lacquer-thinner suspension agent will sometimes attack the enamel and cause it to wrinkle and blister. Therefore, if your base paint is enamel, you'd better spray it with several coats of paint sealer before applying lacquer over it. If there's any doubt as to the type of paint you're about to cover with lacquer, we suggest you conduct a small patch test on some obscure area first.

Since few primer-sealer solutions are available in spray cans, one may be forced to buy a primer-sealer in bulk form and apply it with a spray pack. An efficient primer-sealer is offered by Ditzler (DL-1970) in neutral gray, ready to spray, properly diluted for ease of application. Regular primers are readily obtained in all-in-one spray cans, and will suffice—provided that the surface underneath is properly prepared. In a nutshell, proper surface preparation includes: (1) Sanding—to give the surface a roughness or tooth while breaking down the protective top coat glaze. (2) An overall wash with *Prep-Sol, Cle-Sol* or similar wax and oil eradicating medium—which can be applied with a rag; then a dry-off period, followed by a secondary surface washdown with warm water. (3) Application of a primer, preferably a primer-sealer.

Once the primer has been applied and has dried, check it for scratches, dirt, dust, etc., and if any surface imperfections (including paint runs, sags, orange peeling) are apparent, sand lightly with 400-grit sandpaper,

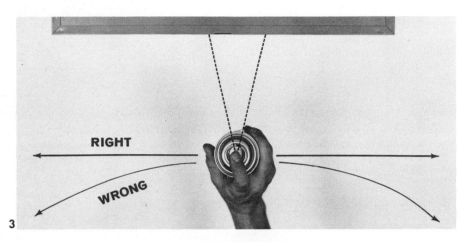

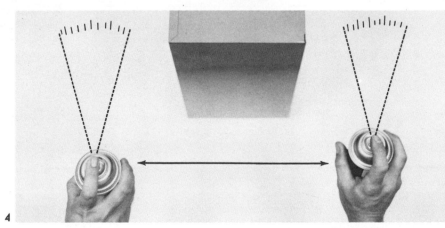

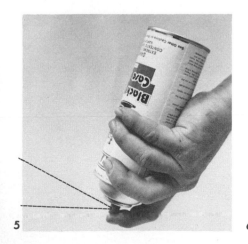

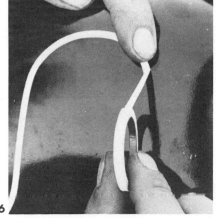

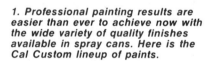

1. Professional painting results are easier than ever to achieve now with the wide variety of quality finishes available in spray cans. Here is the Cal Custom lineup of paints.

2. As shown in this cutaway, most spray cans have curved siphon tubes. If a near-empty can fails to spray when tilted, turn the nozzle 90° or 180° and try again—the end of the curved tube may not be in the paint.

3. To ensure uniform paint thickness, the nozzle should be moved parallel to the surface (except as noted in the next caption) for uniform effect.

4. While doing long panels that can't be covered with one sweep, ''arc'' away from the surface at the end of each sweep to avoid a double thickness of paint where the sweeps overlap.

5. After use, invert the can and trigger its nozzle for a second or two. The end of the siphon tube will be uncovered, allowing the propellant to purge the nozzle of paint which could dry up and clog the nozzle.

6. Narrow masking tape, available at art supply stores, is the friend of trick painters, both amateur and pro. It can be used for tight-radius bends such as in flames, but use regular-width tape for straight line taping.

Spray-Can Trickery

wet, to final-finish the primed surface and prepare it for base coat color painting.

Patience is all-important. If you spot a run, wait till it dries, sand it down as described and reprimer. The color or base coat is then applied with the spray can (or pack), holding the spray tool a distance of 12 to 18 ins. from the surface to be painted.

To apply the paint, depress the finger spray-valve tip and come across the surface in a sweeping motion, letting off on the valve after passing over the painted area. Make the passes evenly, from side to side, with slightly overlapping spray strokes, until the area displays an even, solid coating of paint. Each pass should be allowed to "flash" or surface-dry before the next consecutive coat is administered. If one coat is laid on using horizontal strokes, the following

coat should be applied utilizing vertical strokes. This assists in assuring evenness in color and coating. If by chance a run, sag or pebbling (orange peeling) occurs, allow an hour or so drying time and then sand out the blemish(es) and recoat. These minor goofs can be remedied if you are spraying opaque colors. If you run or sag with candy, you've had the course. You must take the paint off down to the base coat or primer and start anew. Runs and sags are

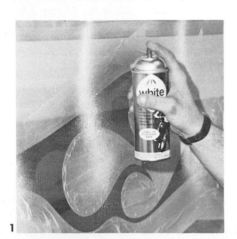

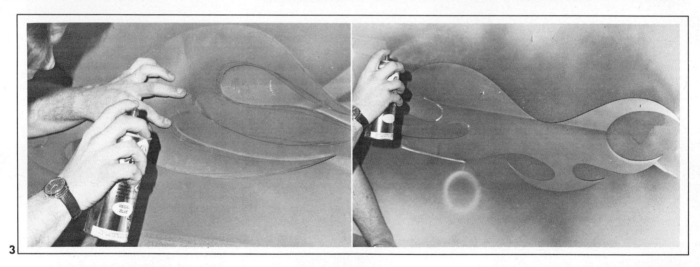

caused by holding the can too close to the surface, moving the can too slowly or by trying to apply too much paint without allowing the previous coat to "flash." Surface orange peel or pebbling manifests itself when the can is held too far from the surface. Practice on a piece of cardboard or waste metal until you achieve proper control and rhythm.

FINISHING

Assuming that all transpires well in the execution of the overall paint job, and the painting is completed in terms of color, design, composition, etc., the painted panel (after a top-coat application of clear acrylic) should be allowed to dry and harden for at least 48 hours. For maximum effect and a superglossy fine finish, acrylics require a final fine-sanding before the surface is fully rubbed out. Final sanding also does away with surface imperfections such as dust and dirt particles which may have settled onto the surface. The last sanding is done with 600-grit wet sandpaper; surface sludge and residue which accumulates is chased down with water-soaked sponges or rags. The final step, rubbing out the surface, can be done by hand or by machine (buffer). A rag, slightly damp, or a lamb's wool buffing bonnet is impregnated with rubbing compound and vigorously applied to the surface until the waxy compound dries—to a lucid, glasslike finish.

1. Once your pattern is masked off and scuffed, spray with whatever paints you desire, but remember that both candies and pearls require a base coat like white, gold or silver.

2. You can get as tricky as you want. By repeatedly masking patterns that overlap and then spraying them, you can provide dimension with layers of different colors contrasting.

3. Whether you just want to keep both side of your car the same or plan to do trick paint for others, you can use cardboard cutouts of some design elements, either spraying around them or through them.

4. When your trickery is all done and the edges are pinstriped, no one will ever know that you did it yourself, or that it wasn't done with a spraybooth and expensive gun.

5. Besides the canned trick paints available from Metalflake and others, there are also spray-paks with cups that are removeable so you can spray any available paint with them. Thus, you're not limited to what your local paint store carries in spray cans.

6. Sperex Corporation, the pioneer of high-temperature paints, now has numerous colors and finishes in their vast line of "VHT" areosol paints.

7. The Starburst enamels are from Nason Automotive Finishes, a division of Fuller O'Brien Corp. Two shades of primer are offered, along with the solids, metallics and candy flake.

8. Sem Products, Inc. manufactures the "Aerolac" paints. Automotive-quality acrylic lacquers, they are available in lead-free colors of mini-flake, pearl and candy finishes.

5

6

7

8

Two-Part Paints

Carport queens belong to yesteryear; for today's action, jet-plane paints have swooped to the rescue.

There once was a time when you could tell whose street rod was a bona fide carport queen. It was the one with the fewest rock chips on its front axle—because its owner never drove the little darling unless the weather was clear and dry and the roads free of debris. On the other side of the spectrum was the fool with the fuel. This motor moron was so careless with the nitro and alky that the paint on his digger looked as if it had come out second best in a battle with an acid tank. As for Freddy Flatbottom, the stroke with his custom-painted boat, it would take only two trips to the river before his dandy candy had faded off into the sunset. But all that can be changed now, thanks to the glistening material that covers commercial jet aircraft.

About 10 years ago—15 if you lump in epoxies—a totally new type of paint system was introduced. The prime market for the material was the various airline companies which were replacing their piston-driven airliners with the then-new commercial jets. The products were the first of the two-part paints, a system developed to combat a number of paint longevity problems caused by the pistonless aircraft. It seems that the new fire-resistant hydraulic fluids, introduced because of their safety features were lifting the existing alkyd enamels right off the aluminum. Further aggravating the problem was the fact that these planes were flying higher, faster and longer than ever before, and the paints couldn't cope. The higher altitudes brought on fade from ultraviolet light and 50-below-zero temperatures. Faster landings and takeoffs sandblasted surfaces and affected panel expansion-contraction rates. To top it off, longer periods between major overhauls increased the chances for nicks, scratches and corrosive liquid contamination. So here was a need to develop a new type of paint—a finish that was tough, durable, fade-resistant, fuelproof and one that would have a high gloss to decrease dirt buildup and lower wind drag. The final answer came in two cans.

TWO-PART SECRET

What generally constitutes a two-part paint system is an acrylic-type enamel mixed with a catalyst. The binders and solvents within the paint are specifically formulated to mix with the catalyst, making it unwise to try to crossbreed the various paint systems. In other words, don't combine Sherwin-Williams' Polasol catalyst with Bostik-Finch's Cat-A-Last polyurethane base or you'll be sorry.

In the meantime, the paint is cured by the chemical reaction between the base and its catalyst. It usually takes the epoxies a couple of hours to dry to the touch. Should the epoxy be used as a filler in fiberglass, it must be left overnight to dry before sanding. Generally, polyurethanes will dry to the touch in about an hour and a half and should be allowed to sit approximately 4 to 6 hours before they can be masked. However, the polyurethanes won't reach full hardness for up to 7 days after application.

As you might have guessed, epoxies and polyurethanes are not one and the same. Epoxies tend to be primers and fillers. They are formulated to provide excellent adhesion qualities, as well as to fill surface imperfections. Naturally, those epox-

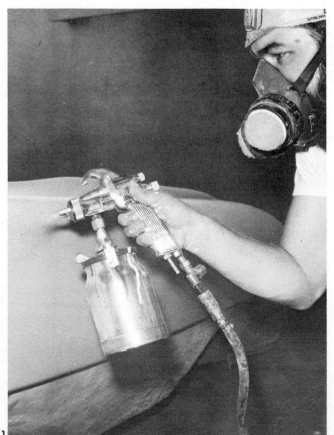

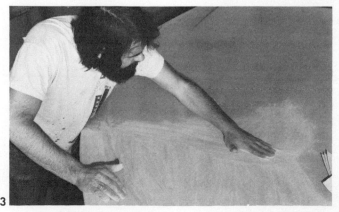

ies which possess good filling abilities are perfect for fiberglass and old Ford I-beam axles. Those which are non-filler or corrosion-resistant are used to prime smooth surfaces. Epoxies can also be used as top coats (engines or frames), but they do not have the fade-resistant qualities that polyurethanes have. And epoxies are cheaper to buy, usually costing from $10 to $15 a gallon. It's the pure polyurethanes that are the really impervious systems. They are for top coats and feature all the designed-in characteristics of fade resistance, extremely high gloss, great durability, terrific flexibility, toughness and the ability to ward off the effects of corrosive fuels or liquids.

CAREFUL, NOW!

But the pure polyurethanes do have their drawbacks. First, they are heck-on-wheels to strip. You just don't decide to change your mind midway through painting your car, motorcycle, boat, plane or go-kart, and opt for a different color or finish. The stuff, once it's dried, just won't come off—unless you're willing to expend a considerable amount of elbow grease or some money for a serious session with the chemical paint stripper. You're also faced with a relatively narrow selection of base colors. Now this is generally okay with the street rodders or those enthusiasts who like their paint schemes simple and straightforward. But many of the racers go in for the pop art, glow-biz world of candies, pearls, metallics and flakes, which many of the pure systems don't offer. Then there is the matter of cost. Depending upon color—and reds tend to be the highest—you can expect to pay upwards of $50 a gallon for the top-of-the-line polyurethanes.

Remember now, we're talking about pure polyurethanes and not the less-costly and less-restrictive systems which combine a high-grade acrylic enamel with an add-in catalyst. These two-part paints would be termed the in-betweens. They consist of standard automotive colors, say a '75 Ford blue metallic, which will take on all the polyurethane characteristics when augmented with an accompanying catalyst. Many of the major paint manufacturers offer these systems, but like the pure polyurethanes, they can only be used in conjunction with that particular company's base paint, catalyst, reducer, primer and retarder. No crossbreeding is allowed.

BILL'S BASIC RULES

According to Bill Carter (Carter's Custom Paints, 13218 Burbank Boulevard, Van Nuys, Calif.), two-part paints are just as easy to apply, using the same spraying techniques, as acrylic enamel or lacquer. "Guys tend to stay away from things they don't know about," says bearded Bill, a man who has spent half of his 30 years custom-painting trucks, boats, airplanes and racing cars. "Naturally I want a clean surface, free of any old paint or material that will lift off the new coat. I also want a surface with a good tooth, so I tend to have the frame rails or bodies sandblasted or roughed up to get the paint to really stick to the metal or 'glass."

Throughout the years, Bill has found that the "in-betweens," such as Ditzler's Delstar/Delthane combination, can be applied right over a bare frame without any primer and will ultimately dry so hard that even a hammer blow won't chip it. "Not only that, the stuff dries with an unbelievable gloss, and it really covers and fills surface imperfections, plus offering a vast color selection that my customers demand. When a racer is planning to run nitro and alky in his motor, I use a pure polyurethane clear (like Delclear) to fuelproof colors."

Obviously there are two ways of approaching the job of shooting two-part paints. The easiest is having someone else do it . . . and then there is you, pal! Most professional automobile painters haven't dealt with the material and, consequently, as Carter said, "are leery about using it." Yet there may be a couple of ways out. Although the two-part paints were originally designed for large commercial jets, many of today's private aircraft are covered with polyurethanes. The idea we want to get across is to drop by your local airport and see if any of the painters there can help you out. Another avenue could be the guys who paint the high-rollin' line rigs. Those are the things that seem a mile long when they gutter-ball you on the right. Most of them are also covered by two-part paint systems. And then we can get back to you. Take it from Bill Carter, you *can* do it yourself! But beware of the harmful side effects from the material. Prolonged inhalation and contact with the skin can cause some pretty ugly problems. The government requires that the manufacturers provide a warning on the label if the paint/catalyst is toxic. So read the printed instructions carefully, heed the advice, and proceed with caution—it's your body. Carter uses a special paint spray respirator/filter arrangement because, in his words, "some of the stuff is so nasty that it can foul up your whole breathing system."

1. Bill Carter uses a number of pure polyurethane and epoxy finishes in his boat and race-car painting shop, as well as the easy-to-use two-part paints that are less expensive and come in more colors. Bill recommends a respirator/filter like this when spraying any of these toxic paints.

2. The two-part paints for those on a limited budget combine a standard acrylic enamel with a catalyst agent to harden it. Most major paint shops will sell you these, but they must be mixed exactly as directions read.

3. On 'glass surfaces or car frames, 80-grit sandpaper should be used so the primer will adhere well. Epoxy primer dries hard enough that it can be sanded in 24 hours without fear of future shrinkage ruining job.

4. Use of the "in-between" acrylic enamels allows a wider color choice for trick paint jobs, and can still be covered with a "fuel-proof" clear.

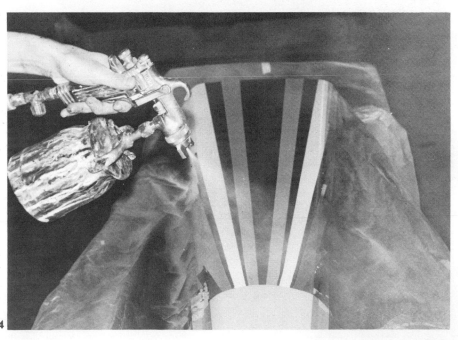

Transfer Film Replacement

The new "woodies" one sees today are really all steel just like a sedan. The wagon look comes from adhesive-backed film. Here's how damage is repaired.

Nostalgia sells well these days, and the '30's and '40's seem to be the most popular periods at the present. As usual, modern technology has been able to recreate the effect at a fraction of what it would cost to duplicate the original and give it a modernized touch at the same time. Everyone seems to recall the "woodies" of the past with great affection, but few would be willing to pay for the real thing and, safety regulations notwithstanding, fewer would risk a high-speed collision in one.

So the ideal compromise—simulate the wood grain effect with pressure-sensitive transfer film and accentuate modern body lines at the same time. Transfer film in patterns has been around for several years, but it's never been quite as popular as on the '72 and '73 models, especially wagons. In the past, its application has been somewhat tricky, partly because of the adhesion problem, but most of the misgivings associated with it in the past seem to have been conquered now—you don't even hear a body or paint man groan when a repair drives up these days. The wit will suggest that perhaps he's been up to his knees in sticky paper for so long that one more doesn't add to the pain, but watching our expert do a 5-minute door panel repair recently convinced us that some advances have really been made.

For those of you who like the bold, adventuresome way of life, we put the entire procedure on film and then elicited some handy tricks of the trade from Larry Davidson, who's fast enough these days to think about trying a panel with one hand tied behind his back. Follow along, and there's no reason why you shouldn't be able to do the same job just as neatly—just forget Larry's elapsed time, and use as much of your *own* as you need to work comfortably without making a mistake.

1. The door handle, top, and bottom chrome strips and clips were removed and the damaged spot repaired with body putty. Hand sanding for smooth body contour finishes preparation for the new transfer film.

2. Some manufacturers supply pre-cut transfer film panels but Larry prefers to use it from a roll as shown. Hang the roll up with masking tape to overlap the door joint by a couple of inches.

3. Use a razor blade to cut along the rear of the door edge as shown. Work carefully and you can duplicate the line of the door exactly. Then move the cut panel 1¼ inch to your right, retape and cut front edge. This provides overlap for door edges.

4,5. Tape is also used as a cutting guide. Start tape correctly by placing the bottom edge so that it's in center of adjacent trim strip. If old transfer panel top isn't perfectly straight, curve tape to conform to old panel by feeling clip holes and running bottom edge of tape through them. Cut along bottom of tape for new panel contour. Do the same to bottom of new panel, but this time, run tape to use top edge for cutting guide. These two cutting tricks allow you to complete the replacement without a template.

6. Remove new transfer panel and masking tape. Rub old panel with a cloth soaked in liquid detergent until you have a nice slippery surface. This will let you position the new panel exactly without worrying about the adhesive sticking.

7. Separate the transfer film from its paper backing. Be careful at this point and pull at the angle shown to avoid stretching film out of shape.

8. By the time the transfer film is positioned, the detergent should be dry enough to let the adhesive take hold. Knowing just the correct amount is secret of fast work. Use heat gun to complete job; go carefully, apply heat evenly and don't stay in one place for more than a few seconds, or film will stretch permanently.

9. Now place the transfer film on the door panel over the damaged area and slide into correct position. Top and bottom should intersect clip holes, with equal overhang at ends.

10. Rubber squeegee is useful in forcing air bubbles from under transfer film surface. By this time, adhesive will have taken over completely from detergent.

11. Heat gun comes in handy to seal transfer film around the door edge. With careful use of gun, you can shrink or expand film to fit a contour perfectly.

12. Without access to a regular heat gun, a light socket with heat lamp or even a ladies' hair drier will serve the same purpose, but don't attempt transfer film application without a source of heat if you expect a perfect job like this. Bolt on chrome, and it's like new.

6

7

9

8

10

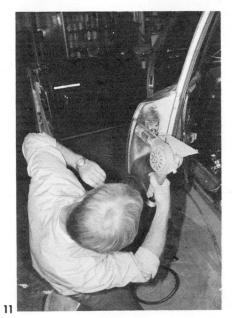

11

12

Auto Cosmetics

Keeping your car spic-and-span inside and out will prolong its life and upgrade its potential resale value.

There have been a lot of advances made in automotive finishes over the past few years; some new cars even claim a ''no-wax'' feature for their factory-applied paint. But despite the advances in both paint technology and press releases, one fact still remains—no painted surface will ever retain its like-new condition for very long without help from you. Almost as soon as the paint is dry, it begins to oxidize, or ''chalk,'' and so the showroom look gradually fades—along with the color of the paint. And there's another fact that's of equal importance to any car owner, enthusiast or not—the better you care for your automobile's appearance, the greater its value when you eventually dispose of it. After all, would you buy a used car with a dull, faded coat of paint, torn upholstery and stained carpets? As we all understand dollars and cents when it's put to us that way, let's take a close look at some of the fundamen-

tals involved in caring for the exterior and interior of your car.

Whether your car has one of the ''no-wax'' finishes, or one of the older kind for which no such statements are made, you'll have to periodically wash, polish and wax the finish to keep it at its best. To help you maintain the paint's appearance in tip-top condition, dozens of companies make a very handsome living by mixing, blending, bottling and marketing hundreds of concoctions designed to beautify and protect your paint job. As might be expected, some do the job better than others, and some cost more than their competitors; but there's no direct relationship between cost and how well a product works—you'll have to discover this by trial and error.

WASHING IS FIRST STEP

To begin with, the surface should be thoroughly cleaned to remove all traces of old wax, road film, dirt, etc.

Wash the car weekly if you're unable to garage it and must park outdoors where tree sap, leaf stains and bird droppings will fall on it, as these substances can have an adverse effect upon the paint surface in a relatively brief time. As a first step, rinse the car's surface with plenty of cold running water to wash off the loose dirt, and then go over the surface with a sponge and lots of plain cold water. Avoid using those sponges or cloths sold for dry car cleaning, as moving dirt or grime around on the paint surface without benefit of water or other liquids is bound to cause some scratching. Unless the surface is just plain filthy, avoid the use of detergents, but if you've let the condition run down that far, one sold specifically for washing cars will outperform the common household detergent you keep under the kitchen sink. Once you've finished washing the car, use a chamois or clean terry towel to damp dry it until all water is gone.

CLEANERS AND POLISHES

Although still available as individual items, cleaners and polishes are now often combined with a protective wax, allowing you to do the rest of the job in a single operation. While many regard a cleaner and a polish as being one and the same thing, there is a difference. A cleaner contains a harsher abrasive than that found in a polish and so it removes road film and paint oxidation resulting from the chalking of the finish. The milder abrasive of a polish is primarily designed just to cut through a light dirt

1. More and more cosmetic care is being handled by professional car-washes. While such care doesn't really prolong the finish, it doesn't break it down as some critics contend.

2. To show us the correct methods, we went to the pros. As a painter, Larry Davidson knows how to keep that finish in top shape. Start by rinsing surface with cold running water.

3. Go over entire surface with sponge and cold water; if it's really dirty, use a little detergent in the water.

4. Dry surface with chamois or terry towel, but don't rub or scrub.

5. Use polish or cleaner on small sections if you plan to hand-rub car.

coating and restore the paint's original luster. But whether you're cleaning a new car finish or a recent repaint job, it's best to start off with a polish, even if you have to go over the surface more than once.

MACHINE VS. HAND POLISHING

A hand-rubbed car sounds delightfully exotic, but to many, it's a perfect waste of time. Reasoning that they'll eventually end up with a hand-rubbed finish anyway, they prefer to do most of the initial work with a machine. The problem here is one of knowing how to use the polisher. If you've never had any experience working with one, I'd suggest you volunteer to do a neighbor's car first—but pick one you're not too fond of. Until you become familiar with the feel and technique of using a mechanical polisher, it's fairly easy to cut right through the paint to the bare metal. This is especially true on a new car, as factory-applied paint is *very* thin to begin with.

Once you get the knack of handling a polisher, work one panel at a time until the paint begins to shine, then use more polish with a folded piece of terry cloth to get around the little places where the polisher won't

go—door handles, grille moldings, fender corners, etc. Doing these areas will take you almost as long as machine polishing the panel, and you'll soon understand why many feel that hand-rubbing the entire car is so futile. After completing the polishing, wipe the panels with clean soft rags, hand-rubbing any areas that do not sparkle until the shine comes up.

USE A PROTECTIVE COATING

Once you've washed and cleaned/polished the painted surface, your car is as naked as a jaybird, as the old saying goes. Used by itself, a polish or cleaner will not provide any significant protection against further deterioration of the finish; you'll need a protective coating of wax or silicone to do this job. Such a coating provides a protective shield against the elements and fills in those fine scratches and lines that tend to accumulate despite your best efforts to prevent them. The wax or silicone coating thus prolongs the newly restored luster of the finish, while making it easier to remove dirt and grime without injury to the paint. Apply the protective coating as soon as possible after completing the polishing operation. If you use one of the one-step, wipe-on/wipe-off combination

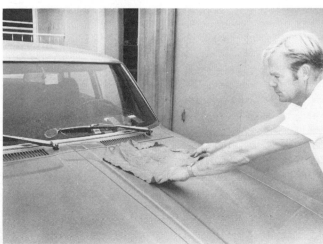

Auto Cosmetics

cleaner-wax compounds, the job is already finished.

You can always count on striking up a heated argument among car enthusiasts when you inquire which is best—a paste or a liquid wax. The old concept of a wax job was that the better the protection a wax offered, the more difficult it was to correctly apply and rub out. In fact, there was a time-honored cause-and-effect relationship between the amount of elbow grease and the degree of shine, to which many car buffs automatically subscribed. While it may have been true at one time, today's waxes and polishes disprove the idea that waxing one's car must be a labor of love. Choose your paste or liquid wax/polish on the basis of durability of the finish it produces—they're all fairly easy to use.

HOW LONG WILL IT LAST?

This depends upon a combination of factors: the quality of the wax you apply, the color and type of paint to which it's applied, where you live, and the weather conditions. While black is the neatest color when it's finished, it's also the hardest to maintain satisfactorily; and white is almost as difficult to keep up properly because of its greater tendency toward chalking. Metallics do not stand up as well as non-metallics, and tend to fade at a faster rate. Salt-laden air near the ocean, chemical fumes from nearby industrial areas, fuel particles from jet planes passing overhead enroute to the local airport—these and many other forms of natural and man-made "pollution" attack a wax/silicone paint finish, as does evening dew and early morning sunlight when cars cannot be garaged.

While separate polishing and wax-

ing can often last from 6 months to a year, users of the combination products will find it advisable to repolish the vehicle approximately every 3 months. But, as it's really impossible to set a hard-and-fast rule as to how long the coating will remain effective, here's a rule of thumb you can follow: Automotive polishes, waxes and silicone coatings form a film across the paint surface. When water strikes this film, it breaks up into bead-like droplets and rolls off. As the film progressively deteriorates, or wears away, water striking the surface will form in sheets or streaks instead of drops. Hosing the car down with clean water every weekend will show you just how well the coating is holding up; when the water starts sheeting instead of beading, it's time to redo the surface with a new coat. Once you've cycled into the habit of a weekly rinse and wash job, restoring the protective coating will require

1. *It's not a bad idea to spray a coat of clear acrylic over large chrome areas for rust protection. Use cardboard to prevent overspray.*

2. *Don't overlook antenna. Chrome polish or Glass Wax not only cleans it for easier up/down operation, but removing oxidation improves reception.*

3. *A light application of steel wool and cleansing powder is usually sufficient to restore whitewalls and remove scuff marks.*

4. *Most people find brush touch-up kit as good as anything devised to date. Carefully fill chipped area with paint to build it up to original thickness. After it's dried, blend new with old by rubbing or lightly sanding.*

5. *Touch-up compound comes in matching colors, is very thick. A drop on edge of squeegee provided is applied much as with a brush—you fill chipped spot and then run squeegee across surface to smooth and blend.*

only a quick pass with the polish and wax (or combination product), unless you've been off-road or driving under other severe conditions.

HOW ABOUT CAR WASHES?

The automatic car wash has become the busy driver's substitute for tender loving weekend care these days, but, surprisingly, most modern wax and silicone coatings will withstand the car wash detergent with surprising vigor. The greatest damage you're likely to suffer comes from repeated scrubbings by the automatic brushes and buffers which tend to leave an increasing number of fine scratches on your car. But if you wax well enough and often enough, the majority of the scratching will be surface lines in the wax coating, easily removed with a good polishing; if not, the scratching will take place on the paint's surface and then you're in trouble. About all you can hope to do once this happens is to fill them in with a new coat of wax.

VINYL ROOF CARE

Since vinyl is subject to both drying and fading, vinyl roof care is as important as keeping the painted surface in good condition. When you wash the car, use a vinyl cleaner or a solution of mild detergent and water on the roof, rinsing with plain cold water. After the top has dried, follow with a thin, even coating of vinyl roof dressing—available in both aerosol sprays and cans. Again, the spray idea sounds great, but as you'll have to mask off the area around the roof to prevent overspray, you might as well consider using the brush-on variety from the can. It does just as neat a job, and in less time.

Vinyl dressings serve two purposes: they keep the material supple to prevent it from drying out and cracking, and they enhance or change the color if you wish. While the dressing used should be the same color as that of the roof, you can apply a different color if you're tired of the old one. It's even possible to go from white to black or black to white—but expect that it will take two or more coats for such a drastic color change. Even application here is a must, if you expect a neat, non-streaked job to result. And be sure to do it inside or in the shade; if you apply vinyl dressing in bright sunlight, it will dry too fast and streak.

TOUCH-UP PAINTS

No matter how carefully you drive, or how gingerly you treat your car, its painted surface is bound to suffer from little chips, nicks and the like. While the front end and lower sides generally receive their share of rock nicks, the edges of doors, the deck lid and hood are most susceptible to chipping. It's just a coincidence that you happen to discover most of these defects in a parking lot as the guy next to you drives away. The only solution is to forget the tantrum you'd love to throw and repair the chipped/ nicked area as soon as possible. While few of these defects are worth the trouble and expense of refinishing the entire panel, it's unfortunate that no one has yet come up with a completely satisfactory and foolproof method of touching up these kinds of spots and scratches so they are unnoticeable to the eye.

A wide variety of different touch-up kits can be obtained from your dealer or local auto store; if you don't know the paint number (usually located on a metal plate under the hood or inside the door jamb), they can determine the exact color by make, model and year of your car. You'll find touch-up compound in small tubes with special applicators provided, while paint is packaged in various ways, from small cans and bottles with a brush attached inside the cap, to aerosol spray cans. Again, the spray can is a dandy idea in theory, but the novice touch-up artist should approach their use with extreme caution or he'll wind up repainting the entire panel anyway; they're quite difficult to control properly where only a tiny nick or scratch is involved, especially when working on lighter color paints that have begun to fade.

Follow the directions provided with the touch-up kit you use to the letter, if you expect decent results; improvisation seldom works well here, unless you're a natural-born artist. While some owners will be content to merely cover the offending area and let it go at that, others will want to apply the paint in successive layers until it has built up nearly to the original

4

5

Auto Cosmetics

thickness, then very carefully sand and/or rub the area until the edges are blended smooth. Very large scratches as well as deep nicks can be repaired in this way, and while the results probably won't satisfy the perfectionists among us, even the most amateur job often turns out looking quite good.

CHROME CARE

Keeping chrome bright and shiny isn't half the battle it was just a few years ago; today's cars just don't use it in the same quantities as those of the '50's. In addition, the chrome plating has disappeared from many modern bumpers, replaced by colored plastics coordinated to match the body color and trimmed with a silver Mylar® strip. Body moldings have gone much the same way, vent windows have disappeared, etc.

But if your car does have chrome plating on the trim, and you live in a climate like that of So. Calif., caring for it requires little more than an occasional treatment with chrome polish or Glass Wax. In winter climates and near the seashore, where corrosion becomes a major enemy, the problem remains much as it's always been. Various chrome renewers are sold to dissolve the rust and pitting, but their use is only temporary—after a few days of driving in slush, the rust and pitting returns. If it's really bad, you can use steel wool and a kitchen cleanser powder like Bon Ami to remove the corrosion, but you're likely to scratch the surrounding surface unless you work carefully.

In the good old days, sports car addicts used to paint the affected areas with clear fingernail polish after thoroughly cleaning them of corrosion

1. Machine polishing is much faster, but do one panel at a time, and don't let the machine get away from you if you're a novice at polishing.

2. Use care if you're a beginner at the art. Too much pressure on crown and contour surfaces can cause pad to buckle, allowing machine to cut right through the paint.

3. Don't attempt to work around door handles, etc., with machine; polish these areas by hand.

4. Today's paste waxes are almost as easy to apply as the liquid wax/polish. Be sure to follow instructions on can and cover surface thoroughly.

5. Don't neglect that vinyl roof— use a mild detergent and scrub the roof with a brush. Let dry and then apply a coat of dressing.

6. Clean chrome areas with a chrome polish or Glass Wax. Remove any pitting or rust spots and cover with clear fingernail polish.

1

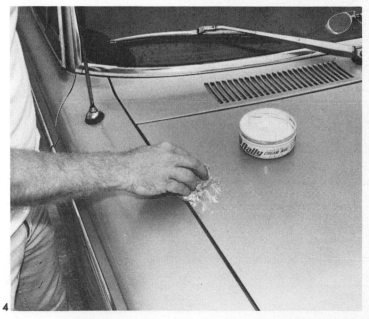

2

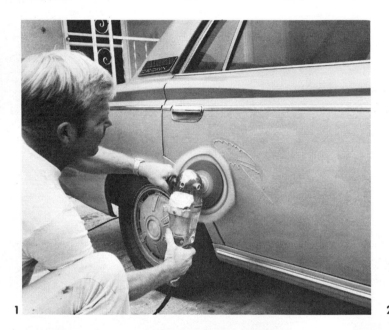

3

4

with vinegar and baking soda. Today, a coat or two of acrylic clear will serve much the same purpose. The best advice for chrome preservation in winter weather areas is to begin treatments as soon as you get the car (assuming that you buy it new). While this won't prevent eventual deterioration, it'll slow the process down considerably.

TIRE CLEANERS

Some readers have probably used, or at least remember, the small cans sold to renew the appearance of tires. Containing a little tar and lots of thinner, a can of this goop and a 49-cent brush did the same for aging rubber that a bottle of hair coloring did for its graying owner. And when you were finished with it, the tires didn't really look like new, they looked more like early-day retreads— black and shiny beyond reality. Well, the stuff is still available for those who are nostalgic for the '50's.

But there's a better cleaner/preservative on the market. Those who live in urban areas where smog and air pollution are a problem have probably noticed that tires don't seem to stand up as well these days as they appeared to only a few years ago. Most of us tend to blame this on "cheaper materials," but the fact is that pollution and smog attack tires, causing them to discolor and the sidewalls to check. Of course, once this happens, there's little you can do but grin and bear it—or paint on a coat or two of the "black goop." But if you have a relatively new car, or are considering the purchase of one, pick up a can of Armor-All at your local auto parts emporium and apply it. The end result is a retention of the natural appearance plus a slightly increased gloss; and, in addition, the tires won't check at all.

If you have whitewalls, scuffs can be removed with a little kitchen cleanser and steel wool, although cleanser-impregnated pads are sold at highly inflated prices for the same purpose. You can also buy whitewall cleaner, which really amounts to a solvent that will remove the dirt; but the least expensive method will do the job just as well. Of course, if you've beaten the white to death by driving along curbs too often, you can pick up a can of tire whitener and paint them back in place; but you'd be just as well off painting over them with the black goop and letting it go at that.

INSIDE THE CAR

Now that we've managed to spruce up the outside, let's open the door and take a look at the interior. If the nylon carpeting has a few stains from careless eating at the local drive-in or roadside stand, they should be removed. Even if you use floor mats and have managed to avoid the problems of spills and stains, the carpet has probably been waiting for a good cleaning. Run a vacuum cleaner around the floor first to remove as much dirt as you can. If the carpeting is extremely filthy, it might be a good idea to remove it from the car where you can work on it easier, but we hope that you haven't let things go *that* far.

All kinds of carpet cleaning agents are sold, most of which promise various miracles; but while their ease of application is attractive for a quick job, the results that most of them deliver aren't, despite the TV commercials showing the little lady spraying the foam on only to vacuum it up a few minutes later—with a spotless carpet underneath. What they don't show you is the part where the stains gradually reappear a few hours later. You'll get better and faster results if you pick up one of the small plastic applicator bottles with a combination sponge/scrub brush that screws on in place of a cap. Use FabricMagic or HR_2 rug shampoo concentrate, mixing with water according to the directions. Scrub the carpeting with this and you'll lift almost anything you've had the misfortune to spill, except ammonia or bleach. When you're done, vacuum the damp carpeting again, leaving the doors open for awhile in order to let air circulation finish the job.

The upholstery comes next, and this includes the seats, door panels and headliner. On late-model cars, these are covered with either a smooth or textured vinyl. While you can use one of those special upholstery cleaners which brushes, sprays or foams on, you'll have just as good results on seats and panels with a solution of mild dishwashing detergent and lukewarm water. Wipe on with a sponge and then dry off with a terry towel.

Removing scuff or dirt marks from the headliner is a slightly different problem; this usually means cleaning the entire area, not just the dirty spot. It's absolutely amazing just how much filth will collect up there, often changing the color so slowly that you don't really notice it. You can usually get a good idea of the amount of change that's taken place by simply pulling the sun visors from their clip and comparing the area behind them with the rest of the headliner. The difference will be especially noticeable if

Auto Cosmetics

you smoke a lot and drive with the vent window open.

As dirt, smoke and road film combine to form a rather greasy coating, you'll need something with a little more oomph to remove it completely and easily. While you can try the automotive upholstery cleaners previously mentioned, nothing to date has turned out to be more effective than a few squirts of Big Wally or Fantastik, common household cleaners used in most homes. Spray or squirt a moderate amount on a small clean sponge and gently wipe the headliner surface; you'll be surprised at how quickly the clean sponge and dirty headliner change colors. This even works well for scuffs on light-colored door panels, etc.

REPAIRING UPHOLSTERY

Not too many years ago, leather and vinyl were extra-cost options, with a variety of cloth fabrics used to cover most car seats. They were murder to keep clean, especially those with a basket-weave pattern which had the misfortune to catch a gob of catsup or some other staining substance. To prevent this kind of damage—as well as rips and tears—most of us bought seat covers; the buggy may have been a physical wreck when it was traded in, but by gosh, the seats were just like new. Well, time has worked its changes; leather is now very expensive and almost unobtainable in all but the most exotic cars, vinyl has replaced cloth as the workaday covering for upholstery, and the demand for seat covers peaked some years back. Interestingly enough, cloth has made a slight comeback recently, this time as an extra-cost option or in cars like the Levi's Gremlin.

If you've had the misfortune to forget that screwdriver in your back pocket as you slid behind the wheel in one of these, you've probably got a beautiful rip or tear somewhere in the upholstery. But you're also in luck, because the denim fabric is fashionable today, with or without patches. And that's the answer—all you need are a couple of pieces of brightly colored denim and someone who's handy with a needle and thread. Have her (him?) neatly hand sew a patch over the damaged area with a black nylon thread, and then put a matching one on the other seat just for balance; not even your best friends will know what's under the patches, and you'll probably even pick up a number of compliments for your mod taste.

Rips and tears in vinyl upholstery are a different matter, and not as

easily repaired. While some use a patch of automotive electrical tape or one of the colored Mystik tapes as a quick remedy, it's difficult to hide the fact that you've done it. And if the rip/tear happens to be on a part of the seat that supports weight, your patch won't last very long, as it'll flex under the weight and movement of sitting on it. In addition, such patches can be messy, since the tape's adhesive will often bleed and run during hot weather.

There are a number of different vinyl fabric repair kits on the market; a popular one recalls the days when we used to patch inner tubes. It comes with a piece of repair fabric (colors can usually be matched fairly closely) and a tube of vinyl solvent, which acts something like a glue. The idea is to cut a patch sufficient to cover the damaged area and then taper the edges so that it'll blend into the seat without notice. Once the patch is cut to size and tapered, just apply the solvent/glue and put it in place. The major difficulty in using this type of kit comes in featheredging the patch properly to make it blend in well.

Another variety uses a solvent and a foil mold to restore cigarette-burned areas and can be adapted for your use, provided the damaged area is not too large. The solvent is used to fill the hole and soften the area around a tear. Then the foil mold which matches the surrounding material is applied. Once it's dry, the mold is removed, leaving the repaired area almost invisible. Both of these kits, and the other types that continue to appear and disappear from the market, can do the job, but only if the rip/tear to be repaired is not too

1

1. If you use a spray bomb, use a cardboard mask with small opening cut out. This keeps overspray to limited area, makes blending easier.

2. Remove carpet stains with rug shampoo concentrate, good scrubbing.

3. Before the carpet dries, vacuum the area to remove all traces of shampoo. This will lift almost any stain except bleach or ammonia.

4. Common household cleanser and sponge will remove road film, smoke, and greasy fingermarks from headliner and light-colored upholstery as fast as anything sold for that purpose.

5. Tired of dirty, scuffed door panels? Mask them off and shoot the panels with a can of Vinyl Spray. You can also change colors with it.

large, and does not have to support weight and movement. In the case of a gash or slit across the bottom of the seat, your best bet is a set of seat covers; the only remaining alternatives are to either forget it and let things go, or to go ahead and have the seat reupholstered.

VINYL RESTORATION

The best way to handle a vinyl surface that's discolored or stained is to spray it with Vinyl-Spray. This product is obtainable from auto supply stores under a variety of other trade names and comes in an aerosol can. It's available in many colors as well as black and white, and renews (not repairs) the vinyl's finish while allowing the original pattern (if any) to show through.

Don't try to use one of these sprays without first masking off all surrounding areas; newspapers—and plenty of them—will do the job adequately. When working with the spray

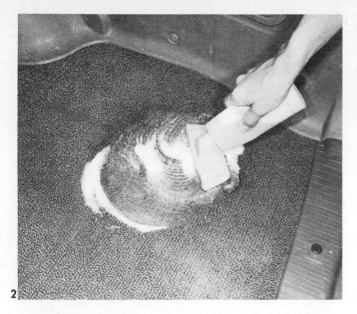

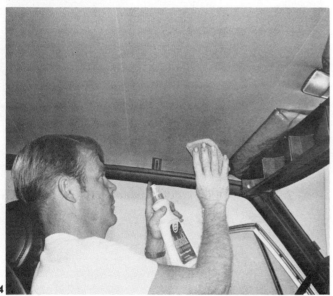

can, be sure to open all the doors for proper ventilation and pick a fairly cool day—if you're working in the sun or on a hot day, the surface of the spray dries too fast. Since Vinyl-Spray is quite thin, a very light mist coat works best; it's very easy to over-apply and then you'll have a problem with runs and sags. Let the first coat dry for about 30 mins. and then mist on another light coat. Two coats should be about perfect—but wait a couple of hours before removing the masking just to make sure that everything has set up properly.

You can use Vinyl-Spray to change the color of the seats, door panels, dashboard, headliner, etc., if you're tired of the present color scheme. Depending upon the color you're trying to cover, and the color you want, you'll find two to four coats required. As you'd expect, it's easier to go from a light color to a darker one; but this stuff has pretty good covering power and you can turn black into

white with much less difficulty than you'd think.

TOUCHING UP INTERIOR TRIM

Late-model cars use considerably less interior metallic trim than in the past; dashboards, door panels, arm-rest supports and the like have been increasingly replaced by—or faced with—vinyl. Vinyl-Spray will restore or change their appearance as you de-sire. But for those cars with metal trim, interior touch-up paints are readily available to match all original factory colors.

Unlike touching up exterior nicks and chips, the use of an aerosol can is most suitable for working on interi-or trim, as the best job results from redoing the entire trim area, whether dash, glove compartment door or armrest support. You'll have to mask off the surrounding area if you want a neat job, but a few newspapers and a roll of masking tape will do the job in a matter of minutes. Scratches, nicks,

chips, etc., should be smoothed out with light sanding strokes using a fine grit (#400) paper to minimize scratching of the surrounding paint.

If you want to go all the way, you can sand the trim to bare metal and prime before repainting, but this ap-proach may mean more bother than it's really worth, as trim contours are usually many and sharp, and can present time-consuming problems. You'll get just as good results if you simply featheredge the damaged area as you would with any other spot re-pair and then lightly scuff up the rest of the surface to be refinished.

Keep the spray can moving once you begin to spray, and apply several light coats, waiting after each one un-til it becomes tacky before applying the next. This will eliminate the prob-lem of sags and runs, and can be followed by a coat of Leveler to smooth out the sprayed area. Leveler will also blend overspray into the sur-

Auto Cosmetics

rounding area if you attempt to make the repair without masking.

WRINKLES FOR A DIFFERENT EFFECT

Older cars and pickups often used a baked enamel crackle finish on the trim, an effect simulated by today's grained or pebbled vinyl. The stuff was tougher than an elephant's hide and resisted scratching and other damage very well, but when damage did occur, there was very little you could do to restore it. If you're an enthusiast, or just think you'd like to try something different for a change, you might consider redoing your interior metal trim with wrinkle paint.

This can be bought wherever you buy auto supplies and comes in various colors. Properly applied, it imparts a rich and distinctive textured finish that can be felt as well as seen. Wrinkle paint is both durable and long-lasting, and it does a spectacular job of customizing under the hood if you've become tired of chrome. It will also provide a good deal of protection when used on metal kick plates or the metal areas around window glass, etc. And by varying the method of application, you can determine the exact amount and degree of texture necessary.

Unlike other spray paints, this one is designed to go on in heavy coats, since you need a coat that's sufficiently thick for the wrinkling process to take place. You'll need at least two coats applied 3 mins. apart to achieve the fine texture. Spray one coat horizontally and the other vertically; this will ensure that wrinkling will be uniform. And if you want a coarse finish, then simply spray a third one diagonally.

Don't get too excited if the wrinkling effect doesn't take place as soon as you've set the spray can down; it's a function of drying and will take between 20 mins. and 2 hours to fully appear, depending upon the temperature and the amount you applied. If you're in a hurry to see your artistry, you can use a heat lamp to reduce this period considerably—but keep it a couple of feet away from the painted surface for best results. If wrinkling does not appear within this time, you (1) sprayed the coats too thin, (2) tried to spray too large an area at one time, (3) waited too long between coats or, (4) held the spray can too far from the trim when applying.

As you can see, working with wrinkle paint is a little like working in the dark until you've used it enough to become acquainted with its eccentricities; so it's best to practice spraying on a scrap piece of metal to establish both the touch and spray pattern. If you practice on two or three different pieces, you'll find that the resulting wrinkle pattern will vary, primarily because of the way you hold and move the spray can, and the thickness of the coats applied. Keep a rag and a can of thinner nearby to wipe it all off if your coat is too heavy and begins to run; nothing looks worse than a wrinkled run or sag.

CLEANING UP THE TRUNK

Wrinkle-finish paint is great for de-tailing small pieces, but there's always difficulty in doing large areas, even on a part only as large as a dashboard panel. The problem with large parts is that it's difficult to keep the wrinkling *uniform*. While the durability of a wrinkle finish would seem ideal for a trunk area, there's a better way to do the job.

Going by several different names, including Zolotone and Spatter Paint, trunk paint is available from several manufacturers in bulk or in spray cans. Trunk paint is thick and is usually a mixture of two colors, so the result is a mottled finish of contrasting-colored specks, such as grey and black. These trunk finishes come in several color combinations and are often a good match for the factory finish in your trunk area. It's easy to repair in the future, should you get a scratch on it, because the random effect makes spot repairs blend in perfectly. Redoing your entire trunk area sheetmetal with trunk paint and then recarpeting or matting will make it like new again. If your car is old enough that you can't get a factory trunk mat at your dealership, then consider the ribbed vinyl floor matting sold in hardware and carpet stores for protecting household carpets from muddy feet in wet weather. Just cut it to fit the floor of your trunk and glue it down.

But suppose your trunk area came equipped with carpeting and the adhesive has dried out—now you've got pieces flopping all over inside. The best way to stick them back in place for good is to use contact cement. Clean the old adhesive from the metal area with a good solvent;

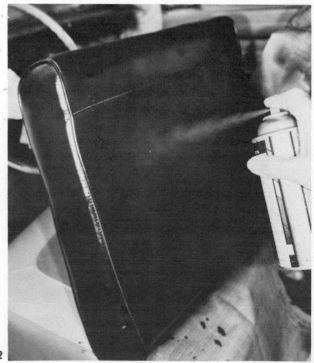

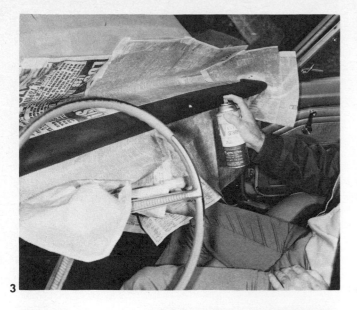

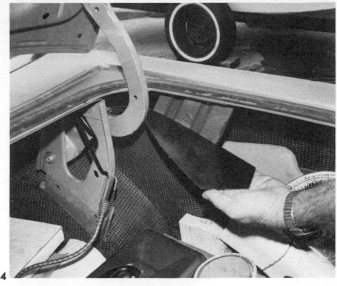

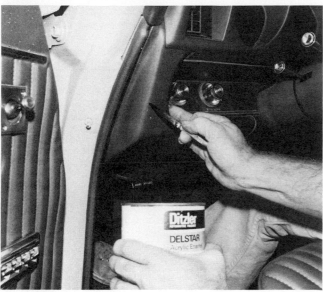

3

4

5

6

1. Dark over light goes on just fine with only two coats; light over dark is trickier, requires more spraying. Use care to avoid runs and sags.

2. Four to six cans will do average interior completely. When working with split seats, be sure to fold forward and shoot area in back.

3. Vinyl Spray works well on modern dashboards, as they're mostly vinyl. You'll have to mask off the instruments and windshield as the overspray is tough to get off.

4. To reseal trunk carpeting, apply a thin coat of contact cement to both surfaces. Let everything dry until tacky and then join together.

5. Pinstriping brush works well for touching up small scrapes, scuffs on metal dash areas. If nicks or chips are large, refinishing entire panel usually gives best results.

6. Trunk restoration can be easily accomplished in an afternoon with a can of spatter-paint and a roll of black, ribbed rubber matting. Use your old trunk mat as a pattern.

this will prevent the stuff from forming lumps once the carpet is glued back in place. Then apply the contact cement with a brush to the metal surface as well as the back of the carpeting and let it dry until tacky. Starting at one end, gently press the carpeting back in place and it'll stick just as if it had been welded there in the first place. Be sure to clean up any excess cement that might ooze out along the edges, or it'll make a grand mess that's difficult to clean up later.

RESTORING FLOOR MATS

About the only thing left to do is to clean up those vinyl floor mats. Once that's done, the car should be in A-1 condition, inside and out. As floor and trunk mats are designed to protect the surface on which they're placed, a certain amount of staining, streaking, cracking and even fading is to be expected. There are all kinds of vinyl and rubber dressings designed to care for them, but most will just

sink in and disappear, as if by magic.

The best method we've come across to date is to apply a coat of Armor-All as soon as you get the mats. This will help prevent cracking and rotting, especially if you live in damp or wintry weather areas. Then, to assure that their color retains its brightness, use Rubber-New. This transparent spray will even cover water spots, and it keeps the mat's original sparkle intact.

If you've got old, faded mats that need to be brought back to life, clean them thoroughly with a stiff brush and warm soapy water, then rinse and dry. Shoot a light coat of Vinyl-Spray to restore the color and cover with Rubber-New a few hours later.

Car appearance care isn't the one-time affair, but, like the lubrication and preventive maintenance given the operating parts, should be done on a regular basis. When you trade for that new car, the salesman just isn't going to believe his eyes!

Tailgating

That vast expanse of metal across the back of a pickup is a great place for the individualist to play.

Many of the vehicles running around on the streets today, but which haven't appeared elsewhere in this book, are not cars, but pickup trucks. Naturally, they're subject to as much exterior damage as their passenger-carrying counterparts and probably even more so, since by their very nature they are exposed to more than their fair share of dings and clobbers.

The main reason we haven't delved into pickups is that the straightening of damaged sheetmetal on a pickup is identical to the hammering out that's done on an ordinary car—maybe it's even easier since pickups are *designed* for the hard knocks right from the start, and doors, hoods, fenders, and so on, are generally very easy to replace. Too, there is frequently much more working room under truck fenders for swinging hammers and dollies, and interior door trim is held by simple screws or snaps instead of the trickery that plusher cars contain. Component parts exposed to superficial parking lot damage, like grilles and bumpers, usually require only the unwinding of visible or at least easily accessible nuts and bolts for total removal. Any-

one who can remove a front fender from a late Cadillac in half an hour, for example, can pull one off a pickup in a handful of minutes.

By the same token, painting a pickup is easier than painting a car. There's less trim and fewer windows to mask off—though the painter will likely have to stand on a box or low ladder to run tape across the upper part of the windshield, and to sand and spray the turret top. But then, factory pickup colors are generally not metallics, and this makes it easier to blend or match color.

This isn't to say that a complete repaint job can't be done in Metalflake or a deep, transluscent hue just to set the hauler apart from all of its look-alikes on the highway. In fact, the panel breakup on a truck is such that a great many color tricks can be devised without detracting at all from overall vehicle design. Pickups are great, too, for the expression of individualism through color fogging, paneling, cobwebbing, striping, flames, or whatever else might come to the painter's mind.

But no matter the extent of special bodywork or trick painting that the novice—or the pro—might like to try

on a pickup, he'll finally come to the one huge panel that's going to tax his imagination. That's the tailgate; that vast, rectangular advertising billboard that runs very nearly the full rear width of the truck and stands some 2 feet high.

Few people embarking on a pickup customizing project want to retain those foot-high letters spelling out F-O-R-D, C-H-E-V-R-O-L-E-T, D-O-D-G-E or the others, but how to get rid of them is a special problem. Sometimes the clever use of striping or paneling will diminish the boldness of the lettering without really eliminating it. In other cases a plain flat piece can be cut from light sheetmetal and pop-riveted or metal-screwed right over the factory's deeply embossed letters which are next to impossible to hammer out.

At any rate, a truck tailgate is a good place for the imaginative truck enthusiast to play. There are no guidelines, no limits for what's possible. But here is a random sampling of some of the tricks that are being currently employed to stun, startle, amaze, or humor following motorists.

1. If you can't lick 'em, join 'em. Stock Chevy LUV tailgate lettering is empasized by its owner by shadowing. Added touch is simple striping.

2. 1958 Chevy Cameo Carrier tailgate was factory rehashed to set it apart from run-of-the-mill pickups of the same year, but this one carries dark contrasting striping to enhance it.

3. Here's a pickup whose owner didn't mind touting the manufacturer's name; in fact, he emphasized it even more by paneling the tailgate in wood, gluing on wooden letters, then finishing the whole thing with clear and going wild with his pinstriping brush.

4. Clean and simple, that's the way John Westerfield likes his '56 Ford. Tailgate is painted to match rest of the truck, but with lettering done in contrasting color with a striping "squibble" below it.

5. One thing you may have missed in the preceding photo, is that the latches and restraining chains were eliminated from the 'gate. One way to do this is with hook 'n' latch tie-downs mounted on the inside.

6. Tailgates make a great place to boldly acclaim a truck's title. The stiffening ridges in stock 'gate were covered with an inset metal panel.

7. See where imagination can lead you? This owner preferred re-doing his tailgate with fluted panels found in an unpainted furniture store, gluing them over wooden inset panel, adding numbers to identify truck's year.

8. If expense is no object and you kinda like the stock lettering, simply have the whole tailgate chrome plated, then mask off the letters and stiffening ribs before spraying the paint.

9. Ed Rettedal got rid of the stock 'gate trim on his '66 Ranchero, livened area up with bold striping, script.

10. Center portion of embossed Chevy tailgate was panel painted to help make identifying letters even more vividly pronounced.

11. While we're at it, we couldn't help but consider the inside of a tailgate. This Ranchero's owner paneled his in clear-finished veneer, used chrome headed screws to secure it.

3

4

5

6

7

8

9

10

11

Vinyl Put-On's

Behold! A quick and easy way to add delicate murals to the exterior of your favorite conveyance.

The mural painting fad has been with us for several years now, but odds are if you've tried to do it yourself, you've found it more of a challenge than you realized. And, if you've been lucky enough to have a custom painter in your area who is capable of doing good airbrush mural work, you've been astounded when he told you how expensive it was. Well, there is now a quick and easy way to add murals to the exterior (or interior, if you wish) of your van, car, bike, dune buggy, bus, airplane, truck, boat, dragster, glider, rhino, etc., and it doesn't cost you an arm and a leg.

Greg, the custom painter from Akron, Ohio, who is credited with starting the whole mural painting craze, has been doing development work on a medium-hard vinyl "stick-on" mural which can be applied to any relatively smooth and flat surface. Actually, the murals are made of a new material known as Acroart, the same material used on a popular brand of extremely durable indoor/outdoor toys. You simply select the mural of your choice, cut around the border with a razor, an X-Acto knife or a pair of scissors, peel off the paper backing to reveal the sticky backside, and put it on where you want it.

While the murals can be applied to any dry surface, to facilitate positioning Greg suggests that you wash the surface which is to receive the mural with a soap and water mix and apply the mural while the surface is still wet. This has several advantages, as it allows "slip," permitting you to move the mural around and position it exactly where you want it. It also provides a clean surface for maximum adhesion. Once the mural is positioned, you work the water out with a squeegee and let it dry. A wet surface is not required, but if you apply the mural to a dry surface, you had better get the position right on

These new stick-on murals for vans and cars are printed on sturdy vinyl and come in a wide variety of styles, all designed by master mural-painter Greg of Akron. Here, Greg himself is caught applying one of his murals for a customer at the Van Fair East. It's easiest to install by first washing the area with soapy water. Results are very satisfying.

the first try as it can't be moved around.

HIGH RESISTANCE

Although the murals are relatively impervious to weather, have a high degree of resistance to color fading (to the ultraviolet rays of the sun), and are generally moisture-resistant, you can put a coat of clear over them if you wish to afford them additional protection against the elements. You can do this with clear epoxy, clear lacquer, clear enamel or even varnish, but it is not mandatory. After the mural has been applied to your vehicle (or snow shovel or washing machine), you can pinstripe the edge for an added touch of professionalism. Again, like the clearing process, the pinstripe is not required, as the mural comes with a stripe printed around the edge. You may also choose to apply the murals and then paint your van, fogging over the edges to make it more a part of the paint scheme.

Altogether a total of 13 different murals are available in a variety of

sizes, which vary from 7½x7½ ins. all the way up to 14½x36 ins. They are all full-color and generally are on dark backgrounds. Presently, Greg is working on vinyl murals on a clear background which will allow your existing paint to show through, but these are still in the development stage and will not be available for an undisclosed period. The pricing of the Acroart murals is very reasonable, as the small 9x6-in. ovals are $5.95 each while the largest murals—14x36 ins.—are $29.95. When you consider the high quality of the artwork, the durability of the product and the relatively low cost, you can see that Greg's pressure-sensitive murals are a good buy. You can write to Greg for further information at 1750 Wadsworth Road, Akron, Ohio 44320, or you can purchase the murals at your local speed shop. They are now being marketed through the Trimbrite Corp. of Holt, Mich. In addition, a new line of vinyl "Van-Decs" is currently offered by the Nordec company at 100 Northfield Rd., Bedford, Ohio 44146. You're in luck.

Vinyl Top Installation

Meeting a very trying challenge.

Ever have a yen to put a snappy vinyl top on the roof of that old buggy? If so, maybe you've been turned off by the prices pro shops ask. Well, because of the nature of the installation, we can't help you save much money, but if you insist on doing it yourself, we can show you how to meet the challenge.

First of all, forget about buying the vinyl and making your own top—only a glutton for punishment would take this route. Hustle down to your nearest top shop, select the color and pattern you want and let the guys cut and stitch it together for you. This way, you'll get a perfect top to apply, cut exactly for your car and with professionally sewn seams. Incidentally, you'll have a choice of a ridged or flat seam—choose the one that best matches what you think the car's personality is.

Next, find a pressure feed Binks 69 (or equivalent) spray gun with a gallon tank. You'll need a good grade of contact cement—pros seem to like Fulgrip, and an air compressor. Trying to brush the adhesive on is about as self-defeating as anything we can think of. It brushes on too thick here, too thin there, and leaves all kinds of bumps underneath the vinyl. In addition, you can't coat a large enough area to work with before the brush becomes a semi-rigid club.

Once you've got these essentials, pick a good warm day on which to work or position a couple of heat lamps about 3 feet above the roof of the car. The warmth is needed to keep the vinyl supple enough to stretch properly. Working without heat on a day that's below 75° F will give you a nice job, as long as the weather remains cool, but wait until the first hot day comes along! Now, if you're still determined, follow along as Art Keyes of Speight Buick in Hollywood, Calif. shows you how a pro does it. Oh, yes . . . good luck!

HOW-TO

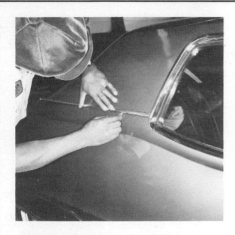

1. Vinyl top installation begins by establishing line where top will meet body. A straight edge and a felt tip marker do the job just fine.

2. Establishing the top line is easy where you can measure against a fixed point, but curves must be templated unless you're a free-hand artist.

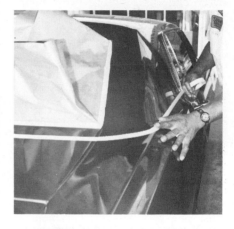

3. Windows and trim are masked off. Tape covers pen line; area is masked. Late models have glue under trim, so vinyl cannot be tucked underneath.

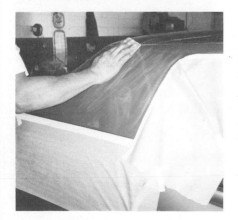

4. Art scuffs the finish with #40 grit paper and then blows the sanding debris off with a shot of compressed air. Top is now ready for adhesive application.

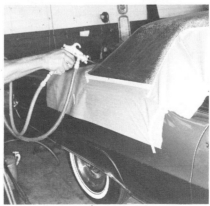

5. A pressure feed gun and 55 lbs. of air puts the adhesive on evenly. If you try to brush it on, you'll wind up with lots of little lumps under the vinyl.

6. After top area has been sprayed, masking paper is removed and adhesive allowed to set. This coat won't lose adhesiveness for 24 hours.

HOW-TO

7. A cup of adhesive and a small brush are used to coat inside of gutter, as it's difficult to spray and we want top to stick perfectly.

8. Art then measures the width of both top and windshield, then decides where the top seams will look best. Ink marks are replaced with masking tape.

9. The vinyl top is laid out on the top and positioned. Masking tape from the ink guide marks help him to line up the seams correctly.

10. Once seam lines are established, the vinyl is secured at both front and rear with tape to keep it from moving. Error like this could ruin everything.

11. One half of the vinyl is folded over, and masking tape is run along its seam line. This gives Art an edge in positioning the vinyl correctly.

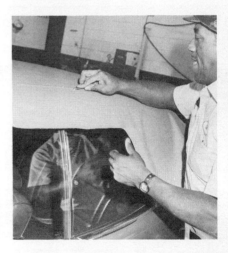

12. Once the adhesive is no longer tacky, Art unrolls half of vinyl across car top, taking great pains to smooth out the seam line so it lies just right.

13. It takes a good deal of muscle to pull and stretch that vinyl so it's perfectly taut before you let the adhesive touch. This is the secret of a good installation.

14. Top overlap gives plenty of vinyl to work with. Tool is used to press vinyl down tightly near chrome, and to provide a cutting guideline.

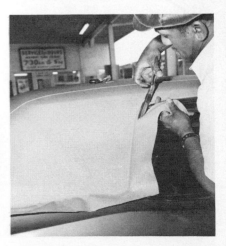

15. The excess vinyl is cut away with shears. You can see the value of the guideline—one wrong cut here and the entire top is spoiled.

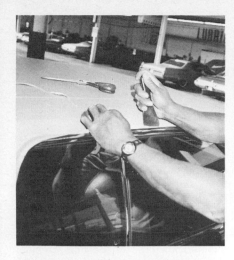

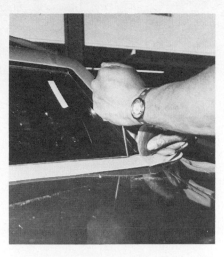

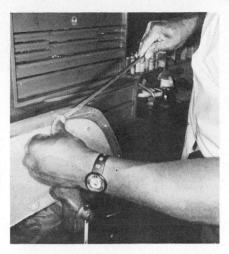

16. After the excess is removed, the vinyl is then tucked into the gutter line for a completely waterproof fit. Extra cement applied here comes in handy.

17. The window trim is lifted up and the vinyl material tucked underneath. If trim springs out too far, a rubber mallet is used to tap it back in place.

18. Now we're ready for the predrilled moulding application. Art bends the moulding (which comes in two pieces) to general body curvature.

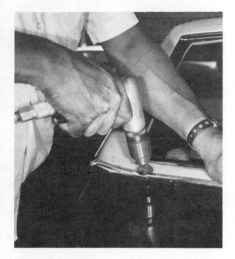

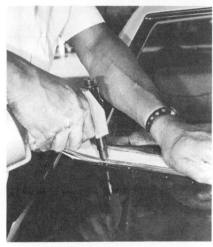

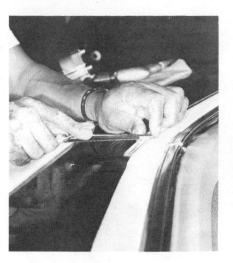

19. A power drill is used after the moulding is conformed to body lines. This finishing touch sets top off from body and really makes it stand out.

20. A pneumatic pop-rivet gun makes the job of fastening the moulding in place fast, easy, and permanent; no mistakes are allowed here, either.

21. The moulding end is cut exactly in the center of the window trim and it's squared off for a good fit. A steady hand and a good file help here.

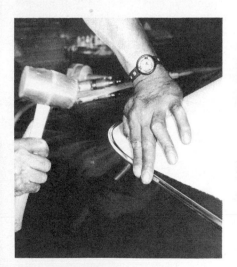

22. The exact body curvature of the trim moulding is established with the help of a rubber mallet and several gentle taps on the aluminum moulding.

23. Edging tool is run through moulding channel so plastic insert can slide through. If channel is opened too much, it can be tapped back in place.

24. Moulding insert is started at one end and pushed through the moulding. Drill a small hole through insert at each end; screws will hold insert in place.

'Blast 'Em!

Sandblasting its way into an ultimate personal touch, comes frosted windows for trucks and vans.

Whenever the term "sandblasting" is brought up in car enthusiast circles, with regard to body parts, a shudder usually can be felt rippling through most of the listeners. Many have had the sad experience of bringing a treasured fender from their projects to be stripped of paint and rust by sandblasting; only to get back a clean, but ripple-warped panel that looked like it had been through a major hailstorm. But such need not be the case if the job is done properly: with low pressure and fine sand. That's a rule with Steve Straw of Associated Sandblasting and Abrasive Co. (8315 Hindry Ave., Los Angeles, Calif., 90045). Steve's a hot rodder who's had metal-stripping problems in the past, too, but didn't find the answer 'til he got into his own sandblasting company. It's while we were there shooting a few pictures for this book that Steve turned us on to an old/new sandblasting technique that really caught our attention . . . *frosted window designs for trucks and vans.*

Now while the idea is far from new (designs have been frosted on windows for perhaps 100 years or more), the application of the technique to cars of today is certainly novel and refreshing. You've probably seen decoratively frosted glass in the front doors of very old homes or stores decorated with an antique decor; with a floral pattern usually frosted around the edges of a window, or the name of the store frosted into the glass. The technique was once very popular on cars, too, as you'll notice on many

windwings at antique car gatherings. Some of the decorative glass treatments you've seen are probably *etched* into glass rather than *frosted,* but that is another whole ballgame. Etched glass designs are created by using acids or strong chemicals to actually eat away part of the glass surface while frosted glass is done by *sandblasting* the surface.

Steve explained that while the frosting technique can be used on any type of glass, it seems particularly applicable for creating designs on the expansive windows of vans. Since pickup and van owners are the types of enthusiasts who can't be satisfied until their vehicle shows the personal touch, especially in the area of custom paint and bodywork, this new trend will certainly be showing up more frequently. While most custom vans don't have the large side windows and thus have more room to apply painted murals and designs, the guys with the windowed vans no longer need to feel left out of customizing opportunities when they can create murals of their own right on the window glass!

STEVE DOES IT

We followed Steve as he executed a simple Chevy emblem in the back window of a pickup. The pickup is the shop truck for Alphabet's Custom West, a custom van and bike company. Joe Alphabet just naturally digs using letters and designs, and feels that this definitely could become the next trend in the innovative van crowd. After the emblem design had been drawn to scale for the pickup's

rear window, Steve taped it to the *inside* of the window, to act as a guide for his masking. Steve says the best material for masking designs is the duct tape used in air-conditioning shops, but among car enthusiasts it is also called "racer tape" and just plain "silver tape." With the design taped to the inside of the window, Steve could follow it on the outside as he masked off the glass and trimmed the tape to the final emblem size with an X-Acto knife. Since the pressure of the air and sand may tend to lift the edges of the tape, be sure to press it firmly into contact with the glass all the way around. The truck was masked off with thin sheets of rubber (the sand bounces off of rubber rather than eating through it), but you could use newspaper if you have many folds of paper around the window.

All that was left, was for Steve to don his protective gear and blast the part of the window that wasn't masked off. It doesn't take much pressure to frost glass, and Steve said that even the small home sandblasters advertised in car magazines would be adequate for doing glass if you have your own compressor. Even with the low pressure and fine sand (actually ground-up walnut shells instead of true sand), it took only a few minutes for Steve to completely do the pickup window. This act completed the job except for removing the tape and the masking rubber. Incidentally, don't worry if you haven't done a perfect job of taping off the rubber modling around the glass. Not

1

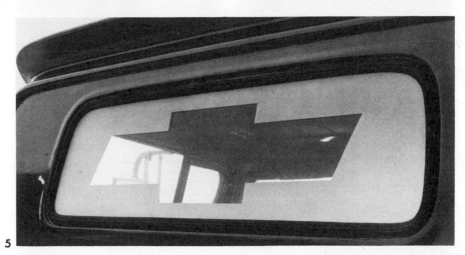

1. Depending on your tastes and the design you choose, sandblasting your pickup or van windows can lend them a touch of imagination or nostalgia. These artistic roses were designed by Frank Mendeola of Long Beach, Calif.

2. Steve Straw of Associated Sand Blasting and Abrasives shows us how to do a simple Chevy logo in the rear window of Joe Alphabet's truck. The design is drawn on white paper, which is taped to the inside of the window as a guide for Steve's masking with duct tape, trimmed to design.

3. The body is masked off with sheets of rubber (sand bounces off rubber), and more duct tape. Don't worry about rubber molding around the glass; the blasting won't hurt it a bit.

4. Wearing a protective mask, Steve blasts the pickup window with fairly low air pressure and fine-grit sand.

5. Strip off the masking and you've got the finished rear window, which is simple and clean, but different.

6. Here's another set of van rear windows done by Frank Mendeola; this time with old-fashioned scroll look.

7. Just how far you can go depends on your local laws regarding visibility, as you can see on this van by Graham Enterprises—with the rose theme in bloom on every piece of glass on the van, including the windwings.

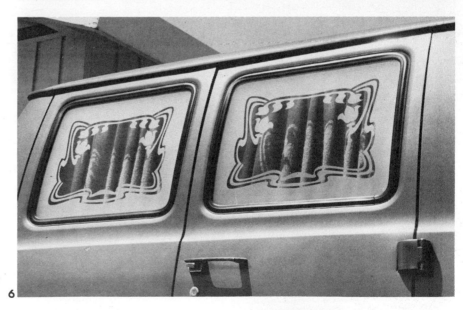

only won't the sandblasting hurt the rubber, it can actually *renew* its appearance. Out o' sight!

The design we used was a simple one, but you can get as complicated as you like, depending only on your skill in masking. You can use cutout patterns for flames, shapes and mural scenes just as you would do for painting; only now you're working on glass. Speaking of painting, have you ever tried to make paint stick to glass? Sandblasting the glass provides the perfect roughed-up surface for primer and paint to adhere to; and can be done over the whole window (to make your two-door station wagon into a home-made sedan delivery); or just over a portion of the window, in a design. You should be able to find an outfit in your area that does sandblasting, and if there's not one

listed under that heading in the phone book, try a local gravestone company. That's how they do most of the designs and lettering on the stones—with sandblasting. If you do your rear window though, we'd caution you to check with the local vehicle requirements first, as it may be illegal to obstruct the rear window unless you have rear-view mirrors on both sides of the truck. You'd better get your design finalized now, though, or everyone else will beat you to the punch—this fad is going to catch on. ✑ 7

Instant Flames

Flames are adaptable to nearly every car shape for pennies a flicker—with "hot licks."

Flame paint jobs have been a customizing staple for over 20 years now. Some years this kind of paint trickery is more "in" than other years; however, the technique has never faded completely from the street and car show scene and probably never will—simply because flame jobs are adaptable and good-looking on nearly every size and shape of car.

But if you happen to live hundreds of miles from the nearest custom painting studio, you are still in good shape, provided that the local speed emporium carries the new "Hot Licks" vinyl flaming kits. These kits use die-cut vinyl sheets with backing to provide durable, nonfading flame patterns that are good-looking and easy to work with—even if you've never touched a vinyl applique before in your life.

"Hot Licks" flames come six to a sheet, with one very large pattern, one very small one and two each of intermediate sizes; with some basic suggestions as to flame layout on the back of the package. The flames can be overlapped, cut in two—for those instances where the designer wants to cross a door opening. Or, they can be trimmed to shape where a flame cuts into a fender line.

Just to show you how easy to work with "Hot Licks" flames are, we cajoled former-pinstriper-turned-magazine-editor Terry Cook into doing the layout and application, and at the same time we talked TC's assistant, Diane Lewis, into letting us use her VW as a showcase/guinea pig for the flaming, since the VW's body shape offers a challenge, even to one as experienced as Terry. Note that the flames on the sides of Diane's VW are interrupted in a couple of places as they cross body panels. These simple matchups were made with scissors and a careful eye, to preserve the continuity of line.

If the idea of removable, inexpensive flame patterns that you can design and lay out yourself is appealing, "Hot Licks" are available at your speed shop.

1. These new vinyl flames from Racing Graphics provide the answer for flame paint jobs without the hassles or expense; and no taping or sanding!

2. Each Hot Licks package contains one large lick, three medium-sized licks and two smaller ones, so you can start small and go big, or just the opposite. Here Terry is lapping a smaller lick over a large one.

3. The stout vinyl construction allows painless cutting and trimming for fit across door-edge gaps and other breaks in a car's body lines. Trimming can be easily done with razor or X-Acto.

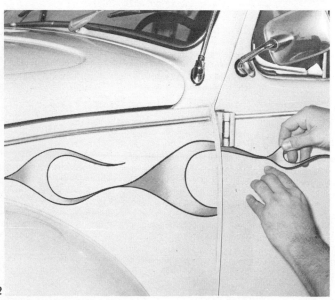